SCIENCE FRONTIERS

The History of SCIENCE

SCIENCE FRONTIERS

1946 to the Present

Ray Spangenburg

Diane Kit Moser

☑® Facts On File, Inc.

Science Frontiers: 1946 to the Present

Facts On File, Inc.
132 West 31st Street
New York NY 10001

Library of Congress Cataloging-in-Publication Data

Spangenburg, Ray, 1939–
    Science Frontiers, 1946 to the present / Ray Spangenburg and Diane Kit Moser.
      p. cm. — (History of science)
    Revised ed. of: The history of science from 1946 to the 1990s.
    Includes bibliographical references and index.
    ISBN 0-8160-4855-X
    1. Science—History—Juvenile literature. 2. Life sciences—History—Juvenile literature. [1. Science—History.] I. Moser, Diane, 1944– II. Spangenburg, Ray, 1939– History of science from 1946 to the 1990s. III. Title.
    Q126.4.S63 2004
    509'.045—dc22   2003024290

Facts On File books are available at special discounts when purchased in bulk quantities for businesses, associations, institutions, or sales promotions. Please call our Special Sales Department in New York at (212) 967-8800 or (800) 322-8755.

You can find Facts On File on the World Wide Web at http://www.factsonfile.com

Text design by Erika K. Arroyo
Cover design by Kelly Parr
Illustrations by Sholto Ainslie

Printed in the United States of America

MP Hermitage 10 9 8 7 6 5 4 3 2 1

This book is printed on acid-free paper.

In Memory of
Morgan Sherwood
and his love of the ever–human
struggle to become rational

CONTENTS

PREFACE

What I see in Nature is a magnificent structure that we can comprehend only very imperfectly, and that must fill a thinking person with a feeling of "humility."

—Albert Einstein

SCIENCE, OF ALL HUMAN ENDEAVORS, is one of the greatest adventures: Its job is to explore that "magnificent structure" we call nature and its awesome unknown regions. It probes the great mysteries of the universe such as black holes, star nurseries, and quasars, as well as the perplexities of miniscule subatomic particles, such as quarks and antiquarks. Science seeks to understand the secrets of the human body and the redwood tree and the retrovirus. The realms of its inquiry embrace the entire universe and everything in it, from the smallest speck of dust on a tiny asteroid to the fleck of color in a girl's eye, and from the vast structure of a far-off galaxy millions of light years away to the complex dynamics that keep the rings of Saturn suspended in space.

Some people tend to think that science is a musty, dusty set of facts and statistics to be memorized and soon forgotten. Others contend that science is the antithesis of poetry, magic, and all things human. Both groups have it wrong—nothing could be more growth-oriented or more filled with wonder or more human. Science is constantly evolving, undergoing revolutions, always producing "new words set to the old music," and constantly refocusing what has gone before into fresh, new understanding.

Asking questions and trying to understand how things work are among the most fundamental of human characteristics, and the history of science is the story of how a varied array of individuals,

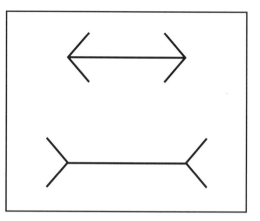

Looks can be deceiving. These two lines are the same length.

teams, and groups have gone about finding answers to some of the most fundamental questions. When, for example, did people begin wondering what Earth is made of and what its shape might be? How could they find answers? What methods did they devise for coming to conclusions and how good were those methods? At what point did their inquiries become *scientific*—and what does that mean?

Science is so much more than the strange test tubes and odd apparatus we see in movies. It goes far beyond frog dissections or the names of plant species that we learn in biology classes. Science is actually a way of thinking, a vital, ever-growing way of looking at the world. It is a way of discovering how the world works—a very particular way that uses a set of rules devised by scientists to help them also discover their own mistakes because it is so easy to mis-construe what one sees or hears or perceives in other ways.

If you find that hard to believe, look at the two horizontal lines in the figure above. One looks like a two-way arrow; the other has inverted arrowheads. Which one do you think is longer (not includ-ing the "arrowheads")? Now measure them both. Right, they are exactly the same length. Because it is so easy to go wrong in mak-ing observations and drawing conclusions, people developed a sys-tem, a "scientific method," for asking "How can I be sure?" If you actually took the time to measure the two lines in our example, instead of just taking our word that both lines are the same length, then you were thinking like a scientist. You were testing your own observation. You were testing the information that both lines "are exactly the same length." And you were employing one of the strongest tools of science to perform your test: You were quantifying, or measuring, the lines.

More than 2,300 years ago, Aristotle, a Greek philosopher, told the world that when two objects of different weights were dropped from a height, the heaviest would hit the ground first. It was a commonsense argument. After all, anyone who wanted to try a test could make an "observation" and see that if you dropped a leaf and a stone together that the stone would land first. Try it yourself with a sheet of notebook paper and a paperweight in your living room. (There is something wrong with this test. Do you know what it is?) However, not many Greek thinkers tried any sort of test. Why bother when the answer was already known? And, since they were philosophers who believed in the power of the human mind to simply "reason" such things out without having to resort to "tests," they considered observation and experiments intellectually and socially beneath them.

Centuries later, though, Galileo Galilei came along, a brilliant Italian pioneer in physics and telescopic astronomy. Galileo liked to figure things out for himself, and he did run some tests, even though he had to work around some limitations. Like today's scientists, Galileo was never content just to watch. He used two balls of different weights, a time-keeping device, and an inclined plane, or ramp. Accurate clocks and watches were not yet invented, but he worked around that problem by rigging his own device. One at a time, he allowed the balls to roll down the ramp and carefully *measured* the time they took to reach the end of the ramp. He did this not once but many times, inclining planes at many different angles. His results, which still offend the common sense of many people today, indicated that, in Aristotle's example, after adjusting for differences in air resistance, all objects released at the same time from the same height would hit the ground at the same time. In a perfect vacuum (which scientists could not create in Galileo's time), all objects would fall at the same rate! You can run a rough test yourself (although it is by no means a really accurate experiment) by crumpling notebook paper into a ball and then dropping it at the same time as the paperweight.

"Wait!" you might justifiably say. Just a minute ago, you dropped a piece of paper and a paperweight and so demonstrated Aristotle's premise when the two objects hit the ground at different times. Now when we do the same thing over again, the two objects hit the ground at about the same time and we demonstrate that Galileo was right and Aristotle was wrong. What makes the difference? You have it: The second time, you crumpled the paper so that it had the same shape as the paperweight. Without crumpling the paper, you would have to make an adjustment for the increased air resistance of an 8½-by-11-inch sheet of paper as opposed to a paperweight that had less surface area.

Galileo's experiments (which he carefully recorded step by step) and his conclusions based on these experiments demonstrate an important attribute of science. Anyone who wanted to could duplicate the experiments and either verify his results or, by showing flaws or errors in the experiments, prove him partially or wholly incorrect. Since his time, many, many scientists have repeated his experiment and, even though they tried, no one ever proved Galileo wrong. There is more. Years later, when it was possible to create a vacuum (even though his experiments had been accurate enough to win everybody over long before that), his prediction proved true. Without any air resistance at all and even with much more sophisticated timing devices, his experiment came out as predicted.

Galileo had not only shown that Aristotle had been wrong. He demonstrated how, by observation, experiment, and quantification, Aristotle, if he had so wished, might have proved himself wrong—and thus changed his own opinion! Above all else the scientific way of thinking is a way to keep yourself from fooling yourself—or from letting nature (or others) fool you.

Of course, science is much more than observation, experimentation, and presentation of results. No one today can read a newspaper or a magazine without becoming quickly aware of the fact that science is always bubbling with "theories." "Astronomer Finds Evidence That Challenges Einstein's Theory of Relativity," announces a magazine cover. "State Board of Education Condemns Books That Teach Darwin's Theory of Evolution," reads a newspaper headline. What is this thing called a "theory"? The answer lies in a process known as the "scientific method."

Few scientists pretend anymore that they have the completely "detached" and objective scientific method proposed by the philosopher Francis Bacon and others at the dawn of the Scientific Revolution in the 17th century. Bacon's method, in its simplest form, proposed that an investigator trying to find out about nature's secrets had an obligation to think objectively and proceed without preformed opinions, basing conclusions on observation, experiments, and collection of data about the phenomena under inquiry. "I make no hypothesis," Isaac Newton announced after demonstrating the universal law of gravity when it was suggested that he might have an idea *what gravity was.* Historians have noted that Newton apparently did have a couple of ideas, or "hypotheses," as to the possible nature of gravity, but for the most part he kept these conjectures private. As far as Newton was concerned, there had already been enough hypothesizing and too little attention paid to the careful gathering of testable facts and figures.

Today, though, we know that scientists may not always follow along the simple and neat pathways laid out by the trail guide known as the "scientific method." Sometimes, either before or after experiments, a scientist will get an idea or a hunch (that is, a somewhat less than well thought out hypothesis) that suggests a new approach or a different way of looking at a problem. Then the researcher will run experiments and gather data to attempt to prove or disprove this hypothesis. Sometimes the word *hypothesis* is used loosely in everyday conversation, but in science it must meet an important requirement: To be valid scientifically a hypothesis must have a built-in way it can be proved wrong if, in fact, it is wrong. That is, it must be falsifiable.

Not all scientists actually run experiments themselves. Most theoreticians, for instance, map out their arguments mathematically. But hypotheses, to be taken seriously by the scientific community, must always carry with them the seeds of falsifiability by experiment and observation.

That brings us to the word *theory.* To become a theory, a hypothesis has to pass several tests. It has to hold up under repeated experiments and not done just by one scientist. Other scientists, working separately from the first, must also perform experiments and observations to test the hypothesis. Then, when thoroughly reinforced by continual testing and appraising, the hypothesis may become known to the scientific and popular world as a "theory."

It is important to remember that even a theory is also subject to falsification or correction. A good theory, for instance, will suggest "predictions"—events that its testers can look for as further tests of its validity. By the time most well-known theories, such as Einstein's theory of relativity or Darwin's theory of evolution, reach the textbook stage, they have survived the gamut of verification to the extent that they have become productive working tools for other scientists. But in science, no theory can be accepted as completely "proved"; it must remain always open to further tests and scrutiny as new facts or observations emerge. It is this insistently self-correcting nature of science that makes it both the most demanding and the most productive of humankind's attempts to understand the workings of nature. This kind of critical thinking is the key element of doing science.

The cartoon-version scientist, portrayed as a bespectacled, rigid man in a white coat and certain of his own infallibility, couldn't be further from reality. Scientists, both men and women, are as human as the rest of us—and they come in all races, sizes, and appearances, with and without eyeglasses. As a group, because their methodology focuses so specifically on fallibility and critical thinking, they are probably even more aware than the rest of us of how easy it is to be wrong. But they like being right whenever possible, and they like working toward finding the right answers to questions. That's usually why they became scientists.

Science Frontiers: 1946 to the Present and the four other volumes in The History of Science look at how people have developed this system for finding out how the world works, making use of both success and failure. Throughout the series, we look at the theories scientists have put forth, sometimes right and sometimes wrong. And we look at how we have learned to test, accept, and build upon those theories—or to correct, expand, or simplify them.

We also examine how scientists have learned from others' mistakes, sometimes having to discard theories that once seemed logical but later proved to be incorrect, misleading, too limited, or unfruitful. In all these ways they have built upon the accomplishments of the men and women of science who went before them and left a long, bountiful legacy from which others could set out for new discoveries and fresh insights.

Each volume of this new edition offers expanded coverage, including more about women in science; many new photographs and illustrations; and a new section, "Science and Society" that examines the interface between science and cultural and social mores and historical events. Sidebars called "Side Roads of Science" examine weird beliefs and pseudoscientific claims of the times. Each volume concludes with a glossary, a chronology, and expanded sources for further exploration, including Web sites, CD-ROMs, and other multimedia resources, as well as recent related books and other print resources.

ACKNOWLEDGMENTS

WE COULD NOT HAVE WRITTEN this book or the others in this series without the help, inspiration, and guidance offered by many generous individuals over nearly two decades of writing about science and science history. We would like to name a few of them; for those we have not space to name please accept our heartfelt thanks, including the many scientists we have interviewed. Their work has helped us better understand the overall nature of science.

We would like to express our heartfelt appreciation to James Warren, formerly of Facts On File, whose vision and enthusiastic encouragement helped shape the first edition; Frank K. Darmstadt, executive editor, whose boundless energy and support made all this book and its companions happen against impossible odds; and the rest of the Facts On File staff. A special thank you as well to Heather Lindsay of AIP Emilio Segrè Visual Archives, Lynne Farrington of the Annenberg Rare Book and Manuscript Library, Tracy Elizabeth Robinson and David Burgevin of the Smithsonian, and Shirley Neiman of Stock Montage, Inc. Our heartfelt gratitude also to Frances Spangenburg, even though she will never read this one, for her unflagging encouragement at every step of our writing careers.

And finally, our gratitude and affection to the late Morgan Sherwood and his wife, Jeanie Sherwood, for their warmth and generosity and their gift of Morgan's fine, extensive library on pseudoscience and the history of science.

INTRODUCTION

From 1946 to the Present:
The Continuing Quest

THE YEAR 1945 WAS BOTH A BITTER and jubilant time. A terrible war had finally ground to an end—a world war that had annihilated millions of Jews, destroyed much of Europe, unhinged large parts of Asia and the Pacific, decimated two cities of Japan, and killed millions of other soldiers and civilians. At last, with great relief, the world could get back to the business of living. And scientists could get back to doing science.

But the political ambience in which they worked was not peaceful, and the world psyche after World War II was deeply shaken. The atomic bomb, with its enormous destructive capacity and its deadly radiation aftermath, had been unleashed, and the world could not escape the new anxieties created by the bomb's existence. By 1949 the Soviet Union, with its declared aggressive policies, had tested an atomic bomb, and a race began between the United States and the USSR to see who could stockpile the most arms. In the United States some people began building bomb shelters in their backyards, and air raid drills remained part of every public school routine throughout the 1950s. The Soviet Union established what came to be called an Iron Curtain in Eastern Europe, a closed-door policy of noncooperation, whereby freedom of travel and economic exchange were prohibited. So, though World War II had finally ended, a new kind of conflict, known as the cold war, began almost immediately.

In 1950 war broke out when North Korean troops, bolstered by China, invaded South Korea, which was defended by United Nations troops. The 1950s and 1960s were a time of many civil wars and coups in Latin America and Africa, in many cases encouraged either by the Soviet Union or the United States. Throughout the second half-century, independence was won, for the most part bloodlessly, by former colonies in Africa, Asia, and Latin America. But many—such as Cuba, Tibet, North Korea, and several Latin America countries—replaced colonial rule with commitments to the Soviet Union or Communist China. And in 1962 the whole world caught its breath as the United States confronted the Soviet Union with evidence of Soviet missile bases in Cuba, only about 90 miles from the coast of Florida—and breathed a sigh of relief when the Soviet Union backed down. Just a few months later, the two governments installed a communications "hot line" between Moscow and Washington, D.C., to reduce the risk of accidental war between the two nations.

For science, this pervasive atmosphere of unease had both positive and negative effects. The free exchange of ideas, theories, and results among scientists—so hard fought for over the centuries—now fell by the wayside as communication fell silent between Moscow, its satellites, and the West. Soviet newspapers, journals and books were not available in the West, and vice versa. Travel between the two regions was severely limited. But, on the positive side, the United States, Europe, and England early recognized the need to keep apace with Soviet advances. And in the United States especially, the tradition begun by the scientists who built the atomic bomb during the Manhattan Project was continued after the war by scientists who coupled their search for scientific knowledge with the need to build advanced military aircraft and weapons for their governments.

Then science in the West received a huge jolt. On October 4, 1957, the Russians launched *Sputnik I,* the first artificial satellite, into orbit around Earth. No other countries were so close to launching anything into orbit, except the United States, where rocket scientists imported from Germany after World War II had been working steadily both on military missiles and on the raw beginnings of a civilian space program. Suddenly, math and science moved center stage. Spurred by competition with the Russians, Western educators put new emphasis on grooming young scientists, while in the United States, the precursor of the National Aeronautics and Space Administration (NASA) scrambled to catch up. By 1961 both the Soviet Union and the United States had sent more than one human into space (with the Russians again first), and by 1961 U.S. president John F. Kennedy had announced plans to send Americans to land on the Moon. To the arms race the two nations now added a race to the Moon, and the Space Age had begun in earnest.

For planetary scientists and astronomers, the boon was enormous. Between 1958 and 1976, scientists sent 80 missions to the Moon's far side (which always turns away from the Earth). Probes to Venus, Mars, Mercury, and the far-flung outer planets followed, both from Cape Canaveral (later briefly renamed Cape Kennedy) and Russia's "Star City." These roaming robots sent radio signals earthward, returning photographs and data that revolutionized human understanding of the solar system and the universe beyond.

By 1971 the Soviet Union had begun a marathon of experiments in living in space, in a series of space stations culminating in the big *Mir* space station, launched in 1986. The United States, meanwhile, sent three teams of astronauts in 1973–74 to a space station called *Skylab* to study the Sun. And in 1981 the United States launched the first of a fleet of Earth-orbiting vehicles called space shuttles. In addition to deployment of countless satellites having a variety of purposes, ranging from scientific to military to business, the space programs of these two countries have collected extensive data about the effects of weightlessness on living organisms (including humans), crystal formation, and countless other areas of inquiry. By the 1980s many other countries, including China, Japan, and India, had developed space programs of their own.

All this was, in a way, positive fallout from the cold war. As the cold war drew toward end in 1989, and with the breakup of the Soviet Union in 1991, some of the spur for this surge of interest in space exploration and science dissipated. At the same time, a spirit of international cooperation in space has emerged, despite a lack of funding in Russia and the deterioration and finally the demise of Russia's *Mir* space station, when Russian space scientists concluded its 15-year service record by bringing it back to Earth in a fiery blaze. The *International Space Station* continued to carry an international crew onboard, despite a fatal shuttle accident in February 2003. However, the shuttle program was grounded during investigations, and economic pressures and military expenses in the United States severely hampered further development and use of the space station.

Nevertheless, scientists throughout the world eagerly resumed communication and collaboration with scientists from Russia and other former citizens of the Soviet Union. Ironically, the new flow of information came at a time when funds dwindled worldwide in the face of terrorism, war, and new nuclear threats.

And if any single fact of life has haunted science in the last half of the 20th century, it is the greatly increased cost of doing science. Gone are the days when Galileo, in the 17th century, could hear about a new optical instrument, gather together a few materials, build his own telescope, and shortly be making astronomical observations that no one had ever made before. With 1945 dawned the age of "big science." Particle physics, the study of subatomic particles, could only be conducted with the aid of giant machines, called particle accelerators, that began to be built, one by one, in Stanford and Berkeley, California; in Batavia, Illinois; in Geneva, Switzerland; and elsewhere. As Europe struggled to recover from the devastation of war, most early post–World War II work was done in the United States, and physicists flocked there from Japan, China, and Europe.

Only well-endowed universities and institutions, with the help of government funding, could afford to build the big machines. The giant computer and semiconductor industry, as well, spun off from advances made by physicists and engineers—discoveries about the behavior of electrons and quantum mechanics and the discovery of the transistor by a team of scientists at Bell Laboratories (again, through research funded by a large corporation, not the individual enterprise of a single curious mind). The first commercial computer to go into service was the UNIVAC I, a giant machine built in 1951 and purchased by the U.S. Bureau of the Census. Again, only the enormous needs and financial capabilities of government could justify and finance the start-up. (Today, for under $1000, any individual can buy a personal computer the size of a briefcase with greater capacity than the UNIVAC I, which filled an entire room the size of a gym.) The period from 1945 to the present has been a time of turbulence and change, a time both of violence and social progress.

Civil rights and liberties have become a matter of worldwide concern, and some progress was made in the United States under the leadership of Martin Luther King, Jr., and others in the 1960s— but not without high costs. Martin Luther King, Jr., was assassinated in 1968. The U.S. Supreme Court ordered integration of schools in 1954 and federal troops enforced it in Little Rock, Arkansas, in 1957. In the 1960s civil rights legislation in the United States established the principle of equal opportunity for all in jobs and housing. And by 1991 even South Africa had abandoned apartheid laws and had begun to integrate schools.

Political assassinations also haunted the times. President John F. Kennedy and his brother Robert F. Kennedy were assassinated—John in Dallas, Texas, in 1963 and his brother on the night he won the California presidential primary four and a half years later, in 1968. In India a fanatic assassinated pacifist leader Mahatma Gandhi, who had led India successfully in a fight for independence from Britain, in 1948. Extremists struck again, nearly 40 years later, in 1984, assassinating Prime Minister Indira Gandhi (unrelated to Mahatma Gandhi), and seven years later her son Rajiv Gandhi, who had succeeded her, was also killed. Other assassinations, terrorist bombings, and hijackings worldwide reflected an atmosphere of turbulence. But at the same time, forces for peace, national independence, and self-rule often triumphed as well.

The fight for democratic process and self-rule had its ups and downs, with several significant changes in addition to the breakup of the Soviet Union. In 1986 Corazón Aquino was elected president of the Philippines, putting an end to 15 years of martial law and 20 years of rule by the graft-ridden government of Ferdinand Marcos. East Germany and West Germany were reunited in 1990 and held the first democratic elections in a unified Germany since 1932.

Science, meanwhile, could not stand apart from these political, social, and moral issues. Many scientists took a stand after World War II against the continued development of weapons, among them Albert Einstein, whose sphere of influence is legendary, and Danish physicist Niels Bohr. Andrei Sakharov, in the former Soviet Union, who helped his nation develop a hydrogen bomb, spoke out in 1967–68 against testing of nuclear weapons in the USSR and for worldwide disarmament—an act for which he was unjustly discredited, persecuted, and threatened. Finally, in 1980, when he criticized the Soviet Union for its invasion of Afghanistan, he and his wife, Elena Bonner, were placed under house arrest. There he remained imprisoned until 1986, when the growing spirit of *glasnost,* or openness, led to his release.

As expanding knowledge creates new areas of concern for ethics and new decisions to be made, science walks close to the heart and soul of society on many issues. Is a cloned tomato better than a natural tomato, or should it be suspect in some way? When donor organs can save lives, when and under what circumstances can they be taken from the donor? Given the nuclear accidents at Three Mile Island (in Pennsylvania) in 1979 and at Chernobyl (near Kiev, in the Soviet Union) in 1986, can nuclear power plants be considered safe?

Science is often viewed as both hero and villain in the second half of the 20th century. While science has enabled enormous technological advances—from electricity to compact discs, from automobiles to airplanes to space exploration, from satellite communication to fax machines—science also sometimes gets blamed for the loss of the "simple, natural life." But the cycle continues: discovery spawning new technology, which in turn makes new discoveries possible, in a series of leap-frog jumps into the future. The process required new understanding of the effects of what we do, new attitudes of stewardship toward our planet, and a new sense of responsibility for the effects of our actions upon our neighbors—responsibilities that our forebears, with their "simpler life" of timber harvesting and poor crop planning, often failed at.

The second half of the 20th century was a time for exploring the most fundamental components of the universe, the essence of which things are made. Leucippus and Democritus, among the Greeks, believed that all matter was composed of atoms, which they imagined to be tiny, hard, indivisible particles. In the 19th century John Dalton believed he knew what an atom was: the smallest unit of a chemical element. But in the last years of the 1800s, chemists and physicists such as Marie and Pierre Curie and Henri Becquerel noticed that the atoms of certain elements seemed to give off a part of themselves in a process that we now call radioactive decay. They asked themselves, if an atom was indivisible, how could it emit part of itself? Here was a clear contradiction, and in the first years of the 20th century, the stage was set for revolutionary changes in the way scientists understood the atom. Electrons were discovered, followed by a nucleus composed of protons and neutrons.

But by 1945 exploration of the new world within the atom had only just begun. Today some 200 subatomic particles are known, and more are believed to exist. The story of their discovery has been an intricate and intriguing whodunit that has absorbed some of the best minds of the century.

Meanwhile, enormous technological breakthroughs in rocket technology and space science have enabled astronomers, cosmologists, and planetary scientists to explore the universe more closely than Galileo, Kepler, or any of the great observers of the past could ever have dreamed possible.

At the same time, in the life sciences, researchers were eagerly racing to discover the structure of the fundamental constituents that control the shapes and forms of life. By 1946 it had been clear for two years that the ultimate architect of living things was a molecule known as deoxyribonucleic acid, or DNA—a substance that had been completely unknown before the first half of the 20th century. And its structure still remained a mystery as the second half of the century began. But James Watson and Francis Crick would soon unravel it, and the new field of molecular biology would become the cutting edge of the life sciences for the rest of the century.

In this book, it is possible only to explore *some* of the exciting discoveries made in the second half of the 20th century—in light of the explosion of new finds and intriguing questions raised every day. At the end of the book, we've suggested several more books for further exploration, as well as other resources, such as Web sites and organizations. We hope you'll plunge into these, too, and discover for yourself some of the fascinating complexities and delightful questions our universe poses. For science provides us all, whether we are professional scientists or not, with a special window on the world that enables us to see in ways we might not otherwise see and understand in ways we would not otherwise understand. It is a special, and uniquely human, way of thinking.

Like the other four books in The History of Science, *Science Frontiers* follows the adventures of scientists as they probe, question, experiment, build theories, and engage in trying to understand the universe. We follow them as they develop the process of science—meeting with new ethical issues, world politics, and the challenges of a generally politicized arena. Scientists made breakthroughs in nearly every field during the latter half of the 1900s, followed by exciting prospects in the 21st century. It was a time of many beginnings: the space age, the human genome, a cloned ewe, the structure of DNA—and a time of vastly increased possibilities, thanks to microchips, rockets, computer databases and modeling, advanced and spaceborne telescopes, electron microscopes, and particle accelerators. This may be the most exciting time ever in which to do science—and in some ways the most difficult. This book examines some of these stories.

For exploring related topics, a bibliography at the end of this volume provides Internet addresses, multimedia references, and an updated list of books reflecting recent research and interpretations, as well as a few classics. A chronology and glossary round out the reference tools at the conclusion of the volume.

PART I
The Physical Sciences, 1946 to the Present

1

The Subatomic World
A Swarm of Particles

BENEATH A LONG, CURVING OVERPASS of Interstate 280 on the San Francisco peninsula, a four-mile-long building cuts through the gently rolling Los Gatos Hills. Most people never notice the unimportant-looking brown concrete slab, or if they do notice as they whiz by, they have no sense of its extraordinary length. Nor are they aware of the millions of high-speed electrons speeding through its tunnels at a pace that makes the vehicles on the freeway look like they're traveling in megaslow motion. This great gash of brown concrete cutting across the manzanita brush and grassy slopes looks unremarkable even to those who do notice it, except that it is a great deal longer than normal buildings and strangely lacking in corners or bends.

But it is remarkable. This building, known casually to its friends as SLAC, houses one of modern physicists' answers to an age-old question, How do you see the smallest conceivable constituents of matter—the tiny building blocks of which everything is made? SLAC (the Stanford Linear Accelerator Center), huge as it is, provides a window for seeing the infinitesimally tiny particles that make up the atom.

Beginning the Search

But let's back up a little. At the outset (or close to it, as far as the history of science is concerned), back in the time of the ancient

3

In this aerial photograph of the Stanford Linear Accelerator Center (SLAC) in California, the two-mile-long linear accelerator extends diagonally westward. Electrons or other subatomic particles are fired like tiny bullets from the near end, accelerating as they travel the length of the accelerator, under the freeway, to smash into their miniscule targets in the experimental area at the far end. Results of such experiments reveal secrets of the atomic nucleus and related mysteries. *(© Stanford Linear Accelerator Center/Photo Researchers, Inc.)*

Greeks, a man named Leucippus [lyoo-SIP-us] (ca. 450–ca. 370 B.C.E.) and his disciple, Democritus [de-MOK-rih-tus] (ca. 460–ca. 370 B.C.E.), came up with the idea that everything must be made of some very small universal building block. They called this tiny, hard, indivisible particle an atom (from the Greek word *atomos,* meaning "indivisible," or, put another way, "unsmashable"). Too small to see, these atoms, they said, were what you would get if you kept splitting any material into its component parts until it was impossible to split it any further.

That was about 2,400 years ago, and the idea caught on slowly. Most other thinkers of their time and for many centuries afterward did not think much of the idea, but by the late 1600s, it began to attract more interest. The British chemist Robert Boyle was an atomist, and Isaac Newton also liked the idea. In *Opticks,* published in 1704, Newton wrote that he believed all matter was composed of "solid, massy, hard, impenetrable moveable Particles" that he thought must be solids "incomparably harder than any porous Bodies compounded of them." But even Newton had no idea how to look at these particles he thought must exist. So physicists went on studying the relationships of energy and matter, cause and effect. Chemists, meanwhile, continued searching for what came to be called "elements."

A little less than a century later, an eccentric, headstrong chemist named John Dalton proposed, for the first time, an atomic theory that could be tested quantitatively. Dalton defined atoms as the smallest unit of an element, and he published the first list of atomic weights for the known elements of his time. His work provided the keystone for several dozen discoveries of new elements in the century that followed. But what Dalton and his contemporaries did not yet realize was that Dalton's "atom" was *not* the same as Leucippus and Democritus's indivisible "atom," the smallest fundamental particle to be found in nature.

The first clues of this difference began to become evident at the end of the 19th century with the discovery of X-rays and other forms of radiation. Scientists discovered that these various types of radiation were composed of particles given off by atoms—Dalton's atoms, that is. If atoms could release particles, then, plainly, atoms were not indivisible: There was *something* smaller. In 1896 English physicist J. J. Thomson demonstrated the existence of the electron, a small, light, negatively charged particle that had a mass equal to only a small fraction of the mass of hydrogen atoms. This did not explain where radioactive particles came from, but it was a start. And so began the field of subatomic particle physics.

In 1911 Ernest Rutherford was the first to describe the atom as composed of a dense, positively charged nucleus surrounded by negatively charged particles (electrons) orbiting in mostly empty space. *(Edgar Fahs Smith Collection—University of Pennsylvania Library)*

In 1911 New Zealander Ernest Rutherford concluded, from experiments he and his research teams did at McGill University in Canada and at Manchester University in England, that the atom was mostly empty space, with Thomson's negatively charged electrons in orbit around the perimeter, like tiny planets in a miniature solar system, and a nucleus at its center, composed of positive particles (soon named *protons*).

Danish physicist Niels Bohr, who arrived in England to study in 1912, was one of the few physicists who liked this idea of an atom composed mostly of empty space. By 1913 he proposed an updated version of Rutherford's model—a central positive nucleus surrounded by electrons orbiting at various specific energy levels. Bohr's model combined all the pieces of evidence so far: Thomson's electrons, Rutherford's positive nucleus, and quantum theory, first proposed by Max Planck in 1900. The basic idea behind Planck's theory is that you can explain how atoms behave—and how subatomic particles interact—based on seeing the photon, or quantum (the tiny packet of energy that light and all electromagnetic energy travel in), as both a wave and a particle, not one or the other. While this idea seems strange, the theory of the quantum explains a great many phenomena that otherwise had no explanation, and in the end revolutionized physics.

By the third decade of the 20th century, rapid-fire changes began to occur in physics; one after another, new particles were discovered, and with each new discovery another revision had to be made to the concept of the atom and what it was really like. The new view of Dalton's atom soon bore no resemblance at all to Leucippus and Democritus's unsplittable, billiard-ball-shaped fundamental particle. It was not unsplittable. It was not a solid spherical mass. However, it still was arguably the smallest fundamental particle of an element.

In 1930, based on his study of experimental data, Wolfgang Pauli came up with the idea that a strange unknown particle must be given off in radioactive beta emissions, a particle having no mass (or nearly so), no charge, and practically no interaction with anything else. He thought such a particle must exist in order to explain the loss of energy in the reaction—otherwise the law of conservation of energy would have to be abandoned, a move he did not want to suggest. Four years later, Enrico Fermi gave his stamp of approval by naming the tiny particle *neutrino*, which means "little neutral one" in Italian, Fermi's native language.

Almost impossible to detect, the neutrino eluded observation for years, and no one could prove that it existed. There were those, at first, who suspected that Pauli had just pulled a sort of bookkeeping trick—made something up to make the energy books look balanced. But in 1956, through the use of a nuclear power station, an elaborate experiment was completed that proved the existence of the ghostly neutrino, and Pauli was vindicated. Recent experiments, one completed in 1995 at the Sudbury Neutrino Observatory (SNO) in Ontario and another in 1998 at the Institute for Cosmic Ray Research at the University of Tokyo, have resolved the ongoing mystery of the neutrino: Why do only about half the predicted neutrinos apparently reach Earth? The answer appears to be that neutrinos have mass—sometimes. That is, some of them change character on the way to Earth, and consequently are not detected. These experiments serve as a compelling reminder of the interdependence of cosmic and atomic realms.

Also in 1930, from a theory proposed by Paul Dirac, a 28-year-old British physicist, came the idea of another hypothetical particle similar to an electron but having a positive charge. In fact, based on Dirac's efforts to get quantum and relativity to work together, physicists came to the astonishing conclusion that wherever matter exists, its mirror—antimatter—must also exist. This idea of antimatter, according to fellow Nobel-winning physicist Werner Heisenberg, was "perhaps the biggest of all the big jumps in physics in the [20th] century." The idea met with some opposition, despite Dirac's mathematical prowess. Then, in 1932, a young American physicist named Carl Anderson was working with a powerful magnet and a cloud chamber at the California Institute of Technology, when he saw it—

at least he saw the tracks of a subatomic particle that seemed to be an electron, but was pulled in the opposite direction by the magnet. He called his new particle a *positron*.

Also in 1932, meanwhile, James Chadwick at Cambridge University found undeniable evidence of the existence of yet another particle, one that had no charge and was located in the nucleus of most atoms. He called it the *neutron*. This particle was easily detectable and it explained a lot, including the discrepancy that no one had ever understood between atomic number and atomic weight. The number of negatively charged electrons balanced the number of positively charged protons in the nucleus, but all atoms except hydrogen had at least twice as much mass as these particles could account for. So where did all the mass come from? Now the answer seemed clear: neutrally charged particles in the nucleus.

The existence of neutrons seemed readily substantiated, and it was hard to argue with Carl Anderson's evidence for the positron. A few scientists at this stage were still skeptical about Pauli's neutrino. But, in any case, even with these additions, the number of fundamental particles within the atom still seemed manageable.

Carl D. Anderson with the cloud chamber he used in 1932 to establish the existence of the positron, substantiated by the tracks shown at right *(NARA, courtesy AIP Emilio Segrè Visual Archives; photo by C.D. Anderson, courtesy AIP Emilio Segrè Visual Archives)*

In the coming years all that was about to change. In 1935 Hideki Yukawa (1907–81), a young Japanese physicist at the University of Kyoto, proposed a solution to a major problem: What held these neutrons and protons so closely together in the nucleus? If the nucleus contained only protons, having a positive charge, and Chadwick's chargeless neutrons, Heisenberg had suggested, then the only electrical charge in the nucleus was positive. And since like-charged particles repel each other, why did not the tiny particles fly apart in opposite directions? Maybe, suggested Yukawa, some sort of "exchange forces" were at work in the nucleus—but what they were and how they worked he never said.

Hideki Yukawa (1907–81) set physicists on a long and fruitful search for fundamental particles. *(AIP Emilio Segrè Visual Archives, W. F. Meggers Gallery of Nobel Laureates)*

Yukawa figured that, since ordinary electromagnetic forces involved the transfer of photons, then some kind of "nuclear force" must operate within the nucleus, involving the transfer of some other entity. This nuclear force must operate only over very short ranges—ranges, that is, the size of the diameter of a nucleus (measuring about ten trillionths of a centimeter). It must also be remarkably strong—strong enough to hold together protons whose positive charges would ordinarily force them apart. And, based on the results of experiments, this force must drop off very quickly as distance increases, so that beyond the perimeter of the nucleus, it would not be felt at all.

Yukawa worked out a theory that evidence of this force appeared when particles were transferred back and forth among the neutrons and protons. The mass of these particles, he said, would depend on the range over which the force operated. The shorter the range, the greater the mass would have to be. To function across the width of a nucleus, transported particles would have to be about 200 times the mass of an electron and about one-ninth the mass of a neutron or proton.

The short-range force that carried these particles came to be called, logically enough, the *strong* force. As for Yukawa's particle,

Triumph of the Chip
and the Digital Computer

In 1948 three researchers at Bell Laboratories in New Jersey made an amazing discovery. William Bradford Shockley, John Bardeen, and Walter Brattain found that they could use certain impure crystals to work the same way Thomas Alva Edison had used vacuum tubes: as electronic devices, or transistors, that control the flow of electrons. And so solid-state semiconductor electronics was born. The result has affected nearly every aspect of our lives, from the kitchen to automobiles to business, communication, and space exploration. Before long, radios were transformed from large pieces of furniture that people gathered around in their living rooms to a tiny packet and earphones that transmit a private world of music, talk shows, and news into the ears of joggers, shoppers, and skateboarders. Soon TVs got small enough to slip into a shirt pocket. But the influence on digital computing was phenomenal. In the late 1940s only giant institutions such as the U.S. Bureau of the Census, banks, and big corporations used these enormous, room-sized number-crunching devices. Digital computing had by this time found a place for itself in the handling of millions of transactions and records. But vacuum-tube computers used vast amounts of energy, required huge, air-conditioned rooms, and were notoriously unreliable—down more often than they were operational.

The reliable descendant of the transistor—the microchip—soon made computers both dramatically cheaper, incredibly smaller, and more dependable. Today, for under $800, people buy computers to set on a desk at home or in offices that have hundreds of times more memory and speed than the room-sized, multimillion-dollar computers of the 1940s. They're vastly more efficient and simpler to use, as well. The computers of the 1940s were hard-wired to perform specific functions only. Information was stored on big magnetic core devices and data was entered using cards that were tediously pre-punched by "keypunch machine" operators. By 2003 hard drives with storage capacity up to several billion bytes became common on desktop computers, or PCs, and literally millions of software programs made the PC nearly endlessly adaptable. Today few businesses—even small, family-owned shops or sole-proprietor contractors—get along without the use of at least one computer. Millions of households have them. And for scientists, the PC and also the more capacious and powerful mid-range and main-frame computers have become great assets in building theories and exploring possibilities through the use of computer modeling. By building a model, scientists can play out complicated "what-if" scenarios for everything from planetary formation to predictions about the movement of tectonic plates or the future course of our planet's greenhouse effect.

Computers received the greatest impact of solid-state electronics technology, but solid-state devices, or microprocessors, are everywhere—in cell phones and telephones, radios, TVs, microwave ovens, automobiles, videocassette recorders, audiocassette recorders, CD and DVD players and burners, programmable thermostats, and on and on. New gadgets, tools, and devices are added to the list every day.

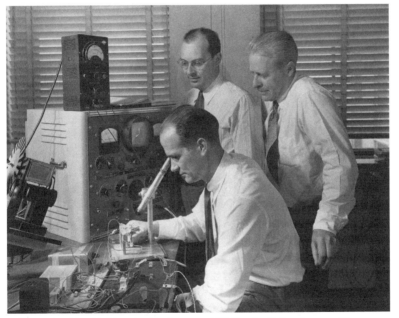

William Shockley (left), John Bardeen, and Walter Brattain, shown with equipment at Bell Laboratories, where they worked. For their discovery of the transistor effect (1948) and work on semiconductors, the three inventors shared the 1956 Nobel Prize in physics. *(Lucent Technologies' Bell Laboratories, courtesy AIP Emilio Segrè Visual Archives)*

for several years it was known as the Yukon in his honor, but the term *meson* is the one that stuck, referring to the fact that mesons, as understood at the time, had a mass intermediate between the proton's and the electron's. (More recently, it has become known as the "Yukawa particle.") The following year, using the very same equipment he had used to track the telltale path of the positron, Carl Anderson found evidence of what he thought was the meson. As it later turned out, Anderson's new particle was not a meson but another particle, called the *muon*, and Yukawa's meson was not actually confirmed until 1947, about where this book's tale begins.

By 1947 the list of ultimate building blocks of matter and radiation had expanded to include the electron and its reverse twin, the positron, along with the proton, the neutron, the muon, the pion, the neutrino, and the photon. As it turned out, these were not all as elementary as physicists thought at the time; before long, they would discover that protons, neutrons, and mesons all broke down into even smaller constituents. Yukawa had set physicists on a search for the small and fundamental that would expand the number of subatomic particles to the hundreds. Dalton would have been amazed to see his ultimate fundamental particle now.

And so began our entrance into the subatomic world—bizarre, absurd, and astounding. Before long, physicists had a new inventory of extraordinary names to describe the minuscule world of subatomic particles and the forces at work there. They began to talk of tiny particles with whimsical-sounding names such as Anderson's *muon*, joined by the *lepton, pion, gluon*, and, most fantastic of all, the *quark*—which they discussed in terms of *strangeness, charm, colors*, and *flavors*.

Quantum Joined to Maxwell's Theory

During World War II, between 1941 and 1945, the United States had gathered together at Los Alamos in north central New Mexico the most prodigious group of physicists ever gathered for a project. Their objective: to build an atomic—or, more accurately, a nuclear fission—bomb before physicists in Nazi Germany could do the same. The Manhattan Project, as it was called, succeeded, making its first test in July 1945. The U.S. government used its deadly products, however, not to defeat Germany, which had already surrendered two months earlier, but to end the war with Japan.

Out of the closely knit, highly focused teamwork that built the atomic bomb came a group of physicists that included both seasoned senior scientists (such as Enrico Fermi and Hans Bethe) and young, innovative minds (such as Richard Feynman).

Richard Feynman earned fame early as one of the rising stars who fought the good fight in what was informally known as the "War Against Infinities"—the struggle to find a theory that united quantum theory with James Clerk Maxwell's highly successful 19th-century electromagnetic field theory.

Paul Dirac (left) and Richard Feynman, deep in discussion at the 1963 International Conference on Relativistic Theories of Gravitation in Warsaw, Poland *(AIP Emilio Segrè Visual Archives, Physics Today Collection)*

By 1946 the two great revolutions of 20th-century physics—that is, quantum mechanics and relativity—had already produced a profound effect on our mental images of subatomic particles. Werner Heisenberg, with his "uncertainty principle," had established that an electron could not be thought of as having both a particular velocity and a location at exactly some point in space; instead we know only a probability of where it might be. Also, according to quantum rules, a phenomenon known as "virtual particles" can be created by borrowing the necessary energy—coming into existence for the barest sliver of a second and then, just as suddenly, disappearing. So there can be a real electron, whose exact position we can never know, surrounded by a swarm of transient virtual photons. The photons (messenger particles of light) let us know that the electron is there. They also ever-so-slightly modify its properties, and these modifications can be measured with careful, precise measurements and analyzed by patient, determined theoretical calculations. All of this enormously complicates the process of measuring the physical, observable electron in an experiment.

If you find this confusing, you have lots of very intelligent company. "[Electrons and light] behave in a way that is like nothing you have ever seen before," Richard Feynman would tell his students a few decades later. "Your experience with things that you have seen before is incomplete. The behavior of things on a very tiny scale is simply different." Simplifications and metaphors do not really work, Feynman added. Atoms are not really like solar systems or springs or clouds. Only one simplification really works, he said: "Electrons behave in this respect in exactly the same way as photons; they are both screwy, but in exactly the same way . . .

"I think I can safely say that nobody understands quantum mechanics. . . . I am going to tell you what nature behaves like. If you simply admit that maybe she does behave like this, you will find her a delightful, entrancing thing. Do not keep saying to yourself, if you can possibly avoid it, 'But how can it be like that?' because you will get 'down the drain,' into a blind alley from which nobody yet has escaped. Nobody knows how it can be like that."

And then Feynman would go on to show how the experiments, the calculations, all the evidence point to the fact that indeed this tiny world that works like nothing we know does in fact work like that. In fact, Feynman's work, quantum electrodynamics (known as QED for short), tied together in a theoretically tidy package all the phenomena at work in light, radio, magnetism, and electricity. At the same time, independently and separately, two other people were working on the same theories: New York–born Julian Seymour Schwinger and Japan's Shin'ichiro Tomonaga.

Schwinger (1918–94), a child prodigy, entered the City College of New York at the age of 14. By the age of 21 he had completed his Ph.D. at Columbia University and at 29 he was promoted to full professor at Harvard University. He was the youngest in the long history of the university to attain that rank. Tomonaga (1906–79), meanwhile, a classmate of Yukawa's at the University of Kyoto, had studied for a time with Heisenberg in Germany, returning to Japan to finish his doctorate in physics, which he received in 1939 from Tokyo Imperial University (later renamed Tokyo University). During World War II, cut off by the strife from American and European physicists, Tomonaga worked on what would eventually become QED while teaching at Tokyo University of Education, of which he became president after the war, in 1956.

In the late 1940s, though, some of the calculations for electrons, as they interacted with virtual particles popping in and out of existence, came up with a result of infinity for the mass of the electron—an obvious error that everyone recognized as absurd for this tiny particle. Feynman, Schwinger, and Tomonaga worked out the behavior of electrons mathematically with new theoretical insight and far greater precision than anyone had done before, and they overcame the error. Their calculations could explain the electromagnetic interactions of electrons, positrons, and photons with stunning accuracy. Could the same

Julian Seymour Schwinger (1918–94) independently worked on QED and shared the 1965 Nobel Prize in physics with Feynman and Tomonaga. *(AIP Emilio Segrè Visual Archives Physics Today Collection)*

Gesturing, Nobel laureate Shin'ichiro Tomonaga (1906–79) in 1948, about the time he was working independently on the theory that would later be called QED, for which he shared the 1965 Nobel with Feynman and Schwinger *(University of Tsukuba, Tomonaga Memorial Room, courtesy AIP Emilio Segrè Visual Archives)*

be done for neutrons and protons, held together in the nucleus by a powerful bond known as the strong force? Hopes were high.

Parade of Particles

The experiments designed to peel away the secrets of the nucleus did not go well. The nucleus and the strong force, it turned out, were much more complicated than anyone had imagined.

As early as 1941, Yukawa and the rest of the scientific community had realized that the meson found in 1936 by Carl Anderson was not the predicted carrier of the strong force. It was something else. Shortly before Japan attacked Pearl Harbor on December 7, 1941, Yukawa, in Kyoto, wrote dejectedly, "The mesotron theory [as he called it] is today at an impasse."

The war had slowed down both communication among scientists and research, although three Italian physicists managed to conduct an experiment secretly in a Roman cellar that proved that Anderson's mesons hardly interacted at all with the nuclei of atoms. When they finally were able to announce their results after the war in 1947, the search was on, again, for Yukawa's meson.

It did not take long. After the war, a British chemical company had begun producing photographic emulsions capable of revealing high-energy cosmic rays, and Cecil F. Powell in Bristol led a team that used these emulsions to trace the tracks of cosmic rays. Because cosmic rays are not visible to the human eye, Powell and his team needed a way to "see" the cosmic rays and what they were doing. A charged particle passing through the emulsion left a trail of ions that induced a series of black grains to form. From the number and density of the grains, Powell and his colleagues could deduce some of the particle's characteristics, such as mass and energy. Also, when they looked at the cosmic-ray particle tracks, they found evidence for some that did use the strong force in interacting with atomic nuclei. What is more, their weight was close to the mass predicted by Yukawa—a little heavier than Anderson's meson. Using the Greek letters *pi* and *mu* to distinguish the two middleweight particles, Powell called the new particle a pi-meson, which soon contracted to *pion*, and Anderson's meson he called a mu-meson, which became *muon*. The year was 1947, about the same time that Feynman and the rest were firming up QED to explain and predict electron behavior, and excitement began to build that perhaps a similar breakthrough was at hand for particles in the atomic nucleus.

Not everyone was ecstatic, though. Powell's discovery meant that Anderson's muon was "extra," apparently unnecessary, according to all current theories. As Columbia University physicist Isidor Rabi put it quizzically, "Who ordered that?"

Instead of clearing up, the story of the nucleus steadily became even more confusing. After the pion, physicists began to discover whole families of particles related to it, or related to the proton. Each new discovery of a particle brought with it a realization that the virtual cloud swarming about the nucleus must be even more complex than previously thought, and the mathematical equations describing the interactions began to become hopelessly complicated. In 1947 two scientists at the University of Manchester spotted a particle in their cloud chamber that they dubbed the K-meson, or

Richard Feynman's Legacy

When Richard Phillips Feynman (1918–88) formulated quantum electro-dynamics (QED) in 1948, he was still in his 20s. This work earned him a share (along with Shin'ichiro Tomonaga and Julian Seymour Schwinger) in the 1965 Nobel Prize in physics. Without question, he was one of the most brilliant, unconventional, and influential physicists of modern times. In general, scientists are cautious about using the word *genius,* but most will apply it to two 20th-century physicists: Albert Einstein and Richard Feynman.

Feynman always had an urge to know how things worked. As a boy he fixed radios, picked locks, learned to speak Portuguese, and deciphered Mayan hieroglyphics. In high school his teacher let him sit in the back and work problems in advanced calculus while the other kids worked conventional physics problems. He was smart. But he was also known for his non-stop bongo playing, and as an adult he once played an impromptu xylophone, made by filling water glasses, and kept up the music nonstop all evening to the great amazement of visiting Danish physicist Niels Bohr. As fellow physicist C. P. Snow described him, Feynman was "a little bizarre . . . a showman . . . rather as though Groucho Marx was suddenly standing in for a great scientist."

After completing studies at the Massachusetts Institute of Technology and Princeton University, he received his Ph.D. in 1942 (having published his dissertation on quantum mechanics). Feynman was immediately commandeered for the atomic bomb project, known by the code name Manhattan Project. He soon became a brash young group leader and gained exposure, at close hand, to some of the finest physicists in the world, including Enrico Fermi, Hans Bethe, Niels Bohr and his son Aage, and J. Robert Oppenheimer.

After the war, while teaching at Cornell University, he worked on QED. Considered to be one of the key architects of quantum theory, he invented a widely used method known as "Feynman diagrams," which gave physi-

kaon, related to the pion. (A cloud chamber is a device in which the paths of charged subatomic particles are made visible as trails of droplets in a supersaturated vapor.) Two years later Cecil Powell's team found tracks in their emulsions of a charged particle that broke down into three pions, and they called their new particle the tau-meson. Not until 1957 did anyone realize that the two were just difcists both a way of visualizing particles and their collisions and a way of talking about them in a common language. Many fellow physicists consider that at least three of Feynman's later achievements were also worthy of a Nobel: a theory of superfluidity (explaining the frictionless behavior of liquid helium); a theory of weak interactions; and a theory of partons (hypothetical subparticles, such as quarks, in hadrons) that helped produce the modern understanding of quarks. Like Einstein, he was always ready to accept the challenge of nature's next riddle.

Feynman's 1985 autobiography, *Surely You're Joking, Mr. Feynman*, was a surprise runaway best-seller. He began another, *What Do You Care What Other People Think?* but was unable to complete it before his death in 1988. However, the published chapters still provide a final glimpse inside a great and original mind.

Perhaps most important of all was Feynman's legacy as a superb lecturer and teacher—his unique approach to problem solving and life influenced many younger scientists at both Cornell and California Institute of Technology (Caltech), where he later taught, and his published lectures have become classics.

Richard Feynman (1918–88), teaching at Caltech (*AIP Emilio Segrè Visual Archives, Physics Today Collection*)

ferent states—positive and negative versions—of the same particle, which finally was called a kaon. In the early 1950s, cosmic ray physicists discovered yet another particle, apparently a neutral cousin of the positively charged proton, which they called a *lambda*.

In the midst of this chaos, a new and powerful tool was about to make its mark. So far, most of the discoveries had been made by cosmic ray physicists tracing particle tracks in their cloud chambers. But to answer the questions now being raised, particle physicists needed more detailed data than the cloud chambers alone could produce. That's where particle accelerators came in. These powerful machines could deliver uniform, controlled beams of high-energy particles—electrons, for example, or protons or pions. By tracing the results when they smashed into each other, they could find out an

Lasers: Quantum Physics at Work

One of the stunning outgrowths of quantum mechanics are lasers, which have only been around in a workable form since Theodore Harold Maiman developed the first laser in 1960. A *laser* (the word stands for *L*ight *A*mplification by *S*timulated *E*mission of *R*adiation) produces a narrow, accurate beam of very bright light—different from ordinary light because it is coherent. That is, all rays of a laser have exactly the same wave length and their waves are perfectly in phase and parallel. Or, put another way, in a laser, the quanta (packets of which the light is composed) are organized end to end, stuck together, in a way, producing a continuous wave. That's why, vibrating together, they produce light of very high intensity.

Laser beams can be either visible light or infrared rays, which are invisible, and both have numerous uses in communications, engineering, science, and medicine. Visible light lasers are used, for example, in recording, CD-ROM players, and fiber-optic communications, while an infrared laser can cut through substances ranging from metal to human tissue with extremely fine accuracy.

A laser beam is produced by exciting atoms in a medium that can absorb and release energy. A surprising variety of substances will work as a medium: a solid crystal such as a ruby, certain liquid dyes, or a gas such as carbon dioxide.

Energy is introduced to excite, or pump, the atoms of the medium, raising them to a high-energy state. For example, electrons from an electric current introduced into a gas medium excite the atoms of gas. Finally, one or more atoms reach a higher energy and release a light ray (or photon). The light ray strikes another atom, which reaches a new level of energy, and it, in turn, emits a light ray, and so on as the light builds up. (This process is known as stimulated emission.) Mirrors—one fully reflective and the other only partially reflective—reflect the light rays back and enormous amount of accurate detail about a particle's properties. In fact, physicists can do two basic types of experiments using an accelerator and a particle detector: scattering experiments and particle-producing experiments.

In scattering, experimenters look for clues about the nucleus by tracking how particles scatter: how many, in what directions, and at what angles. The higher the energy from the accelerator, the better

forth (in the part of the process known as amplification), so that more and more atoms release light.

Each new ray emitted by an atom vibrates in step with the ray that struck the atom. With all the beams in step, the light escapes the tube through the partially silvered mirror, and the energy is released as laser light.

fully reflective mirror

partially reflective mirror

1 Electrons at ground level absorb the pump light.

2 Excited elctrons emit photons in random directions.

3 In-line collisions of photons with other excited electrons start a wave front between mirrors.

4 Back-and-forth reflections between the mirrors build the wave front until it bursts through the less efficient mirror.

How the laser beam is built up within the laser cavity

the structure comes into focus. Using this technique enabled scientists to find out about the composition of nuclei—how the protons and neutrons were arranged and how they jostled within the nucleus to maintain their arrangement. With still higher energy, experimenters could probe even deeper to see how the parts of the protons and neutrons fit together.

The second use of particle accelerators and detectors—the discovery of new particles—proved effective immediately. By 1949 scientists in Berkeley, California, isolated the neutral pion using the big synchro-cyclotron built there under the direction of Ernest O. Lawrence. It was the first new particle to be found at an accelerator instead of in cosmic-ray experiments.

In the fall of 1955, researchers Emilio Segrè and Owen Chamberlain succeeded in spotting the negatively charged antiproton, the proton's antimatter twin. It had been almost 25 years since Carl Anderson had found the electron's twin, the positron, on August 2, 1932. Protons were accelerated at the University of California at Berkeley in the newly built Bevatron and were hurtled at a copper target at an energy of 6 billion electron volts. (This is the minimum level required to coax an antiproton into appearing from a flash of energy.)

In the 1950s and 1960s, a huge swell of new subatomic particles flooded the scientific journals from the accelerators at Berkeley, Brookhaven (on Long Island, New York), Stanford, Fermilab (near Chicago), and CERN (in Geneva). The more particles that physicists found, the more undiscovered particles they found evidence for, and often the particle around the next corner promised to be heavier and more resistant to discovery.

The higher the energy of the accelerator, the more likely the physicists could break the next particle loose, as they moved deeper and deeper into the structure of the nucleus. Lawrence's 1949 synchro-cyclotron wielded a stream of particles at 100 MeV. (*MeV* means "million electron volts," usually pronounced emmeevees. An electron volt is a measure of the amount of energy required to move an electron across a potential difference of one volt.) By the 1990s the Tevatron at Fermilab could bump its energy up to one TeV (a trillion electron volts).

Experimenters also developed a vast supply of variations to get at particular pieces of information—different kinds of detectors,

Emilio Segrè *(Photo by Clyde Wiegand, courtesy AIP Emilio Segrè Visual Archives)*

different kinds and energies of "bullets," to find out a particle's life-time, decay modes, and so on. (All the new particles were very unstable and broke down quickly into other particles.) The data were overwhelming.

Particle physics seemed to be headed for total disorder and confusion.

The Structure of the Nucleus

Meanwhile, two physicists were looking at the atomic nucleus in a different way. One was Maria Goeppert-Mayer (1906–72), who was born in Poland and studied physics in Germany at the University of Göttingen. At a time when women in Germany were not encour-aged to pursue higher education, Goeppert's father, who was a sixth-generation academic, was highly supportive of her career. She completed her doctorate there in 1930, the same year she mar-ried Joe Mayer, an American physicist who was studying in Ger-many on a fellowship. Shortly after their marriage, the Mayers moved to the United States, where Joe Mayer had an offer at Johns Hopkins University. The timing was not good for finding work in the United States, though—in the early years of the Great Depres-

Superconductors

In 1911 a Dutch physicist named Heike Kamerlingh discovered that when mercury is cooled to very low temperatures—close to absolute zero (−273.15°C, −459.67°F, or 0 K)—electrical resistance vanishes. He had discovered a strange phenomenon that became known as superconductivity—one of the most important breakthroughs in modern experimental physics.

Not until 1957, though, did anyone come up with a theory explaining why this works. Three U.S. physicists, John Bardeen, Leon N. Cooper, and John Robert Schrieffer, proposed what is known as the BCS theory (named after them, using their last-name initials). This theory states that the superconducting current is carried by electrons linked together through lattice vibrations that cannot dissipate energy through scattering, the usual cause of electrical resistance in conductors.

Practically speaking, though, superconductivity did not have much use at first, since the temperatures at which this phenomenon went into effect for various substances, known as the "critical temperature," were all extremely low and difficult to achieve. Superconductors were put to use in large, powerful magnets in particle accelerators and magnetic-resonance imaging (MRI) machines used in medicine. However, the cost and inconvenience are high because the superconductors have to be cooled with liquid helium.

Then in 1986 and 1987, two researchers at IBM, K. Alex Muller and Georg Bednorz, reported the development of materials that become superconducting at substantially higher temperatures than liquid helium, which boils at 4.2 K (−268.95°C or −452.07°F). These new materials, which are ceramics, have a critical temperature between 90° and 120°K, another big breakthrough, since these temperatures are above the boiling point of liquid nitrogen—much cheaper and easier to maintain than liquid helium. These high-temperature superconductors lose their superconductive properties, though, at high current levels, a problem that has hampered their use in commercial applications.

sion—and Goeppert-Mayer's field, quantum physics, was still quite unusual in the United States. College rules against nepotism were also applied against her, possibly as a cover for bias. She was unable to obtain a salaried position on a university faculty. Instead, she obtained a position as "Volunteer Associate" at Johns Hopkins University, a sort of research assistanceship, on a meager salary. Later she taught, unsalaried, at several universities, including Columbia University, Sarah Lawrence College, the University of Chicago, and the Enrico Fermi Institute for Nuclear Studies. She also served as a research sci-

Maria Goeppert-Mayer was the first American woman (and the second woman ever) to win the Nobel Prize in physics. *(AIP Emilio Segrè Visual Archives, Physics Today Collection)*

entist on the Manhattan Project, working with Edward Teller, and at the Argonne National Laboratory, as a senior physicist. These were the years when Jewish scientists were fleeing the loss of civil rights and the terrors of the Holocaust in Germany and fascist Italy, and many had come to the United States. As a result, young scientists like Maria Goeppert-Mayer and Richard Feynman gained exposure to some of the finest scientific minds in their field, especially in New York and Chicago. So Goeppert-Mayer was surrounded by a steady flow of fertile ideas, a perfect environment for a theorist.

Working as a half-time research scientist at the Argonne National Laboratory just outside Chicago, Goeppert-Mayer began investigating the nucleus of the atom and the structure of stable isotopes—those that do not break down through radioactive decay. She had access to empirical data from the cyclotron at Argonne through her connections with experimental physicists at the University of Chicago. She collected and analyzed statistics and concluded that certain numbers of protons or neutrons seemed to be consistent in stable isotopes, notably, 2, 8, 20, 28, 50, 82, and 126.

Tools of Science: The Particle Accelerator

1929

▶ British physicists John Cockcroft and Ernest Walton invent the first particle accelerator, a simple machine that enables them to bombard lithium and produce alpha particles (helium nuclei), artificially transforming lithium into helium. They are able to confirm the production of helium nuclei by observing their tracks in a cloud chamber.

1930

▶ Ernest O. Lawrence at the University of California at Berkeley comes up with his idea for the cyclotron, which can accelerate protons or alpha particles in spiral paths between two circular poles of a large electromagnet. The first cyclotron is very small, able to fit in the palm of his hand. The spiral path makes powerful acceleration possible without high voltage or a super-long, straight path. Larger and larger versions follow throughout the 1930s at Berkeley's Radiation Laboratory (now known as the Lawrence Berkeley Laboratory). By 1939 they have a 60-inch-diameter cyclotron that can boost particles up to 10 MeV. Soon Lawrence begins planning a 184-inch cyclotron capable of reaching 100 MeV, an unheard-of energy, and a new "synchro-cyclotron" version follows, capable of hundreds of MeV.

1946

▶ The first synchrocyclotron is built at Berkeley, California.

1952

▶ A consortium of eastern universities builds the first "synchrotron," the Brookhaven National Laboratory's "Cosmotron," on Long Island, New York. The big machine is capable of delivering more than 1 billion electron volts (1,000 MeV or 1 GeV, for giga electron volts, meaning a billion), later as much as three billion. Instead of having huge fixed magnets through which particles are made to orbit, the synchrotron's magnets are smaller and moveable—synchronized to move into position as the particles' orbits intersect them. This means that, while cyclotrons are limited by the size of magnets we can manufacture, the size of the synchrotron is only limited by the consortium's finances and the size of the land parcel it is built on.

1954

▸ The Conseil Européen pour la Recherche Nucléaire (CERN), now called the European Organization for Nuclear Research but still commonly known as CERN, is founded in Geneva, Switzerland.

1959

▸ CERN begins operation of its 25-GeV accelerator.

1965

▸ The SLAC (Stanford Linear Accelerator Center) particle accelerator goes into operation in California.

1969

▸ Robert Wilson founds the Fermi National Accelerator Laboratory, soon known as Fermilab, in Batavia, Illinois, near Chicago.

1972

▸ The large accelerator at Fermilab begins operations at 200 GeV (giga electron volts, or 200 billion electron volts). Later that year it reaches 400 GeV.
▸ The Stanford Positron Electron Accelerating Ring (SPEAR) is completed at SLAC.

1976

▸ CERN begins operation of the Super Proton Synchrotron (SPS), a four-mile ring originally delivering protons at 300 GeV, eventually reaching 450 GeV.

1977

▸ A team at Fermilab finds the bottom quark.

1983

▸ A team headed by Carlo Rubbia at CERN discovers the charged W particles and the neutral Z particle predicted by the electroweak theory.

1984

▸ The particle accelerator at Fermilab reaches 800 GeV.

(continues)

(continued)

1985

▶ The 900-GeV Tevatron particle accelerator at Fermilab begins operation; later it is boosted to 1 TeV (1 trillion electron volts).

1992

▶ CERN releases its hypertext system for physics, and the World Wide Web is born.

1994

▶ A team of Fermilab finds the top quark.

2000

▶ CERN shuts down its successful Large Electron Positron Collider (LEP) to make way for building the more powerful Large Hadron Collider (LHC).

2006

▶ CERN LHC to begin operation.

She called these the "magic numbers." After further investigation, she published the hypothesis that particles in atomic nuclei orbit in shells, or layers, much as electrons seem to do—"like the delicate shells of an onion with nothing in the center."

A conversation with Enrico Fermi set her to thinking about spin-orbit coupling, and she intuitively saw the relationship between her "magic numbers" and the structure of the nucleus. Spin-orbit coupling refers to protons and neutrons spinning on their axes, either counterclockwise or clockwise, while orbiting. One or the other of the spin directions takes very slightly less energy, and this difference accounted for the magic numbers. She concluded that the nucleus of an atom is composed of layers of proton-neutron shells maintained in place by complex forces. Goeppert-Mayer published two papers on her theory in 1950 and later that year she visited with Hans Jensen (1907–73), the other physicist who simultaneously had developed a shell theory for the nuclear structure. They decided to collaborate on a book detailing the structure of the atomic nucleus.

In 1960 Goeppert-Mayer became full professor of physics at the University of California, San Diego. In 1963 Hans Jensen and Maria Goeppert-Mayer shared (with Eugene Wigner) the Nobel Prize in physics. It was a high point, but she said, "If you love science, all you really want is to keep on working. The Nobel Prize thrills you, but it changes nothing."

2
The Realm of Quarks

PATHWAYS THROUGH THE CHAOTIC subatomic particle jungle have not been easy to find. But to one multitalented physicist goes much of the credit for blazing those pathways—ingeniously sensing the topography and insightfully mapping it out, while marking the complicated trail with whimsical names and literary allusions.

Murray Gell-Mann, whose father had left Austria to settle in New York, was born in New York City in 1929. He entered Yale University on his 15th birthday, and that alone reveals much. At age 21, he earned a Ph.D. from Massachusetts Institute of Technology (MIT). After further studies under Enrico Fermi in Chicago, Gell-Mann attained the rank of full professor at Caltech by the time he was 27. Having a razor-sharp intellect, highly eclectic interests, and a gift for languages (fluent in many, including Swahili), he has been known to savor reminding his more "ordinary" colleagues of the "IQ gap."

By the time of his arrival at Caltech, Gell-Mann had already plunged deep into the jungle of particle physics. In addition to Chadwick's neutron, Dirac's positron, and Pauli's neutrino, Yukawa had postulated the meson—of which too many had turned up: not only Anderson's mu-meson, later renamed "muon" because it turned out not to be a meson, but Powell's pi-meson (pion), which was Yukawa's carrier of the strong force. By the 1950s there were also K-mesons, heavier yet, which had about half the mass of a proton. Before long, particles even heavier than protons—called hyperons—began to turn up.

The K-mesons, or kaons, and hyperons especially intrigued Gell-Mann in the early 1950s. These particles, he reasoned, were created

Murray Gell-Mann, November 1969 *(AIP Emilio Segrè Visual Archives, Physics Today Collection)*

by strong interactions and should, by rights, also be broken down by them. But they were not. Instead they were broken down by the weak interactions (the interactions of which radioactive emissions are the evidence).

When Marie and Pierre Curie began studying radioactivity back in the 1890s, they meticulously measured the results of the mysterious "beta ray" emission (release of electrons from the nucleus) that few people—aside from colleagues such as Henri Becquerel—had ever even heard of. By the 1950s, though, a great deal was known about radioactivity and the weak interaction that governed it. Measured at about 1,000 times weaker than the well-known electromagnetic interaction, and weaker yet than the strong interaction that holds nuclear particles together, the weak interaction had become a reasonably well understood phenomenon—or at least most physicists thought so.

Well understood, that is, except for the fact that, by all rights, the definitely weaker and ever-so-slightly slower weak interaction should not prevail over the faster strong interaction. Kaons should have decayed via the strong interaction, according to what was known, but they did not. They only decayed via the weak interaction. These facts seemed really strange to particle physicists. And, as a result, they started calling kaons and hyperons "strange particles."

Looking at Strangeness

So in the early 1950s Gell-Mann became immersed in questions of strangeness. At the same time, Japanese physicists T. Nakano and Kasuhiko Nishijima were working along the same lines independently and came to similar conclusions. In exploring subparticles, Gell-Mann began thinking in terms of groups, instead of thinking of them individually. If you looked at the characteristics of protons and neutrons, for example, they were strikingly similar in every way—except that one group was positively charged and the other was neutral. Gell-Mann found that, if you ignored the charge of the subparticles, most subparticles in the nucleus seemed to fall into groups of two or three.

So Gell-Mann divided the known particles into groups based on all characteristics except charge. Then, based on the total charge of all members of each group, he assigned each group a charge center. The neutron-proton group, for example, had a charge center of $+1/2$ (since the group's total charge was $+1$ and there were 2 members). But for kaons and hyperons, strangely, the charge center was not really in the middle the way it was in other groups—it was off-center. Gell-Mann found that he could measure just how much off-center they were, and he assigned a number to the degree they were off-center—a number he called their "strangeness number." The strangeness number for protons and neutrons was 0, since they are not off-center at all. But he found that some particles had a strangeness number of $+1$, -1, or even -2.

What's more, Gell-Mann noticed a pattern in all particle interactions: The total strangeness number of all particles involved in any interaction is always conserved; that is, it's the same before and after the interaction. Physicists liked this because it illustrated that a kind of symmetry was at work (which nature often displays—so these results seemed plausible). The conservation of the strangeness number in interactions could also be described in quantitative terms (which physicists always like—as quantitative terms are more readily verified than subjective observations). Also, Gell-Mann's observation could be used to explain the unexpectedly long life of the strange particles. Both Gell-Mann and the Nakano-Nishijima team published their ideas along these lines in 1953.

Some mysteries about the weak interaction remained unexplained, though—mysteries that came up one afternoon in 1956 over lunch as Chen Ning (Frank) Yang and Tsung Dao Lee chatted at the White Rose Café in New York City. As these two longtime friends and colleagues talked, they began to have a sneaking suspicion about the weak force that no one had ever thought of before.

A Left-Handed World

Frank Yang, who was born in Hofei, China, in 1922, had traveled to the United States at the age of 23 to study with Enrico Fermi. But he arrived at New York's Columbia University only to find that Fermi had left for the University of Chicago. Unflappable, Yang set off for

Tsung Dao Lee (left) and Chen Ning (Frank) Yang *(Alan W. Richards, Courtesy AIP Emilio Segrè Visual Archives)*

Chicago, where he did study under Fermi, earning his Ph.D. in 1948. That's also where he met up with Tsung Dao Lee, whom he had first encountered in China. By 1956 Yang had already established his reputation when, in 1954 with Robert Mills, he helped set the stage for quantum field theory with the establishment of what are sometimes called Yang-Mills gauge invariant fields.

Tsung Dao Lee was born in Shanghai in 1926 and had traveled to the United States in 1946 to study in a graduate program—even though he had not yet completed an undergraduate degree. The University of Chicago was the only school that would let him enroll; the university's acceptance was lucky for Lee, since some of the best minds in physics were there at the time. He was well prepared to take advantage of that fact and obtained his Ph.D. in 1950, working under hydrogen bomb architect Edward Teller.

Lee and Yang crossed paths again for a time at the Institute for Advanced Study in Princeton, New Jersey, where Yang stayed to become professor of physics in 1955, while Lee accepted a position at Columbia University in 1953. For New Jerseyites, New York is always just a train ride away, and the two generally got together once a week to compare notes.

The topic of conversation on that particular afternoon at the White Rose Café was the "strange particles" called K-mesons, which seemed to break down in two different ways—one, a sort of right-handed way, and the other, a sort of left-handed way.

This ordinarily should not happen—and it did not happen with other particles. The way that the K-mesons broke down seemed to defy an important principle of physics: the law of conservation of parity. Like the laws of conservation of energy and conservation of matter, conservation of parity was a guiding principle that always before had seemed to predict nature consistently.

Imagine yourself standing in front of a mirror. What in reality is on your right is mirrored on your left, and your left side appears to be on the right side of the mirrored image. If your hair is parted on the right, in the mirror it appears to be parted on your left. Now imagine reversing the rest of the image, top to bottom and front to back. The law of conservation of parity says that if you take a system and switch everything around in this way, the system will still exhibit exactly the same behavior.

Parity has two possible values: odd and even. The law of conservation of parity says that if you start out with odd parity before a reaction or change, you should end up with odd parity afterward. That is, when particles interact to form new particles, the parity should come out the same on both sides of the equation.

The problem with the K-mesons was that when they broke down, sometimes they broke down into two pi-mesons, both with odd parity (which combined to give even parity). Other times they broke down into three pi-mesons (which combined to give odd parity). It was as if you looked in the mirror and sometimes your right hand was reflected on your right and sometimes on your left. The two sides of the equation were supposed to mirror each other perfectly, but they did not always. Physicists tried to fix this by saying that there were two different types of kaons, one with odd parity and the other with even parity. But Yang and Lee thought that might not be the right solution. These mesons were exactly the same in every other way. Maybe there was something else at play.

Was it possible, Lee and Yang asked each other, that conservation of parity did not apply to these "strange particles"? Maybe there actually was just one K-meson, not two. Maybe the reason conservation of parity appeared to be broken was that the principle did not apply to the weak interaction. They realized that no one had ever checked out this possibility, and they began to think about the kinds of situations that might test the premise. So began what became known as "the downfall of parity"—not a total demise, but a downfall with respect to one area, the realm of the weak interaction.

Lee and Yang began sketching out a paper, which they shortly published, on "The Question of Parity Conservation in the Weak Force." In it they reviewed a number of reactions and examined the experimental implications of the possibility that parity (that is, mirror symmetry) was not respected by the weak force. How could you test this idea? They thought if you could examine the directions in which an emerging electron is ejected from a spinning nucleus in beta decay (the realm of the weak interaction), and could see, for example, that the electron favored one direction over the other, then that would be a tip-off.

The original idea—the theory—had sprung from the minds of Lee and Yang in collaboration. But a theory is only worth something in science if it stands up to experiment. If it does, it may open up a large new area of research, generating new and provocative questions and putting to bed many old ones.

Chien-shiung Wu (1912–97), whose experiments showed that Lee and Yang's ideas about the conservation of parity were right *(Columbia University)*

Immediately, Chien-shiung Wu, the experimental counterpoint to Lee and Yang, swung into action. Professor of physics at Columbia and a colleague of Lee's, Wu was a well-respected, iron-willed experimentalist, whose specialty was radioactive decay. Known for being tough on her students and demanding, she was equally demanding of her own work and exceedingly energetic. In this case, Wu—or Madame Wu, as she was almost universally known (even though Wu was her own name; her husband's name was Yuan)— ran experiments that were timely, intricate, and clean. Wu decided to use cobalt 60, which decays into a nickel nucleus, a neutrino, and a positron. What Wu wanted to "watch" with her apparatus was the spin of the positron as it sped away from the nucleus—but she had to make sure that the nuclei of her cobalt 60 samples were all spinning in the same direction so that the spin of the nuclei would not affect the spin of the emitted particles. To do this, Wu planned a complicated experiment that involved using cryogenics at the U.S. Bureau of Standards in Washington, D.C., to drop the cobalt to a very low temperature, just above absolute zero.

By early 1957 she had begun to get stunning results. "Wu telephoned," T. D. Lee told his colleagues over the first weekly departmental lunch of the new year, "and said her preliminary data indicated a huge effect!" Before long, Wu's results were in. Parity did not hold for the weak force. And by the end of the year, Lee and Yang had won the Nobel Prize for their insights.

Many physicists were not happy, however. The subatomic world, unlike the disorderly everyday world, had always seemed to have a wonderful elegance, a predictability—a symmetry—about it. Now symmetry seemed to be a sometime thing.

"I cannot believe God is a weak left-hander," Wolfgang Pauli quipped in disgruntlement. (Not that he thought being left-handed was undesirable—just that he had always seen nature as even-handed.) Pauli had voiced an unease that many other physicists also felt. Many began to wonder about the consistency of other laws of conservation. If parity is not consistent, then maybe the other conservation laws are not always consistent. Maybe symmetry cannot be counted on as a principle anywhere. Lee, Wang, and Wu had raised many questions. But for scientists, who thrive on trying to find answers to unanswered questions, it's the sign of good science not only to answer questions and make the pieces fit, but to raise new ones.

The Corker: The Quark

Meanwhile, in California, Murray Gell-Mann had been busy as well. A great theorist has a special talent for synthesizing and spotting patterns amid confusion, and this is exactly what Gell-Mann did. Several things needed to be sorted out and explained, including the mind-boggling number of particles (why so many?) and the apparent groupings into families (what mechanism or principle caused them?).

Building in part on the work of Yang, Lee, and Wu, Gell-Mann came up with some ideas, a system of classification, which he published in a long series of papers in the early 1960s. He called his system the "Eightfold Way," a term he borrowed from an aphorism attributed to Buddha in Chinese literature. (Not, as some enthusiasts have thought, that Gell-Mann meant to imply that physics had become mystical or even philosophical—he just needed a name for a concept that was so new to the world of language that its very name must be invented. Most of the letters of the Greek alphabet were already taken up with the task of naming particles. So he borrowed from one of his many interests.)

Gell-Mann's line of reasoning went like this: As he had already noted, many subatomic particles—including mesons, protons, and neutrons—occurred in families, groups of two or three. There were three pions (pi-mesons), two pairs of kaons, a pair of protons (proton and antiproton), and so on. These were very close-knit families, with strong resemblances. In fact, the members of a family were more alike than they were different. The only differences in each case were charge and mass. And the difference in mass was so small (a few MeVs) that they could be caused simply by the difference in charge. In other words, these particles were in all likelihood identical, since the difference in mass could be caused by the differences in charge alone. So, said Gell-Mann, what if you thought of each of these families as a single particle with another characteristic—"multiplicity"? It was a new and productive way of looking at the variety of particles to be found in an atomic nucleus.

Secondly, he noticed that the strong force pays no attention at all to electric charge. It has equal effect whether a particle is neutral, negative, or positive. A proton is held as strongly as an antiproton. The strong force makes no distinction among the neutral pion, its positive sister, or its negative brother. They are like three sides of an equilateral triangle.

Gell-Mann thought there was a connection between the strangeness found in the strange particles and their multiplicity. Unlike pions, which come in triplets, the strange kaons seemed to come in sets of two pairs. He was sure that some deeper symmetry, not yet discerned, was at play here; these were not just coincidences.

At the time, in late 1960, mathematicians had recently rediscovered the work of a Norwegian mathematician named Marius Sophus Lie, who had explored some areas of an abstract formalism called "group theory." Gell-Mann recognized a particular Lie group—SU(3), or Special Unitary group in 3 dimensions—that seemed to work for both mesons and baryons. (This same stroke of insight, by the way, came to Yuval Ne'eman at the Imperial College in London at about the same time.) Using the group as a sort of template, Gell-Mann arranged the mesons and baryons according to their charge and strangeness. But, while there were eight baryons, which fit perfectly into the pattern, there were only seven mesons.

So, based on the characteristics that an eighth meson should have if it fit the pattern, Gell-Mann predicted its existence, in much the same way that Dmitry Mendeleyev predicted the existence of several as-yet undiscovered elements when he drew up the periodic table of the elements in 1869. In particular, Gell-Mann predicted a particle he called an "omega-minus" particle, and he was right. Just such a particle was found in 1964—and observed again many thousands of times thereafter. Its antiparticle, anti-omega-minus, or "omega-plus," turned up in 1971.

So, the Eightfold Way was born, and order, or at least greater order than before, was brought to the particle jungle.

But Gell-Mann had more up his sleeve. Even with the new order of the Eightfold Way, he thought there must be something more, some deeper and simpler order. There must be some particle more fundamental than anyone had recognized before. What physicists were doing, Gell-Mann recognized, was like looking at molecules of a substance and trying to understand their complexities without realizing they were composed of atoms (which is exactly what chemists did for centuries before Dalton). Baryons (neutrons and protons) were composed of something smaller—but what?

The answer began to emerge over lunch on Monday, March 25, 1963, at the Columbia University Faculty Club in New York City. (Physicists seem to do a lot of thinking while they eat!) Gell-Mann was visiting Columbia to give a series of well-attended lectures on the Eightfold Way and other issues, and some of the theorists of the host university, including Robert Serber, took him to lunch. Serber was a quiet man who had been at Berkeley with Robert Oppenheimer and had worked with him at Los Alamos. Generally, he preferred to work in the background, but on this day he had a question: What about a fundamental threefold group of particles, a triplet?

"That would be a funny quirk!" Gell-Mann replied off-handedly. "A terrible idea," added T. D. Lee, who was also there. Then Gell-Mann began scribbling on a napkin: For a triplet to work, the particles would have to have fractional charges, a phenomenon never observed in nature and practically unimaginable. The particles would have to be +2/3, –1/3, –1/3.

But later he began to think more about it. As long as a particle did not appear in nature with its fractional charge, maybe the idea was not so outlandish. If a truly fundamental nuclear particle, a fundamental hadron, were unobservable, incapable of coming out of the baryons and mesons to be seen individually, if it were forever trapped within the physical protons, neutrons, pions, and so on that physicists had found in nature, then maybe it would work. He mentioned the idea in his next lecture. Back at Caltech, he worked further on the idea, and he mentioned it on the phone while talking to his former thesis adviser, Victor Weisskopf, who was then director at CERN, the particle accelerator in Geneva, Switzerland. Maybe baryons and mesons were made up of fractionally charged particles, Gell-Mann suggested. Weisskopf was not impressed. "Please, Murray, let's be serious," came his immediate reply. "This is an international call."

But Gell-Mann was serious. In 1964 he proposed the existence of an outlandish group of particles that carried fractional electric charges. Once again showing his flare for eccentric names, he named them *quarks,* based on a phrase from *Finnegans Wake* by James Joyce: "Three quarks for Muster Mark!" The one with a 2/3 positive charge he called an *up* quark. The other two he dubbed *down* and *strange.* A proton is composed of two up quarks and one down quark, having a total charge of +1. A neutron is composed of two down quarks and one up quark, resulting in a neutral charge. In the last sentence of his two-page article introducing the idea, he thanked Robert Serber for stimulating these ideas.

At the same time that Gell-Mann came out with his quarks, a young physicist named George Zweig was also working along similar lines. Zweig was an experimental physicist, working at CERN at the time, and he thought of these particles, which he called *aces,* as real, concrete particles, not abstract constructs, as Gell-Mann had. Because Zweig was younger and less well known, he did not succeed in getting his revolutionary idea published (even Gell-Mann had chosen to submit to a lesser-known journal to avoid being turned down). But once word got around that Zweig had written an in-house paper at CERN on the subject, Gell-Mann always made sure Zweig got credit, although he teased Zweig about his "concrete block model."

Eventually, physicists came to the conclusion that, if there was a strange quark, as Gell-Mann had suggested, it must be one of a pair. So they began looking for what they called a "charmed quark," the companion to the strange quark. Amazingly enough, evidence for this idea came from not one, but two investigators at separate institutions: Samuel Chao Chung Ting at Brookhaven National Laboratory and Burton C. Richter at SLAC. Considering the fact that particle experiments usually require months, sometimes years, of planning and require the involvement of large numbers of scientists to carry them out, the possibility of two major facilities working on the same project without either one knowing about the other is very low. Yet, on the very day in November 1974 that Ting turned up at SLAC, planning to announce the birth of what he called the J particle, Richter announced that he and his team had found what he called a psi meson. Ting was astounded and, of course, not at all happy. They compared notes and found that the two teams, completely independently, had discovered the same particle, which they ended up calling the J/psi meson. Before long, investigators realized that, because of the properties possessed by the J/psi meson, it could not exist without the existence of the charmed quark. So Ting and Richter, independently, had not only found a new particle, they had also found evidence for the existence of a quark with charm. The Nobel Prize in physics in 1976 was awarded to both Ting and Richter for their discoveries.

Flavor and Color

While Gell-Mann had sought to bring order to the chaotic jungle of subatomic particles, though, the number of new particles continued to increase. But they also continued to fit into the basic structure he had outlined.

A new view of the truly fundamental, structureless, unsplittable particle emerged: There were basic kinds, quarks and leptons. However, there were three types (known as "flavors") of each. (The name *flavors*, of course, is another example of physicists' sense of humor and has nothing to do with taste.)

The three flavors of leptons were electrons (which scientists had known about for a while), muons (or mu-mesons), and tauons (or tau-mesons). Each flavor of lepton has four members; for example, the electron, the neutrino, the antielectron, and the antineutrino.

Quarks were a little more complicated. Pairs of quarks came to be thought of as "flavors"—a concept that parallels flavors of leptons. So each flavor of quark has four members. For example, the up/down flavor includes the up quark, the down quark, the anti-up quark, and the anti-down quark. If you think of the pairs of quarks as parallel to each of the three flavors of leptons, then the three flavors of quarks are the up/down quarks, strange/charmed quarks, and, to fill out the scheme, a new pair: top/bottom quarks.

One of the key differences between leptons and quarks is that quarks feel the strong force and leptons do not. Also, leptons have integral (whole number) charges or none at all and do not combine. Quarks have fractional charges and apparently exist only in combination.

Now there was still one more big question about quarks in the 1970s. If quarks could never be found separate from the tight combinations they form, then what was binding them so tightly?

One powerful idea that virtually all physicists subscribe to is that each different flavor of quark comes in three varieties of a property that leptons do not possess. This property is called "color" (named by Gell-Mann), and the three varieties are called red, blue, and green. These names are merely figurative; quarks do not literally have color as we know it.

But when quarks combine in groups of three, they always combine one each: red, blue, and green. It's just a way to talk in threes. The red, blue, and green cancel each other out to produce colorlessness (as the three primary colors do on a color wheel when you spin it).

Of course, quarks also combine in pairs to form mesons, and in that case, for example, a red quark will combine with an anti-red quark. The red and anti-red cancel each other out, and you get a colorless result.

So color succeeded in explaining how quarks could sometimes combine in twos, to form mesons, and in threes, to form baryons. The study of this process—the way quarks combine in colors to produce colorlessness—is known as quantum chromodynamics (QCD). (*Chromo* comes from the Greek word meaning "color.") The QCD theory shows that color neutrality can be achieved by various combinations of quarks and antiquarks.

But how is color transported? What are the messenger particles that play the same part for the color force that photons play for the electromagnetic force? Physicists came up with a particle called *gluons* ("glue-ons"), which carry two versions of color: a color (red, green, or blue) and its anticolor. When these gluons are emitted or absorbed by quarks, they change the quark color. The constant shifting back and forth of these gluons serves to hold (or "glue") quarks together with powerful force—made all the more powerful by the fact that as quarks move away from each other, the force *increases,* decreasing when they come close together (exactly the opposite of the electromagnetic force). Try placing your fingers inside a rubber band. As you pull your fingers apart, the force between your fingers increases. The lines of color force act like the strands of rubber in a rubber band. As you move your fingers back together, the tension decreases—and it's the same way with the strong nuclear force carried by gluons.

This complicated model of the atom—its many parts and how they are held together as described (very briefly) in the last two chapters—has become widely accepted among physicists. In addition to all the particles—hadrons and leptons and their subcategories—four forces come into play in the atom: the strong force (which holds the nucleus together), the weak force (the force behind radioactivity), the electromagnetic force (which governs electric charge), and gravity (which operates only at long distances and has negligible effect on the interior of the atom).

Within the atom, messenger particles operate to convey the strong, weak, and electromagnetic force. More recently, physicists have come to call these messengers "elementary bosons": the photon for electromagnetism; W^-, W^+, and Z^0 for the weak force; and eight gluons for the strong force. These elementary bosons are fundamental particles—that is, they cannot be broken down into anything smaller.

Now that quarks are with us, the old idea that protons and neutrons are bound together by a pi-meson turns out to be incomplete. Protons and neutrons, as we have seen, are made up of quarks, and the messengers between these quarks are called gluons—which are a type of boson, operating at a much more fundamental level than was recognized earlier in the century.

The total picture—including all six types of quarks, the six types of leptons (electron, muon, tau, electron neutrino, muon neutrino, and tau neutrino), and the four bosons (the force carriers)—make up what is known as the Standard Model. Up until 1995, though, one important particle was missing: the top quark. During two decade-long experiments, more than 500 people at Fermilab near Chicago searched for the missing particle. Finally, they succeeded, and the success is a certainty because the two experiments were designed to

Quarks	up	charm	top	gluon	Force Carriers
	down	strange	bottom	photon	
Leptons	electron neutrino	muon neutrino	tau neutrino	W boson	
	electron	muon	tau	Z boson	

Elementary particles of the Standard Model

complement and cross-check each other. This project is an excellent example of the large collaborations and complex equipment often required to solve the big questions of science today, compared to the past, which often saw individual scientists working alone. This is one of the big changes in "doing science" that has taken place in the past 100 years. Individual contributions still make a big difference, but in some disciplines—especially particle physics—teamwork is a key part of discovery.

As a result of teamwork, the most threatening problems with the Standard Model that existed a decade ago—the missing top quark and questions about the neutrino—have now been resolved. Still, as you can see, the Standard Model is extremely complicated—usually considered a bad sign in a scientific model. Physicists tend to think that simplicity, not complexity, is the rule in nature, and wherever they have explored this idea thoroughly, nature has proved to prefer simplicity. Why, at the very heart of everything, would things get so complex? Some physicists think that, somehow, we have not quite arrived at the true, unified, and simpler view of the universe.

Grandly Unifying

Several people have tried, though, to come up with this simpler view of the world. Einstein spent the last years of his life trying to come up with a grand unified field theory (often referred to as a GUT) that would tie all the forces of nature together. But he never succeeded.

In the 1960s, American Steven Weinberg and Pakistani-British physicist Abdus Salam independently developed a theory of electroweak interaction that combined theories of electromagnetic interaction and the weak interaction, and Sheldon Glashow, who attended the Bronx High School of Science with Weinberg, refined the theory in 1968.

Abdus Salam in 1955 at a conference in Rochester, New York (*AIP Emilio Segrè Visual Archives, Marshak Collection*)

Their theory provided a mathematical roof over the two interactions, and it was hailed as the first successful step toward the grand unified theory that Einstein had sought. And, while it was not completely proved right away, enough experimental support for it came in that the three men received the Nobel Prize in physics in 1979. Then, in 1983, using the accelerator at the CERN laboratory in Geneva, Carlo Rubbia and Simon van der Meer succeeded in discovering the W particles (W$^-$, W$^+$, and Z^0) predicted by the electroweak theory. It was the final confirmation needed for the electroweak theory.

Since that time, attempts have accelerated to arrive at a unified theory of all four forces, and the search for

Sheldon Glashow, 1980 (*AIP Emilio Segrè Visual Archives, Segrè Collection*)

Steven Weinberg *(AIP Emilio Segrè Visual Archives, Physics Today Collection)*

GUTs has opened up many avenues for exploring what may have happened at the time the universe began—in the first few seconds of its existence and in the time directly following. The breakthroughs in particle physics throughout the last five decades have produced a highly fruitful cross-fertilization between physicists and cosmologists, each group excited about and contributing to cutting-edge theory and experiment in the other's field, as we'll see in the next chapter. But first, let's explore some of the ways in which astronomers and cosmologists have found out more about the universe and its objects in the second half of the 20th century and the early 21st century.

3

Stars, Galaxies, the Universe, and How It All Began

SINCE THE BEGINNING OF HUMAN existence, as far as we know, people have looked with fascination at the far-off objects in the nighttime sky—watched them, learned their habits, plotted out their patterns, and assigned meaning to their arrangements. If you lie on the grass in a mountaintop meadow on a dark, clear night, as many earlier peoples must have done, you can see that the sky holds countless complexities. With only a few instruments to help, the ancient Babylonians and Egyptians made many sophisticated observations. But once Galileo added the use of a telescope to the job of watching stars and planets in the 17th century, information about the world beyond ours began to multiply astoundingly. The planet Jupiter had moons, Galileo discovered, and the planet Saturn, it turned out, had rings. As telescopes improved, astronomers began to spot new structures and discovered, moreover, that there were several more planets in our solar system than anyone had ever thought. By the 19th century they expanded their bag of tricks with photography and spectrography (used to study the distribution of energy emitted by radiant sources, breaking up light into its component colors, arranged in order of wavelengths).

But the 20th century, a continuing interplay between theory and experiment, and a marriage of astronomy and physics, has completely transformed our understanding of the vast realms of the universe. In the first half of the century, Einstein's theory of relativity taught us that we live in a space-time continuum that is shaped by the mass of objects. And the series of advances in quantum theory and nuclear physics in the first few decades of the century set the stage for extraordinary new ideas about how the universe began and what its early history was. Advances in instruments and methods of observing the skies, meanwhile, brought on discoveries of new types of objects never before dreamed of, including planets orbiting other stars, star nurseries, far distant galaxies, and more. More than ever before, the study of astronomy, astrophysics, and cosmology (the study of the origins and structure of the universe) is reserved for those who are stout of heart and daring of mind. The statement, "There are more things in heaven and earth, Horatio, than are dreamt of in your philosophy"—as Shakespeare's Hamlet admonishes his friend—could easily be the motto of astronomers, as well as physicists, in the second half of the 20th century.

More Things Than Are Dreamt Of . . .

In the early 1950s, night after night, astronomer Allan Sandage rode an elevator to a spot high up under the dome of the Hale Observatory on Palomar Mountain, near Pasadena, California, to sit in a contraption known as the prime focus cage, the observer's spot at the big, 200-inch telescope. The cold of the mountain air numbing his fingers and toes, Sandage prized the solitude, the intensity of the work, and the feeling of being in the cockpit of a time machine. It was his nightly date with the stars and he never missed it.

Sandage and his colleagues had at their disposal the best equipment ever built for optical astronomy up to that time. The 200-inch (five-meter) Hale telescope had just been completed in 1948. (It is still one of the largest reflector telescopes in the world.) And Sandage had learned his trade on the excellent 100-inch telescope at nearby Mount Wilson, under the tutelage of Milton Humason. Hired on as an assistant to Edwin P. Hubble, the grand master of galaxy measurement, Sandage had embarked on a project that promised to last a lifetime.

Hubble, who had succeeded in measuring distances to nearby galaxies, had undertaken a long-term observation plan to measure distances to more distant galaxies and, ultimately, to measure the size of the universe. His discovery, called Hubble's law, states that the farther away a galaxy is, the greater the degree to which its light is shifted toward the red end of the spectrum—that is, the faster it is

Edwin P. Hubble *(Palomar Observatory, AIP Emilio Segrè Visual Archives)*

speeding away from us. This "red shift" of light is actually a Doppler shift, like the trailing whistle of a passing train, or the horn of a speeding car, as it races away; in this case a shift in light is produced by the galaxies' motion as they rush away from one another while the universe expands.

Sandage's job was to photograph galaxies and search for variable stars within them so he could measure the distances between them. When Hubble died in 1953, Sandage had only just begun. But Sandage inherited Hubble's time on the 200-inch and all his charts and records, and his whole life became centered on measuring the far reaches of space and time. As British spectroscopist Leonard Searle would later say, "Allan Sandage concentrates so incredibly fiercely. He's a marvelous scientist. He flings himself into things. He seems a man of passion."

On the basis of his examination of the spectral characteristics of certain globular clusters, Sandage would ultimately conclude, many years later, that they and the universe in general are less than 25 billion years old. Using the scale Sandage developed, astronomers were now able to measure distances to galaxies anywhere from millions to billions of light-years away.

For an observational astronomer, it was an exciting time. New evidence kept coming in that astrophysicists and their colleagues in other disciplines used to explore questions such as: Do neutrinos exist? What happens when a star explodes? How do stars evolve? What happens deep inside them? Only now are we beginning to find some of the answers as scientists obtain new tools and find new ways to use old ones.

New Ways of Seeing

As we gaze up from Earth, even from a telescope perched high on a mountain and far from city lights, we peer through a haze of atmosphere that distorts and clouds the view. Many objects can't be seen clearly, and some kinds of radiation outside the visible light range cannot be detected at all. But with the birth of space rocketry in 1957, for the first time in history it became possible to observe from outside that atmospheric shell.

In June 1962 Riccardo Giacconi and his colleagues put an X-ray detector aboard an exploratory rocket to see if they could find evidence of fluorescence on the Moon. In the process the little sounding rocket launched from White Sands, New Mexico, made the first discovery of a cosmic X-ray source, Scorpius X-1. (The name means that it is the first X-ray source discovered in the constellation Scorpius, a constellation in the Southern Hemisphere, located partly in the Milky Way.) Finding an object in a nonvisible range of the electromagnetic spectrum such as X-rays is a lot like hearing someone knocking at the door, but not seeing anyone there; until you open the door, you don't know who's knocking. In 1967 astronomers matched up Scorpius X-1 with a visible object, a variable star known as V 818 Sco. A second source, Taurus X-1, was discovered in 1963 and soon turned out to be the Crab Nebula, a turbulent cloud of expanding gas and dust, left over from the supernova observed by Chinese and Japanese astronomers in 1054. A flurry of rocket and balloon explorations followed these discoveries, and by 1970 astronomers had found 25 or 30 sources spread throughout our galaxy. By December 1970 the first X-ray satellite, *Uhuru,* was launched; it discovered a large number of new sources, most of which turned out to be binary systems (composed of two companion stars).

In 1983 the U.S. National Aeronautics and Space Administration (NASA) cooperated with aerospace programs in the Netherlands and the United Kingdom to launch the *Infrared Astronomical Satellite* (*IRAS*), which surveyed all but 2 percent of the entire sky for sources in the infrared wavelength range of the electromagnetic spectrum. *IRAS,* which contained optics cooled by liquid helium, kept up its survey for nearly 11 months, until it ran out of helium. By the time the data was analyzed and organized, the catalog of *IRAS* observations were extensive, including a dust shell around the star Vega (possibly an early planetary system), five new comets, and extensive information about the kinds of objects that emit infrared radiation.

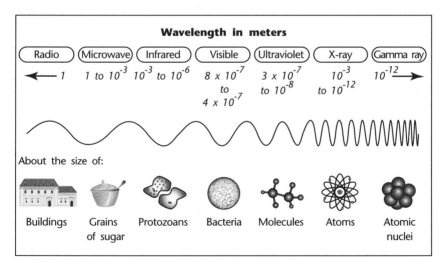

Chart of the electromagnetic spectrum

The U.S. fleet of space shuttles, first launched in 1981, has provided a way to place several complex astronomical observatories into orbit. The first of NASA's Great Observatories series was the *Hubble Space Telescope* (*HST*), launched in 1990. Officially known as the *Edwin P. Hubble Space Telescope*, this observatory was designed to peer far out into space and far back in time and is capable of producing imagery of unprecedented clarity. Still delivering stunning vistas and informative images, *Hubble* started out with a big handicap—and even so brought hundreds of new insights into play about quasars, pulsars, exploding galaxies, the birth of stars, and the age and size of the universe, to name just a few. Most of all, the *Hubble* was designed to engage in a search for primordial galaxies as far as 14 billion light-years away—about the time the universe came into existence—and to perform very deep red-shift studies to determine the large-scale structure of the universe. *HST* was also designed with 10 times the capability of the best Earth-based telescopes for distinguishing fine details in nearby star fields and planetary atmospheres. Orbiting 380 miles above Earth, it became the best hope for obtaining definitive answers to questions about the universe on a large scale, including its size and movement. Unfortunately, after its launch in 1990, a defect was discovered in one of the telescope's mirrors, threatening disappointment to astronomers who had been looking forward to its data for nearly 20 years. While the telescope was still able to gather scientifically worthwhile views, its blurry vision fell far short of plans. However, repair missions performed by shuttle crews solved not only that problem, but have also performed various maintenance repairs and updates that have kept the *Hubble* spaceborne far beyond original plans. With its new optics, *Hubble* can take images of stars some 10 to 11 billion light-years away, and its maintenance and upgrades have extended its life well into the 21st century.

Other space observatories have also joined *HST*. The *Compton Gamma Ray Observatory* (*CGRO*), specializing in gamma ray astronomy, was launched in 1991 and completed its mission in 2000. It carried four large telescopes, some as large as a compact car, each of which recognizes gamma rays within a specific energy range. Because, like all radiation, gamma rays can only be detected when they interact with matter, the *CGRO* detectors converted detected rays to flashes of visible light, which were counted and measured. Gamma rays are the highest-energy radiations in the electromagnetic spectrum, with a range from tens of thousands to tens of billions of electron volts (eVs). (Visible light produces only a few eVs, by contrast.) Cosmic gamma rays cannot be detected at all on Earth because they can't penetrate the atmosphere. But many of the most interesting objects discovered in the past few decades, including quasars, pulsars, and neutron stars, involve large releases of energy, which produce gamma rays, and astronomers hope to gain new insights on these structures and their dynamics through the data rounded up by the *CGRO*. Scientists even think that matter being drawn into a black hole gives off gamma ray radiation, in which case astronomers might catch a glimpse of the matter just before it disappears.

Other "Great Observatories" are also planned, turning their great eyes across the fast sweeps of the universe, looking in various regions of the electromagnetic spectrum. Perhaps NASA's most exciting observatory to date is the *Chandra X-Ray Observatory*, another part of NASA's Great Observatories series. *Chandra* is named after U.S. theoretical physicist Subrahmanyan Chandrasekhar (1910–95), better

Subrahmanyan Chandrasekhar and Henry Norris Russell seen chatting in this photograph taken in 1940 *(AIP Emilio Segrè Visual Archives, Locanthi Collection)*

known as "Chandra." Born in Lahore, India (now in Pakistan), he attended Trinity College in Cambridge, where he earned his Ph.D. in 1933, becoming a U.S. citizen in 1953. A Nobel laureate, Chandrasekhar was known for his rigor and his important studies of white dwarfs, as well as stellar atmospheres, structure, and dynamics.

Launched in 1999, the *Chandra X-Ray Observatory* has delivered brilliant images and many discoveries—including the first full view of a blast wave from an exploding star, a flare emitted by a brown dwarf, and a small galaxy being consumed by a larger one. Only two months after its launch from the space shuttle, the observatory showed that a brilliant ring exists around the center of the Crab Pulsar. Located in the Crab Nebula, the pulsar is the collapsed remains of a massive star gone supernova. The ring provided clues to scientists about how the pulsar energizes the entire nebula.

Also, astronomers know that a massive black hole exists at the center of our Milky Way galaxy, but they have never found the X-ray emission they expect from that region. *Chandra* has found a faint X-ray source near the center of the Milky Way galaxy that may be the long-sought sign.

Chandra also found that a gas funnel pouring into a huge black hole 2 million light-years away turns out to be much cooler than scientists expected. As astronomer Harvey Tananbaum remarked, *"Chandra* is teaching us to expect the unexpected about all sorts of objects ranging from comets in our solar system and relatively nearby brown dwarfs to distant black holes billions of light-years away."

In 2002 *Chandra* was able to provide revealing documentation of the collision of two galaxies. Since many such mergers have probably happened, even in our own galaxy, *Chandra's* imagery may offer insights about how the universe came to look as it does today. From *Chandra's* evidence, scientists think that vast numbers of new stars have formed as a result of a giant merger in the galaxy called Arp 220. The merger also sent vast shock waves through the intergalactic regions of space, and a highly massive black hole may be forming at the center of the merged galaxy. From *Chandra's* information, astronomers conclude that the merger has been taking place for some 10 million years—not long in cosmic terms.

Another exciting observatory, the *Space Infrared Telescope Facility* (*SIRTF* now known as the *Spitzer Space Telescope*), was launched August 25, 2003. *Spitzer* picks up where *IRAS* and *ISO* left off, exam-

Focus on NASA's Great Observatory Series

Telescope	Mission	Date
Hubble Space Telescope (*HST*)	Astronomy in the visible-light region of the electromagnetic spectrum, as well as near infrared and ultraviolet portions of the spectrum	1990; mission extended in 1999
Compton Gamma Ray Observatory (*CGRO*)	Data collection from objects emitting gamma rays, generally the most violent, extremely energetic physical processes in the universe	1991; retired in 2000
Chandra X-Ray Observatory (*CXO*)	To observe in the X-ray region of the spectrum, studying such objects as quasars, black holes, and high-temperature gases	1999
Space InfraRed Telescope Facility (*SIRTF* or the *Spitzer Space Telescope*)	To capture thermal infrared emissions blocked by the atmosphere from solar orbit, trailing Earth's orbit	2003
James Webb Space Telescope (*JWST*)	A large, infrared-optimized telescope, considered a sequel to the *Hubble*	2009 (planned)

ining the infrared region of the spectrum. It is the last planned addition to the Great Observatories (not counting the *Next Generation Space Telescope*). Recent advances in technology should make this observatory one of the greatest and most productive ever. Using its advanced infrared detectors, it is expected to perform complex maps of large areas, and it is equipped to measure spectra 1 million times as fast as any other space-borne infrared telescope. *Spitzer* should be able to help answer key questions about star and planet formation, the origin of energetic objects such as quasars, and the formation and evolution of galaxies and the distribution of matter.

What Happens Inside Stars?

Hans Bethe was a top-flight nuclear physicist who had studied with Arnold Sommerfeld in his native Germany, as well as with Ernest Rutherford at Cambridge and Enrico Fermi in Rome. When Adolf Hitler came to power, Bethe left Germany for the United States, where he helped work on the atomic bomb. But among his greatest contributions to science are his insights into the internal processes and dynamics of stars, which he worked out in 1938. He made use of his extensive knowledge of subatomic physics and Arthur Stanley Eddington's conclusion that the larger a star, the greater the internal pressure and the higher the temperature.

Bethe began with a hydrogen nucleus (a proton) and a carbon nucleus, which started a series of reactions finally resulting in the reformation of the carbon nucleus and the formation of a helium nucleus (an alpha particle). That is, the stellar engine runs on hydrogen fuel, using carbon as a catalyst and leaving helium behind as "ash." Because stars like our Sun are composed mostly of hydrogen, many have enough fuel to last for billions of years. Bethe also outlined a second possible scenario, in which hydrogen nuclei form a union directly (without the carbon catalyst) to form helium in several steps, a mechanism that could take place at lower temperatures. Bethe received the 1967 Nobel Prize in physics for his studies of solar and stellar energy production, which he recognized as fusion.

In 1948 George Gamow became interested in Bethe's idea that nuclear reactions power stars and serve as the source of their radiant energy. Like Bethe, Gamow was also a physicist by training. However, his interest in astronomy dated back to his 13th birthday, when his father gave him a telescope. Born in Russia, Gamow studied at several European universities, where he worked with both Niels Bohr and Ernest Rutherford. Traveling to the United States in the 1930s, he collaborated with atomic physicist Edward Teller, began teaching at George Washington University in St. Louis, and decided to stay. Gamow worked out the consequences of Bethe's idea and found that as a star uses up its basic fuel, hydrogen, in this process, the star gets hotter. He hypothesized that, instead of slowly cooling, our Sun would slowly heat up and eventually destroy life on Earth by baking it and maybe even eventually engulfing it.

Space-based studies of the Sun have confirmed Bethe and Gamow's ideas about fusion-powered stars, in addition to discovering many other facts about the Sun, including the existence of a solar wind of charged atomic particles that constantly rushes past the planets to the edge of the solar system. On three missions of the U.S. *Skylab* space station in 1973–74, astronauts focused primarily

This sequence of close-up images caught a view of an easily identifiable "eruptive prominence" on the lower left side of the Sun. Also known as "solar prominences," such blobs of extremely hot eruptive gas soar to 60,000 degrees F (33,315 degrees C) or more, and this one shot some 80,000 miles (128,747 km) into space traveling more than 15,000 mph (24,140 kph). These images were captured in 1996 by the Extreme Ultraviolet Imaging Telescope, one of 12 instruments onboard the spacecraft known as the *Solar and Heliospheric Observatory* (*SOHO*), a joint project of NASA and the European Space Agency (ESA). *(Courtesy of NASA)*

on the Sun, sending back 75,000 photographs of solar activity, including six solar flares (explosive releases of energy from the Sun).

Stellar Evolution: Cecilia Payne-Gaposchkin

Among the great questions explored by astronomers in the 20th century is, "What is the life history of a star?" Once it became clear that stars are born, burn brightly while young, grow old, and die, astronomers rushed to unfold the details. Among the front-runners in this process early in her career was Cecilia Payne-Gaposchkin (1900–79), a woman who, by the second half of the century, became recognized as one of the finest astronomers in history and the best-known woman astronomer of our time.

Born Cecilia Payne in Wendover, England, she won a scholarship to the University of Cambridge in 1919, where she was inspired by

English-born American astrophysicist Cecilia Payne-Gaposchkin (1900–79) is known for her work on stars in the making, insights into the Sun's place among the stars, and studies on variable stars and the Milky Way. *(AIP Emilio Segrè Visual Archives, Physics Today Collection)*

A. S. Eddington to pursue astronomy. Harlow Shapley invited her to join the staff at the Harvard College Observatory, where she worked on spectra under Annie Jump Cannon, who oversaw the compilation and classification of Harvard's vast catalog of photographic plates of spectra of stars. (Cannon alone classified a third of a million spectra using her own system.) At Harvard, Payne completed her Ph.D. thesis, "Stellar Atmospheres," which Otto Struve described as "the most brilliant Ph.D. thesis ever written on astronomy." At 24, Payne synthesized data from the spectra and her own observations to deduce the temperatures represented by each spectral type, as well as the atmospheric composition of stars. A gifted scientist, Payne-Gaposchkin liked to describe herself as a field naturalist who was good at "bringing together facts that were previously unrelated and seeing a pattern in them." Although she tended to be unassuming and would not have thought of it that way, the trait she described is one of the key qualities of a great theorist.

In 1934 Payne married Sergei I. Gaposchkin, an expert in variable stars who had recently joined the Harvard College Observatory. Together they coauthored many papers. In the 1950s Payne-Gaposchkin also wrote three major texts on stellar evolution, *Stars in the Making* (1952), *Introduction to Astronomy* (1953), and *Galactic Novae* (1957). She became the first woman in Harvard's history to become full professor, a rank she achieved in 1956; she was also the first to become chair of her department, a post she held for 12 years. Her final work, published in 1979, was *Stars and Clusters*.

Like most people intensely involved with their work, scientists are sometimes plagued with attacks of jealousy when a colleague makes a breakthrough. To avoid feelings of jealousy, Payne-Gaposchkin liked to say, she would suggest that scientists should repeatedly ask themselves whether they were thinking of the advancement of knowledge or the advancement of their own careers. Payne, clearly, was more inclined to think about the advancement of knowledge.

New Methods, New Discoveries

In 1931 radio engineer Karl Jansky, from Oklahoma, used an improvised aerial to locate sources of interference in radio telephone links and ended up founding an entirely new branch of astronomy, known as radio astronomy. He published his first results in 1932 and by 1933 had found that the celestial radio emissions he had discovered came from the Milky Way.

The field did not take off right away, though. The first radio astronomy began in Australia in 1946 with solar studies led by E. G. Bowen. By 1947 radio astronomers homed in on the first radio object ever detected that could match up to an object observable with the eyes: the Crab Nebula. Today radio maps of the sky can be used to create images that help us "see" ranges of temperatures and heat divisions in far-off galaxies and stars.

A radio telescope usually gathers radio waves using a dishlike antenna. Possibly, though, one might build a radio wave antenna

Science at Its Worst—and Best: Cold Fusion Fever

Fusion is the engine that drives the internal processes of the Sun—and all stars. It generates enormous heat—the warmth that we feel on Earth, even at our distance of 93 million miles. But what if a *cold* fusion process existed?

The whole point of science is to find ways of knowing the unknown, and all scientists work at uncovering answers both large and small. Of course, many dream of making the spectacular breakthrough that will astound the world and make them famous. But in the latter half of the 20th century, from the viewpoint of those in other disciplines, physicists seem to have had more than their share of cutting-edge discoveries.

So when two well-established chemists, B. Stanley Pons and Martin Fleischmann, saw the results of their experiments in March 1989, they were justifiably elated. They had, it seemed, done the impossible—and outdone physicists at their own game in the bargain. The next thing anyone knew, a press conference had been called, and everything spun out of control from there. They had found, according to their announcement to the press from the University of Utah at Salt Lake City, a method for generating clean heat from nuclear reactions that take place at room temperature and use only sea water as fuel.

Cold fusion, as this process came to be called, would mean cheap power—and could mean a wealth of possibilities for those who held its secrets. It was the alchemist's dream come true. The University of Utah, eager for the funds and stature that this discovery and further research could bring to the institution, promoted the idea of founding a national Cold Fusion Institute. The governor and legislature pledged $5 million for developing the idea further. Testimony before the House Science, Space, and Technology Committee resulted in the suggestion that $25 million in federal funds be set aside for Utah's cold fusion research.

without building a dish, an idea that Jansky pursued. So did a successful group of astronomers in Great Britain under the direction of Anthony Hewish. Usually, though, a radio astronomy antenna uses a scooped reflecting area made of metal or wire mesh. One of the most interesting is the world's largest fixed-dish radio antenna, located at Arecibo, Puerto Rico. Built in 1963, the telescope dish measures 1,000 feet in diameter, spanning some 25 acres. The antenna dish consists of 40,000 individual reflecting panels

But all was not, after all, as good as it looked. Fleischmann and Pons, it turned out, had not run the controls they should have run. (A control in an experiment sets a standard of comparison for verifying the results.) Other laboratories were having trouble duplicating their results. (Another of the necessary facets of a scientific experiment: results must be repeatable.) Fleischmann and Pons said the other scientists weren't doing the experiments correctly, but they were unwilling to provide details. Of course, with so much money riding on their process, their reluctance to be open might be understandable. But in the end, they could not defend their results. Pressured, perhaps, by over-eager administrators at the university or by their own ambition, they had spoken too soon, before they could really be sure of their data. Somewhere, somehow, they had made a mistake. Fleischmann, a visiting professor of electrochemistry from the University of Southampton in England, was a distinguished scientist of considerable repute. Pons was a tenured professor at Utah. The reputations of both were badly tarnished, and Pons left Utah. The president of the University of Utah, who had told the press that cold fusion "ranked right up there with fire, with cultivation of plants, and with electricity," resigned. And the newly founded Cold Fusion Institute closed its doors. The fever was over.

The cold fusion flurry is, most of all, an example of how gullible we all can be. The idea of cold fusion fed the dreams of so many that it won the day, however briefly, against skepticism, underscoring the fact that, as Richard Feynman once said, "The first principle is that you must not fool yourself, and you're the easiest person to fool." The incident also shows that science as a whole is not easily fooled for long; science is a self-correcting process, and sooner or later, when it has gone off on a wrong track, scientists discover their own error, retrace paths previously taken, and look for better answers.

attached to a network of steel cables. The panels focus incoming radio waves from outer space onto a detecting platform suspended above the dish. In recent years radio astronomers have increased the resolution of their equipment by constructing banks of antennas, such as the Very Large Array (VLA) in Socorro, New Mexico, the largest array of radio telescopes in the world—composed of 27 telescope dishes, arranged in a big Y shape stretched across the flat, level plain.

Radio astronomy didn't really begin to catch on until after World War II, but when it did, astronomers became excited about this new way of searching the skies. Radio waves could penetrate the dust clouds that absorb sunlight in space and make optical astronomy difficult. Radio waves are especially helpful, therefore, in studying the center of our galaxy, which cannot see at all by ordinary means.

Radio astronomy was the means used when Allan Sandage and Maarten Schmidt discovered quasars and when Anthony Hewish and Jocelyn Bell discovered pulsars.

Quasars

Several compact radio sources were discovered during the 1950s, but radio telescopes at that time could not pinpoint celestial objects very accurately, so it was difficult to match up these objects with visual images by using an optical telescope. One of these compact sources, known as 3C273, was blocked from vision by the Moon in 1962 and its position could thereby be established. Photos taken by Allan Sandage with the 200-inch Hale telescope atop Mount Palomar showed a dim, starlike object in that position.

But this star had an unusual spectrum. It contained absorption lines that could not be identified. It, and others like it coming later, became called quasi-stellar radio sources (quasi-stellar meaning "starlike"), or quasars for short.

In 1963 Maarten Schmidt discovered that the absorption lines in the spectrum of 3C273 were common ones, but they shifted toward the red end of the spectrum by an extraordinary amount. During the following years, astronomers discovered a large number of quasars with extremely large red shifts.

The spectrum of a star can not only disclose its chemical composition, but from the Doppler shift, or red shift, one can deduce its velocity relative to Earth. Many systems of stars outside our galaxy have a shift in their electromagnetic spectra toward the red end of the spectrum, and astronomers accept this to be a Doppler shift, indicating the velocity with which these systems are moving away from us, a confirmation of the expansion of the universe. Red shifts caused by the expansion of the universe are called cosmological red shifts. If the red shifts of quasars are cosmological, the quasars must be at extraordinary distances—as much as a billion light-years away—making them the farthest objects ever observed in a telescope. Also, because they can be observed over such distances, their energy output must be enormous. As Edwin Hubble had shown, the velocity with which an object is moving away from us is proportional to the distance. This fed into the idea that the universe was created by a huge explosion and that the galaxies are the resultant debris flying in all directions. It also meant that the quasars being observed were very, very far away.

The discovery of quasars caused great bewilderment among astronomers. The consequence of this discovery was that one either had to question the validity of this astronomical yardstick, the red shift, or agree that there are processes out there for which we have no explanation at all. Some quasars have been spotted that are thought to be more than 1 billion light-years away. Probably they are galaxies with extremely active centers, but are so far away that they seem to be very dim single stars.

Not all astronomers, however, believe that quasars exhibit cosmological red shifts. For example, one American astronomer, Halton

Milton Humason: Born Skywatcher

Milton Humason (1891–72), also an astronomer at the Mount Wilson Observatory, truly started out at the foot of the mountain and worked his way up. He began as a mule packer who hauled equipment up the steep trail to the observatory perched on this mountain north of Los Angeles. Later he graduated to busboy in the observatory dining hall and then janitor in the observatory itself. But his love for astronomy won out. The first step was a chance to serve as assistant on one of the small telescopes on the mountain. He augmented his eighth-grade education with avid questions, reading, and studying, and in 1928 he became Edwin Hubble's close collaborator.

Working under Hubble's guidance, then later on his own and with other astronomers at the Mount Wilson and Palomar observatories, Humason measured red shifts in the light of thousands of remote galaxies. Dedicated and skilled as an observer, he was expert at obtaining measurable spectrograms of faint, distant galaxies. His observations established what is still found to be the case today, that Hubble's law holds true throughout the observable universe.

Arp, has discovered a number of systems consisting of a quasar and a galaxy that seem to be physically connected but exhibit very different red shifts in their spectra. He therefore argues that some still unknown mechanism other than the expansion of the universe must cause these red shifts. Most astronomers believe that quasars have cosmological red shifts and that the systems discovered by Arp only appear to be connected, and they in reality are at very different distances from Earth.

A Bug in the Data

In July 1967 Antony Hewish and his students had strung a long antenna in a field near Cavendish Laboratory in England to create a more powerful radio telescope for observing "twinkling," or scintillations, of radio starlight. It was the job of graduate student Jocelyn Bell to check over the charts each day to look for interesting data. In August she noticed a strange twinkling in a spot in the sky where ordinarily there would be nothing like that. Hewish thought it was probably noise in the receiver. They laughingly called this a signal from "little green men"—beings from other worlds—and they continued gathering data. Not only did that signal persist, but Bell found three more, similar pulsating radio resources. They began to realize that their data reflected a real phenomenon: a type of object that had never been detected before. They began to search for explanations in terms of known laws of physics.

What Hewish, Bell, and their colleagues had discovered became known as pulsars (because they pulsate), and the scientists realized that they had detected neutron stars—a type of star that has become so incredibly dense that it may have a mass as large as our Sun crammed into space the size of a mountain. Although it had been thought that neutron stars might exist, no one had ever detected one before.

Listening for Life

Radio astronomy is also a key tool for a small group of dedicated scientists who explore the question, Are we alone? Some—known as exobiologists—are looking for any hint that we are not the only life forms in the universe. Others want to know whether humans are the only intelligent life forms in the universe. Their numbers included respected American astronomer Carl Sagan, coauthor with Ann Druyan of the novel *Contact,* which centers on a woman whose entire career involves the methodical, scientific search—not for UFOs—but for verifiable signs or messages from an extraterrestrial civilization. The novel has imaginative moments—it is fiction, after all—but Sagan knew how scientists have approached this question, and he got the science right when it came to the search for extraterrestrial intelligence (SETI). While the likelihood of "ETs" ever arriving here is slim (such a trip would require many generations from even the closest star beyond our solar system), many scientists think we could someday receive a signal from some Earth-like planet in another solar system somewhere in the universe. But when it arrives, we'll only recognize it if we are listening.

Searching for signals from civilizations beyond the edge of our solar system, though, could be likened to trying to find a needle in a cosmic haystack, or straining to hear a cricket's voice against the roar of Niagara Falls—wondering all the time if there *is* a needle, or a voice, or if, in the end, we'll discover nothing more than a pile of haphazard scrap, or the relentless persistence of unsilent nature. But some questions seem eternal, rooted deep in human consciousness. "Are we alone?" is such a question, and in the 1980s and 1990s, the tools of technology began to come of age enough to enable well-defined experiments aimed at finding the answer. Worldwide, scientists have begun sifting through the wide range of signals from space in a well-organized search. As astrophysicist and SETI scientist Bernard M. Oliver remarked in a 1986 interview, "If we are right, then over the last few billion years, a great number of intelligent civilizations have grown up like islands in this galaxy, and it's inconceivable to me that all of them would go through their entire histories in isolation."

The first great breakthrough in SETI methods came in 1959, when two scientists, Philip Morrison and Giuseppe Cocconi, suggested that radio astronomy could be used to communicate with other worlds. Why radio astronomy? As Oliver explained it, "In the interests of economy and efficiency, a message carrier should meet the following criteria: (1) the energy . . . should be minimized, other things being equal; (2) the velocity should be as high as possible; (3) the particle should be easy to generate, launch, and capture; and (4) the particle should not be appreciably absorbed or deflected by the interstellar medium." These criteria are easily satisfied by radio waves, which are fast, efficient, and relatively cheap. Therefore, it seems only logical that intelligent civilizations (if they exist) would choose the radio spectrum for sending long-range signals across the vast distances of interstellar space.

The first radio-telescope search for extraterrestrial intelligence was a project called Ozma, set up in 1960 by SETI pioneer Frank Drake at the National Radio Astronomy Observatory (NRAO) in Green Bank, West Virginia. Drake chose two nearby solar-type stars, Tau Ceti and Epsilon Eridani, and spent a total of 150 hours "listening." He found nothing, but he had made a beginning.

Since Ozma, more than 30 SETI experiments have been launched in the United States, the former Soviet Union, Australia, and Europe—all without results. Still, despite many hours of combined listening time, they have covered only a tiny slice of the total range of possibilities. Nearly endless combinations of direction, segment of the spectrum, and types of signal modulation remain to be explored.

By the 1980s and 1990s, new technology and the enormous data-handling capabilities of today's computers had revolutionized the search. Multichannel analyzers now can monitor literally millions of radio channels at one time. One project, established by a nonprofit group called the Planetary Society, inaugurated a new 8.4-million channel analyzer in September 1985. NASA's SETI project, which lost funding from Congress in 1993 but has since revived thanks to private funding, uses VLSI (very large-scale integrated) circuitry to pull in as many as 10 million individual frequency channels. Real-time data from the telescopes is analyzed by this equipment for significant data, which is passed on to a signal analyzer that in turn passes it on to a powerful computer.

Without this automated sifting process, the volume of information from the radio telescopes—billions of bits of digital data—would be impossibly daunting. Before the more advanced technology was available, one five-day observation period could produce 300 tapes of data or more. Analyzing the data on those tapes, in turn, could take as long as two and a half years to pump through a computer. After one such experience, astronomer Jill Tarter drew a cartoon of a pair of feet sticking out from beneath a mountain of computer printout, which she labeled "Buried alive!" "You can't do it in non-real-time," she would later explain. That is, if you don't process the data as it comes in—in real time—you'll find "you can't store it, and you can't process it with human intelligence. You've got to have something that is far more dedicated and, once you've told it the rules, plays by the rules consistently and with complete concentration." The task requires equipment that's able to weed out the vast quantities of irrelevant noise and retain only the signals that might be interesting. The new technology does just that.

Astronomer Jill Tarter, whose daughter used to list her mother's occupation as "looks for little green men." But for Tarter, the Search for Extraterrestrial Intelligence (SETI) is both serious and exciting science, and she has spent most of her professional career finding more and more technologically sophisticated ways to "listen" effectively for signals from other worlds. *(Courtesy of Jill Tarter and the SETI Institute; photo by Li Li)*

But having equipment to analyze the data is only part of the challenge. Given the vastness of the universe, where do you look? And what do you search for? SETI researchers usually use one of two approaches: homing in on a few likely stars using sensitive equipment, or using less sensitive equipment in a broader range of frequencies to conduct a broad, full-sky sweep. It is a vast task, one that may have no positive results within our lifetime. It is also a project with a long list of "ifs." For one thing, would extraterrestrial civilizations, if they indeed exist, be likely to follow the same reasoning, choose the same frequencies, and beam in our direction? Perhaps even more important, would they make this costly attempt to reach us? Or would extraterrestrial scientists have trouble convincing some galactic congress to provide funding for such an ambitious, and possibly useless, venture? Also, given the billions of years the universe has existed, this moment when we have reached the ability to search the cosmos for signals from other civilizations may not coincide with the time when signals would arrive. A signal coming from four light-years away would take only four years to arrive here. A signal sent today from a civilization 100 light-years away, though, would not reach us for another 100 years.

But whether the answer is 10 years away, 20, 50, or even 100, most searchers agree that we will learn, not just from the answers that we may or may not find, but from the ways in which we seek.

So the search goes on. Is intelligence an isolated phenomenon, and Earth its only voice? Are we a short-lived quirk of nature, or part of a greater cosmic community? Can civilizations such as ours endure long enough to reach outward toward other worlds, or is humankind doomed to perish, alone and unheeded, a dead end in the handiwork of nature? Are there other voices out there like our own, other searchers in the cosmic darkness, seeking light and companionship? Seeking hope? Only time—and SETI programs throughout the world—will tell.

Extrasolar Planets

Before 1995, scientists rightly postulated there must be other solar systems, but no one had ever seen any proof that planets orbited other stars in the same way Earth does, along with the rest of the planets in our solar system. Then, using Doppler spectroscopy, the first extrasolar planet was discovered orbiting a star called 51 Pegasus. It was a thrilling breakthrough, and since that time, as of September 2003, the number so far has risen to 110 extrasolar planets, all located using the same technology. So far, they have been very large planets, most much larger than the gas giant Jupiter—but those are the easiest to find. Many more probably exist but have so far gone undetected.

Along with evidence that a warm ocean may exist beneath the ice of Europa, one of Jupiter's big moons, and that life-friendly conditions on Saturn's big moon Titan possibly exist (see chapter 4), the rapid discovery of so many planets outside our solar system is an exciting indication that circumstances leading to life forms may indeed exist elsewhere in the universe. It is part of a great unfolding mystery.

In the Beginning . . .

For centuries people have wondered how the universe began and how or whether it might end, and the last half of the 20th century is no exception. But most astronomers in the 1950s tried to sidestep the question when it came to trying to explain it scientifically. George Gamow was an exception. In 1948 Gamow worked out a scenario that would result in the formation of the various elements of the universe from an explosion of the kind of original "cosmic egg" or "superatom" suggested by Lemaître. A widely read popular writer about science, Gamow soon had a widespread reputation for this idea about how the universe began, although it was by no means universally accepted.

In fact, many scientists felt that the question of "the beginning" either was outside the realm of science or was offensive. British physicist Fred Hoyle, also a popularizer of science, numbered among these, and he came out with a competing theory, with Austrians Hermann Bondi and Thomas Gold. Incensed at the idea of an explosive beginning of time, they painted a picture of what they called the "steady-state universe," in which matter is continually being created that, in turn, powers the expansion Hubble observed when he saw that all galaxies are moving away from us. Hoyle poked fun at what he laughingly called Gamow's "big bang" theory. Imagine his amazement when the name caught on.

The Microwave Background

Meanwhile, in 1964, two researchers at Bell Laboratories in New Jersey—Arno A. Penzias (1933–) and Robert W. Wilson (1936–)—were using the lab's big radio antenna to look for weak signals from the sky. But they were having a hard time getting rid of the background noise in order to get a clearer signal. They took the equipment apart. They checked the dish. They checked all the connections. They even found pigeons nesting in the dish, and so they carefully removed the birds and took them miles away to nest somewhere else. The pigeons came back. They removed them again. Nothing would get rid of the microwave background radiation that permeates the universe. Like a great echo, this radiation seemed to imply some great past event that had raised the temperature of the entire universe at a time so long ago that, by now, it has almost, but not quite, entirely dissipated. It was the first real reinforcement for the idea proposed by young Gamow in 1948, who not only predicted this radiation, but figured its exact temperature correctly as 3°K above absolute zero.

Then, in 1992, another piece of evidence came to light. The science team working on data beamed back to Earth by the *Cosmic Background Explorer* (*COBE*) spacecraft announced that, unlike previous evidence, the cosmic background radiation has "ripples." Always before, the data gathered by Wilson and Penzias and all other successive researchers had indicated that the temperature of the background radiation was the same, no matter where in the sky you looked. From this constant temperature, scientists had deduced that the early universe must have been smooth and uniform, completely lacking in what cosmologists now refer to as "lumpiness." Wherever we look in the skies we see clumps of matter—galaxies, nebulae—interspersed with empty space. This spottiness is what cosmologists mean when they talk about lumpiness.

The new data is compelling because of its sheer quantity. *COBE*, launched by NASA in 1989, made several hundred million temperature measurements during the first year in orbit alone. In this enormous pool of data, the *COBE* team discovered tiny variations in temperature, amounting to only 30 millionths of a degree warmer or cooler, in areas where minute fluctuations in the density of gas occurred in the early universe, about 300,000 years after the big bang. (When we talk about a time only 300,000 years after the beginning of time, it's as if, in human terms, we spoke of the first day in the life of a 90-year-old person.)

As the universe expanded, these early areas of temperature fluctuation also grew, so that now, the areas detected by *COBE* are as large as billions of light-years across. They are so large, in fact, that they could not be precursors to even the largest clusters of galaxies we have observed. But their discovery made scientists confident that more density fluctuations of smaller sizes would turn up. And they seem to back up the "inflationary" model of the birth of the universe.

Of course, whether the universe began with a big bang or otherwise, the idea of a creation event always raises the question, Where did the matter come from in the first place? But this, as cosmologist Stephen Hawking once said, is like asking what is located five miles north of the North Pole. Or, put another way, any question about "before the big bang" is unphysical. Time exists inside the universe—the universe does not exist inside time.

Black Holes

Meanwhile, in the 1950s at the University of Cambridge, a very personal battle was taking place. As a young graduate student in physics, Stephen Hawking had just received a chilling piece of news—a diagnosis explaining why, in the past few years, his gait and speech had become less and less coordinated. He had what is commonly known as Lou Gehrig's disease (amyotrophic lateral sclerosis), a degenerative paralyzing affliction that would put him a wheelchair within a few years. In the coming years he could look forward to increasing physical disabilities and, eventually, death. The brilliant young student went into immediate depression. Why pursue the promising career that he had begun? Why go on at all? Several months went by and he made no progress on his work.

Although Hawking's health could not be recovered, luckily for science, his career could. His adviser came up with a plan: Toss a problem into the young man's lap that was so fascinating that he could not resist it. That was how Hawking got started looking into the finer points about black holes and became the most world-renowned expert on the subject, one of the most provocative in modern astronomy.

American physicist John Archibald Wheeler (1911–   ) coined the term *black hole* in the 1960s to describe the structure formed when a star collapses in upon itself and ultimately becomes no larger than a single point in space, a singularity. When this happens, according to Einstein's theory of relativity, nothing can escape the enormous concentration of mass—not even light. So a black hole cannot be seen, except by noticing its effects.

In 1974 Hawking came up with the concept that "black holes aren't black"—that is, he thinks that black holes can slowly bleed radiation. Possibly, he says, black holes may evaporate like snowballs in the sun. This seems to be a contradiction, since a black hole, by definition, is so massive that nothing can escape its gravity, not even light. That's why it's called a black hole. The circumference of a black hole, called the event horizon, allows nothing back out.

But Hawking has pioneered the application of quantum mechanics to black hole theory, and he has come

Stephen Hawking *(AIP Emilio Segrè Visual Archives, Physics Today Collection)*

up with the idea that matter can be created in "virtually" empty space at the event horizon. That is, according to quantum theory, virtual particles can wink in and out of existence so fast that they never disturb the balance required by the laws of conservation of energy and matter. Hawking thinks that this can happen at the event horizon of a black hole and that, while most virtual particles would immediately wink back into the black hole, occasionally some would bleed off in another direction, slowly leaking radiation away from the black hole.

This idea fits well with a theory about how the universe began, proposed in the 1980s by Alan Guth of the Massachusetts Institute of Technology (MIT). Called the inflationary model, Guth's theory proposed that during the first fraction of a second of the existence of the universe, the entire universe expanded enormously in a sudden, ultra-brief (one-trillionth of a second) burst, expanding the universe from the size of an atom to billions of light-years across.

Missing Mass

One of the eeriest phenomena observed in astronomy—rivaling black holes—was introduced by Swiss astronomer Fritz Zwicky (1898–1974) in 1933. The phenomenon is sometimes referred to as "missing mass"

Fritz Zwicky at Caltech *(AIP Emilio Segrè Visual Archives)*

because many clues tell us something is there that we cannot detect with telescopes of any kind. Zwicky called it *dunkle Materie,* or dark matter. Zwicky was an irascible, renegade character, the kind of person that "likes to prove the other guy wrong," as one colleague put it, and it was not surprising that he was one of the first to notice that the universe's ledger books did not balance. He came up with the idea of "missing mass" to describe the dark, invisible mass that must be there— something between 10 to 100 times the amount of matter we can detect in the galaxies and between galaxies.

No one listened to him at first, but by now some astronomers think that the matter we see could not be sufficiently massive to cause the coalescence into the stars and galaxies we see. There seems to be more gravity in the universe than we can account for based on observations of luminous matter.

In fact, the current suspicion is that we have found no way yet to detect as much as 99 percent of the matter in the universe. It does not give off light and is not detectable with X-rays or radio astronomy. But we see its gravitational effects.

Vera C. Rubin at a meeting of the American Astronomical Society in Seattle *(AIP Emilio Segrè Visual Archives, John Irwin Collection)*

For example, in the 1970s Vera Cooper Rubin (1928–   ) and W. Kent Ford at the Carnegie Institution of Washington, D.C., gathered extensive data indicating that in clusters of galaxies, the galaxies far from the center move at too high a speed for the gravitational effects of the mass we see—stars and glowing gas—to hold them within the clusters. Their investigations of the rotation of spiral galaxies revealed the presence of a dark halo around the edge of the galaxies. Within this halo, Rubin and Ford estimate, resides something like 10 times the amount of matter we can actually see in the galaxy. Statistical analysis of the motions of galaxies on a larger scale than clusters backs these ideas up with an estimate that dark matter constitutes 30 times the amount of matter we can detect (except within galaxies, where ordinary matter dominates). Since 1978 a group at Carnegie including Rubin, Ford, David Bursein, and Braley Whitmore has analyzed more than 200 galaxies with confirming results.

What is this dark matter? No one is sure yet; there may be more than one kind. But it is not at all likely that it is mostly ordinary matter—that is, it is not mostly black holes that have formed from stars or dim stars we cannot detect or small chunks of solid matter. By 1984, the candidates were neutrinos (if the mass was greater than zero) or hypothetical particles: photinos, gravitinos, and axions. Some scientists think that dark matter may be slow-moving elementary particles left over from the big bang.

As British solar astrophysicist Martin Rees has remarked, "The most clear-cut way to settle the nature of the hidden mass would of course be to detect the objects that make it up."

Some astrophysicists suggest a connection between brown dwarfs and missing mass, since a brown dwarf is a sort of failed star formed when a lump of gas contracts but has a mass so small that nuclear reactions do not begin in its core. Because there are no nuclear reactions taking place, brown dwarfs are very dark and difficult to detect. In fact, until recently, no one had ever found a brown dwarf, so they were considered hypothetical. However, the first brown dwarf was finally discovered in 1995. As of September 2003, several dozen more had been discovered, thanks to highly sensitive infrared detectors. Many astronomers think that brown dwarfs are most likely as prevalent as regular stars in the universe. Some of the large, gaseous extrasolar planets found near stars may also be brown dwarfs. So brown dwarfs could well explain part of the missing mass.

Much of the mystery has begun to shift to what astrophysicists are calling "dark energy." Astronomers have been intrigued by this possibility for several years, and a 3-D map of the universe completed in October 2003 seems to confirm the presence of dark energy. By detailing the large-scale structure of the universe, the map reveals the interplay of forces over the 13-billion-year evolution of the cosmos and the clustering of galaxies and dark matter. This map offers estimates that ordinary matter accounts for 5 percent of the universe, traditional dark matter makes up some 25 percent, and dark energy, which is all pervasive throughout the cosmos, makes up the remaining 70 percent of the universe. An example of the management complexity of many 21st-century science projects, the international team of 200 scientists from 13 institutes that worked on the map was coordinated by the Sloan Digital Sky Survey (SDSS).

Prior to the mid-1990s, astrophysicists and cosmologists saw gravity as the main sculpting and shaping force in the universe. Then observations of exploding stars in deep space indicated that another force—"dark energy"—might be driving the universe apart. An earlier map in February 2003, studying different galaxies, gave some credence to the dark energy premise. One scientist remarked, "The web of evidence is very strong and all observations are pointing to dark energy." Now the question is, What exactly is dark energy?

Pulling It All Together . . . ?

Most intriguing of all, the recurring question that haunts cosmologists and subatomic physicists alike is, How did it all begin?

Nearly all theorists now agree that there must have been a beginning and that it must have been a big bang, a cataclysmic explosion originating from a particle smaller than the smallest nucleus of any atom. Although some cracks developed in Guth's inflationary theory, newer theories of this inflationary phase of the universe have gained much acceptance among astronomers and cosmologists. Inflationary theory answers many, but not all, of the questions inherent in the "big bang" theory.

Why, for instance, didn't everything just blow apart so violently in those first few fractions of a fraction of a fraction of a millisecond that all matter was evenly dispersed far and wide, with no coalescing objects, no lumpiness, no stars, planets, galaxies, and comets? Or, if not enough momentum was available to blow everything wide open, then why didn't the closely packed infant universe just crush in upon itself? Theorists have actually calculated what the critical value would have to have been for the universe to have avoided either fate, and the calculation works.

Many theorists have tried to figure out exactly what happened in those first few moments, though, trying to reach back in time to a point when the atom's structure was simpler, looking for the simple symmetry behind the complexities we see today. They have looked back to a time when the newborn cosmos for the briefest instant, in one of its earliest, earliest stages, reached temperatures above a billion billion billion degrees, and in this brief moment, the weak, electromagnetic, and strong forces were all just one force. These efforts are the GUTs—grand unified theories—and so far, none of them has worked. Sheldon Glashow once remarked that GUTs are neither grand nor unifying nor theories. So, as particle physicist Leon Lederman puts it, a better term for them than *theories* would be *speculative efforts.*

To carry this force, an ancient messenger particle has been postulated, the Higgs bosons, super-massive particles that played the part of messenger for the grand unified force, just as photons act as messengers today for the electromagnetic force. In the beginning of time, particles and antiparticles could transform themselves rapidly from one to the other. For example, a quark could become an anti-electron (positron) or an antiquark. An antiquark could become a neutrino or a quark, and so on. This process would have been mediated by the Higgs bosons—but these particles have yet to be detected. A team at CERN was on the brink, they thought, of trapping evidence for the Higgs boson, sometimes known as the "God Particle" because it is responsible for conveying all mass to atomic particles. But the results will probably have to wait for the new accelerator to be completed at CERN. If detected, the complex combination of atomic particles including leptons and quarks and described by QCD—the view of the atom known as "The Standard Model"—would be confirmed. For now, though, that confirmation will probably have to wait.

Even more ambitious, and also highly speculative, are the efforts to bring together all four forces, including the gravitational force, combining quantum chromodynamics—the behavior of quarks and their color properties—with gravity. Sometimes referred to as TOEs (theories of everything), these concepts become very complex. One, known as superstring theory, gained great popularity for a while, explaining that in the very earliest flicker of big bang cosmology, there were no point particles, only short segments of string. Ten dimensions are required to make it work—nine space and one time. To explain why we are aware of only three space dimensions, theorists postulate that the other six dimensions are curled in on themselves.

Many scientists are nervous, though, about so much theorizing, building complex theories upon complex theories with little or no chance of subjecting the theories to experiment. Also, the study of smaller and smaller elementary particle structures requires larger and larger accelerators and detectors. The final goal—to understand the fundamental structure of matter through unified symmetry principles—is commendable, but the mathematical complexities required are immense. As a result, many critics worry that cosmological science is in danger of becoming a new kind of mythology, with little possible connection with testable science.

Overall, however, the decades since 1946 have offered astronomers and cosmologists a vast richness of new data, new vistas, and new ideas. Researchers have developed far more sophisticated ways of investigating the universe, its structure and origins, making possible a far greater degree of precision and accuracy than ever before. Also, a highly fruitful cross-fertilization with particle physics has produced important new insights in both fields.

As a result the universe has become vastly larger and more complex than ever before—and ever more intriguing.

4
Exploring the Solar System

WHILE COSMOLOGISTS ENVISIONED the violent first moments of the universe, explored the consequences of evaporating black holes, and pondered dark energy and what it might be, the last half of the 20th century introduced access to a wealth of new knowledge closer to home. With the aid of rocket power, humans could now send emissaries in the form of robot spacecraft powered in part by solar panel "wings" to virtually any planet, moon, or asteroid in the solar system. What once had been purely science fiction became—at least in part—reality. Humans traveled from the safe cradle of Earth to the Moon, hiked its plains, and brought back rocks. Spacecraft visited nearly every planet (only Pluto was left out), uncovered thousands of mysteries, large and small, and discovered a myriad of moons. Some of those voyages continued into the 21st century, new ones began, and many more are in the planning stages. From the late 1950s on, images have streamed back to Earth from the many corners of the solar system in gigantic numbers. The sights have been amazing and the discoveries intriguing. Virtually none of our neighboring planets and their moons has turned out to be exactly what anyone expected.

The catalyst that began it all was *Sputnik I,* launched in 1957 to begin its lonely orbit around Earth. At that moment we became tourists in the solar system for the first time. Satellites orbiting Earth and rocket probes into our atmosphere began to give us new views of our planet and its atmosphere—from outside ourselves. On their heels followed missions to the Moon (both with and without people aboard) and unmanned missions to nearly every planet in the solar system; only Pluto did not receive a visit. What had been tiny, far-away specks focused faintly through the lenses of even the largest telescopes now became rocky surfaces pockmarked with craters, swirling globes of glowing gases, volcanically active nuggets of turbulence, and icy deserts. These were vast and wonderful places, never seen so close before by human eyes. In the vast silence of space, eerie robots whirred near them to send us close-up photographs and data readings that stunned everyone. Nothing was what it had seemed.

Spectacular, brightly colored close-ups of Saturn's rings and the volcanic eruptions on Jupiter's moon, Io, have become so commonplace today that we forget how far away these huge, spinning masses of rock and gases really are—and how impossible such views were to obtain just a few years ago. No one even suspected that Saturn's rings existed until Galileo spied evidence of them in his telescope in the 17th century (and then he could not figure out what these strange "ears" were that protruded on either side of the planet—and then disappeared as the seasons changed). Now we have extensive data about their structure, size, movement, and relationship to the planet and its moons, thanks initially in many cases to data gleaned by a spacecraft named *Pioneer 11*, which flew by in 1979, followed in the 1980s by *Voyager 1* and *Voyager 2*.

Planetary science, which had always, since the time of Galileo, depended upon instruments—ever bigger, more complex, and more expensive—now had an even bigger price tag. The rewards were also vastly greater. We could actually see the surface of these far-off worlds, measure their atmospheres, and study their histories—and compare them to Earth's, thereby learning more about our home planet as well. What we have learned about how the universe works—from the dynamics of atmosphere and meteorology to the presence in space of a solar wind and radiation belts around our planet—not only adds to our basic store of knowledge but also provides priceless lessons about Earth.

The Moon: Closest Neighbor

Locked together in a close cosmic dance, Earth and Moon, planet and satellite, revolve around a common center of gravity, the larger one, green-blue-white, bursting with color, water, and life; the other, smaller by nearly three-quarters, colorless, scarred, cratered, and marked by time. Its hidden face, dark and pitted, is turned perpetually

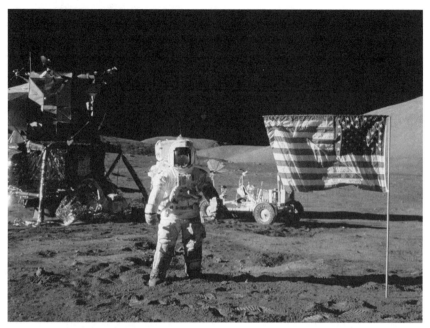

Geologist–astronaut Harrison Schmitt on the Moon's surface during the *Apollo 17* mission in 1972 *(Courtesy of NASA)*

away from Earth, toward the stars. What catastrophe occurred in the long-distant past to leave the Moon so cold and desolate?

At once our most familiar and most mysterious neighbor in space, the Moon has always intrigued the human mind. It is the subject of countless ancient mythologies, legends, and songs. It was the calendar-keeper of the ancients, who depended on its regularity of motion across the sky and its changing phases to mark the passage of the seasons.

For scientists, the questions were many: What was the surface of the Moon really like? Where did it come from and how did it come into being? What was its geology? What did the face that had never been seen look like? When the United States and the Soviet Union (now Russia) developed the ability to leap beyond the confines of Earth's gravity, the Moon was the most natural place to go exploring first. Like the telescope and the camera, the rocket gave us a new tool that could help unravel the Moon's many secrets.

Between 1958 and 1976, the United States and the Soviet Union sent 80 missions to the Moon, although only about 49 of them completed their jobs as planned, and some never really got close. But those that made it—orbiters, soft landings, photo session probes, two astronaut flybys, and six separate astronaut landings—brought or sent back a wealth of information about our closest neighbor in space. More recently, new interest in the Moon has prompted several more missions. *Clementine* in the summer of 1994 was a joint U.S. military/NASA project that sent back some 1.5 million images and mapped 99.9% of the Moon's surface. Laser technology also enabled *Clementine* to generate a detailed topographical map—and in the process the little spacecraft encountered a reflection at the Moon's poles that could indicate the presence of water ice. The possibility raised great excitement, since water on the Moon would simplify support for a colony, an idea that several governments have considered for some time. Four years later, in January 1998, NASA launched another spacecraft, *Lunar Prospector,* to orbit and map the Moon until July 1999, when scientists hoped an intentional crash landing near the pole might send up a detectable spray of water ice; however, no ice was detected. More recently, the European Space Agency (ESA) has launched *SMART-1,* a small craft on a 16-month tour to the Moon, primarily to test its solar electric propulsion technology. Launched in 2003, *SMART-1* is due to arrive at the Moon in 2004. Japan is also launching a mission to the Moon in 2004, and China has plans for a Moon landing. After nearly 30 years of no lunar missions, the Moon has once again become a solar system destination.

We have learned a great deal about the Moon from our visits. It is approximately the same age as Earth: about 4.5 billion years old. The relative abundance and proportions of oxygen isotopes suggest that the two bodies were formed nearby each other, although theories vary about the exact formation process. Did the Moon "spin off" from Earth, like a blob of paint? For this to work, Earth would have had to spin very fast, but the idea has had some supporters. Did it coalesce or condense at roughly the same time and out of the same planetesimal (pre-planet formational material) as Earth? If so, why two "planets" instead of one? Or did Earth "capture" the Moon into its gravitational field as the Moon was passing by? Or maybe, during the early days of Earth's formation, while it was still molten and was slowly building up out of many smaller planetesimals, a large "leftover" planetesimal smashed into it, vaporizing part of both Earth and the planetesimal, and spewing the molten debris into orbit around Earth, where the debris eventually became the Moon.

Perhaps the most important legacies of our lunar exploration were a greater understanding of the Moon, a greater appreciation for our Earth, and a key to some of the mysteries of our solar system. In looking closely at the Moon, we have seen a world barren and desolate, too small and having too little mass to hold on to an atmosphere. Unlike Earth, the Moon is a world stunted and locked into its own past without growth or change—a world now so static (until the next impact) that footprints left by the astronauts on its dusty surface may last a million years. It is a kind of fossil that tells the history of our solar system and our own planet. Our journeys to the Moon have

Gerard Kuiper: Planetary Scientist

Planetary science received a tremendous boost from NASA's programs, and astronomer-planetary scientist Gerard Kuiper (1905–73) was among the early visionaries who helped build a program from the beginning that could provide useful information to scientists.

Born and educated in the Netherlands, Kuiper left his homeland for the United States in 1933, when he joined the staff at Lick Observatory, near San Jose, California. There he studied binary stars and made spectroscopic searches for white dwarf stars. Later at Yerkes Observatory in Wisconsin and its southern outpost, McDonald Observatory in Texas, Kuiper made contributions to the theory of the origin of the solar system.

After World War II, Kuiper pioneered in the new field of radio astronomy, making spectroscopic observations of the planets and late-type stars. Using these techniques, he succeeded in discovering methane in the atmosphere of Saturn's giant moon, Titan, and carbon dioxide in the atmosphere of Mars, as well as water vapor in the Mira variable stars (located in the constellation Cetus). All these discoveries served to tweak the curiosity of those interested in knowing if life existed or had ever existed beyond the atmosphere of our own planet. Kuiper also discovered a new satellite orbiting Uranus and another spinning around Neptune.

In addition to serving as director of both the Yerkes and McDonald observatories, Kuiper later founded and directed the Lunar and Planetary Laboratory at the University of Arizona. For NASA, he served as principal investigator (in charge of scientific responsibilities for a mission (for the already taught us much about ourselves and other members of our biosphere—and have impressed us with the rarity of our existence.

For the next step, naturally, we turned to explore the nearest neighboring planet, Venus, the second planet from the Sun.

Veiled Venus

Often seen brightly gleaming in the early morning sky, or glowing in the early evening dusk, Venus is our closest planetary neighbor. Known as Earth's twin, Venus is close to the same diameter, size, and density as Earth. It is only 26 million miles away and travels a similar orbit around the Sun. But, curious as we naturally were,

Ranger missions to the Moon, an early series of many visits to test and survey the Moon for future astronaut landings). He also made important scientific contributions to early NASA planetary exploration.

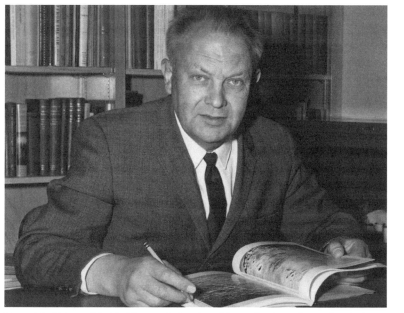

Gerard P. Kuiper (*AIP Emilio Segrè Visual Archives, Physics Today Collection*)

even the most powerful optical telescopes of our biggest observatories could not penetrate the thick veil of clouds that surrounded the planet and blocked our view.

Speculation ran high among science-fiction writers, astronomers, and planetologists alike. Maybe underneath the clouds Venus was a rainy, tropical planet with seas and jungles teeming with life. We could not see the surface—but surely clouds meant water vapor, and water vapor probably meant life, possibly even intelligent life. The idea died hard. But from the 1930s on, radio astronomy and spectroscopy began to give hints that the atmosphere and temperature could not harbor life as we know it. By 1961 microwave astronomy gave us further insights about the planet's direction and rate of rotation, atmospheric temperature, density, and pressure, and a rough idea of topography. But only with the first planetary missions did we begin to confirm fully how unlike Earth Venus really is.

Between 1961 and 1989, more than two dozen U.S. and Soviet missions set off for Venus, most of them successful. Probes tested the upper, middle, and lower atmosphere, analyzing chemistry, cloud movements, pressure and temperature. The Soviet Union launched several landers that penetrated the cloud cover and sent back pictures of the rocky plains of Venus. They relayed back surface temperature readings and more atmospheric analyses, and orbiters mapped the surface.

The U.S. *Mariner 10* spacecraft, launched in 1973, flew past Venus in early 1974 on its way to Mercury, making some interesting observations of Venus, including photos that were 7,000 times better than any we could take from Earth.

In 1978 the United States sent two Pioneer spacecraft, *Pioneer 12* and *Pioneer 13*. The second contained four atmospheric probes that deployed in different parts of the atmosphere and took temperature and pressure readings, plus data on wind patterns. But *Pioneer 12* was the stalwart hero of Venusian research. Designed to orbit Venus for 243 days, *Pioneer 12* continued to transmit scientific data for another *10 years*. By 1988 *Pioneer 12* had sent home more than 10 trillion bits of data, including a description of the extreme greenhouse effect that has trapped the Sun's heat to drive the planet's surface temperature as high as 900°F.

Between 1978 and 1983, the Soviet Union sent six Venera probes (*Venera 11* to *Venera 16*) in pairs, most of them landers. All sent back valuable details about the surface and atmosphere, including the

The Greenhouse Effect on Venus

A victim of the so-called greenhouse effect, Venus's fiery atmosphere is the result of its close proximity to the Sun and its inability to partially disperse its tremendous "heat load" back out into space.

All planets absorb energy from the Sun in the form of solar radiation. This energy (which we call sunlight) is then reradiated outward as longer-wave infrared radiation. The surface temperature of a planet is determined by the balance between the sunlight it absorbs and the infrared energy it emits. The temperature rises if a planet absorbs much more radiation than it gives off.

On Venus the cooling process is particularly hindered by the thick Venusian atmosphere, which acts something like a one-way gate, permitting the visible solar radiation to enter, but preventing the longer-wave infrared radiation from escaping. The atmosphere functions like the lid on a pot, trapping the emitted energy and causing the planet to heat up.

Many scientists fear that an increase of carbon dioxide in Earth's atmosphere, caused by continual burning of fuels such as gasoline and diesel, may also result in a greenhouse effect like our neighbor's and that a gradual accumulation of trapped "heat" may dramatically change Earth's climate and ecological balance.

first color pictures of the Venusian surface, analyses of drilled soil samples, and seismic experimentation. Two more missions launched by the USSR in 1984, *Vega 1* and *Vega 2*, carried experiments from several nations and continued on after the Venus mission to make an internationally choreographed rendezvous with comet Halley—a first-ever visit to a comet.

From all the data collected about Venus, a new picture had begun to form, when the United States sent the *Magellan* spacecraft to Venus in 1989, arriving in August 1990. Despite some technical difficulties, *Magellan* sent back stunning radar images of the surface and completed a 243-day radar mapping cycle during one complete rotation of the planet. *Magellan* revealed a surface torn by tectonic forces, ravaged by searing winds, its crust violently deformed and broken by giant volcanic eruptions.

Overall, the picture of Venus is a far cry from the imagined green, bountiful planet. At the surface, a dim, peachy light filters through the thick Venusian clouds of deadly sulfuric acid. Gentle breezes stir the intense 891°F heat of the barren, dusty high-plains desert. At 217 miles an hour, winds in the upper atmosphere whip clouds overhead 60 times faster than the strange, backward rotation of the planet. In the distance, turbulent flashes of lightning brighten the sky around the conic shape of a volcano spewing smoke and ash. As one technical memorandum from the U.S. *Mariner 5* science team read: "Venus appears to offer roasting heat, a choking atmosphere, crushing pressure, and murky skies, to which forbidding weather and hostile terrain may perhaps be added."

Scorched Mercury

Like a tiny moth circling a bright light, the planet Mercury wings closest of all to the Sun. Darting swiftly along its elliptical path, it defies the optical mirrors of our telescopes and quickly escapes our curious gaze with its forays close to its too-bright neighbor the Sun. Its surface parched by billions of years on this course, Mercury hangs poised, it seems, on the brink of fiery disaster.

But in reality, Mercury is a dense mass of rock and iron baking in the Sun's blazing heat. Once every 88 Earth days, it completes its path around the Sun at an average of 58 million miles from the solar furnace. As a consequence, it is one of the most difficult planets of all to observe from Earth, viewable only for a short time in the morning and evening. Even the invention of the telescope did little to bring Mercury into better focus.

Mariner 10 arrived at Mercury in March 1974. Fitted out with special protection against solar radiation, the spacecraft flew within 437 miles of Mercury's surface to take a close look. Carrying two television cameras with five-foot telescopes, an X-band radio transmitter, infrared radiometer, and equipment for ultraviolet experimentation, it transmitted nearly 2,500 pictures back to Earth. After zipping across Mercury's sky, the spacecraft caromed around the Sun to return twice more for photo sessions in September 1974 and March 1975.

As the first pictures came in from Mercury, scientists were struck by the planet's close resemblance to the Moon. From the evidence strewn across its parched and pitted surface, they concluded that

Mercury's geological history may have been similar in many ways—
the scene of thousands of meteorites smashing against it, some 3.9
billion years back in time.

In fact, the Moon is smooth compared to Mercury. With the
exception of one gigantic flat area known as the Caloris Basin and a
few other small patches, Mercury is almost entirely covered with
craters. Also, while scientists believe that the Moon's *maria* (vast,
flat, dark areas on its surface) were created by lava flows, most hold
an entirely different theory about the formation of the Caloris Basin.
Some evidence points to past volcanic activity on the planet, including some partial infilling of the basin itself, but the great Caloris
Basin was probably formed by the most dramatic and important
event in Mercury's history: collision with a huge asteroid.

From the evidence, planetary scientists surmise that an asteroid—possibly measuring more than 60 miles across—collided long
ago with the tiny world and leveled an area nearly 850 miles across.
As it smashed into Mercury at the speed of more than 315,000 miles
per hour, this huge missile forever changed the face of the planet,
pushing up mountain ranges over a mile and a half high around the
rim of the crater it formed. Even a confused, jumbled surface on
the opposite side of the globe, some specialists believe, may also
have been created by the collision of the impact's gigantic shock
waves as they circled the planet.

This cataclysmic collision, many planetary scientists think, may
have been the last important event in the planet's evolution. Judging from crust fractures and other evidence seen in *Mariner 10*'s photos, they deduce that Mercury had shrunk substantially before the
impact, possibly due to the cooling of the iron core or a slowing of
the planet's spin. After that, the planet evidently ceased to evolve.
Mercury apparently "died" at the end of the same period of great
bombardment that devastated the Moon, some 3.9 billion years ago.

Like a snapshot, the primordial state of Mercury's surface takes
us back in time to glimpse details about the evolution and origins of
our solar system. This is the stuff of which progress in planetary
science is made.

Mars, the Red Planet

Of all the planets in our solar system, Mars has long been a favorite
among science fiction writers and astronomers alike. From the first

days of telescopes, it was the only planet whose surface features could be seen, and in the 1890s it inspired widely respected speculation— stimulated by the observations of astronomer Percival Lowell—that

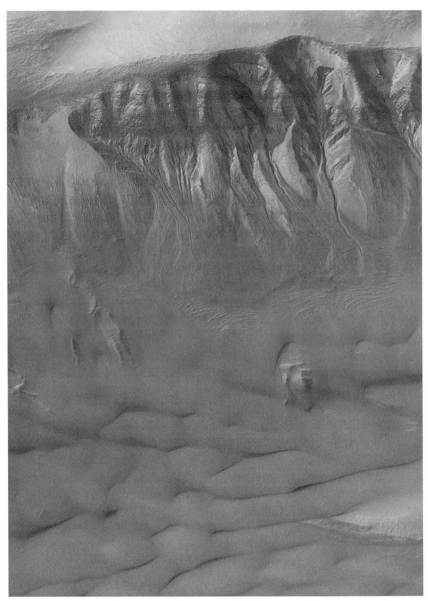

Image of a Martian gully, captured by *Mars Global Surveyor* (*NASA Jet Propulsion Laboratory/Malin Space Science Systems*)

huge artificially made canals criss-crossed its plains, signs of a present or ancient civilization. Seasonal changes in a periodically shrinking and growing ice cap at its north pole encouraged a vision of a planet much like ours, perhaps even with a growing season and a barren winter.

So the first time investigators succeeded in sending a robot spacecraft flying by—the U.S. *Mariner 4* in November 1964—the results were disappointing. From a distance just 6,000 miles above the surface, we saw our first glimpse of a planet that appeared to be flat, featureless, and lacking in life forms. Two more Mariner flyby missions in 1968 did little—except to hint at volcanic action and erosion—to brighten the prospects about what we might find on the surface of Mars.

Then a lonely robot observer called *Mariner 9* entered an orbit around Mars on November 13, 1971, becoming the first human-built object to orbit another planet. Despite a dust storm shortly after the spacecraft's arrival, the Mars of *Mariner 9* was a geologist's paradise. Far from being an ancient inert world, Mars proved to be a world where once rivers may have flowed and volcanoes erupted—a planet whose surface temperature and atmosphere may once have been capable of supporting at least some very simple form of life. Theories flew fast and furiously.

A volcano, which scientists named Olympus Mons (Mount Olympus), rose to more than 79,000 feet above the Martian surface—the largest known mountain in the solar system. Its base was more than 350 miles across, large enough to completely cover the state of Missouri! A huge canyon, of equally giant proportions—Valles Marineris—extended nearly a sixth of the way around the planet, a distance of some 2,800 miles. It was 370 miles wide and nearly 13 times longer than the Grand Canyon (as far as the distance from New York to California). Evidence of water flow abounded with what appeared to be dry river channels, some 600 miles long. As on Mercury and the Moon, asteroid impact had also played an important part in the story, with a crater measuring more than 100 miles in diameter. What did not appear in the photos from Mars was any evidence of an advanced civilization. None of the canals that Percival Lowell thought he had seen. No buildings or satellite dishes. No huts or tilled fields. In fact, no signs of civilization or life.

Intriguing information about the atmosphere arrived in 1974, though, when the Soviet Union's probe *Mars 6* sent back the news of a larger than expected percentage of argon. Because argon is an inert gas, atmospheric scientists surmised that it was left over from an atmosphere—possibly a dense atmosphere, given the large quantities of argon—from which the other gases had since combined with other elements or dissipated into space.

Maybe, given the evidence of running water and a dense atmosphere on Mars sometime in the past, the idea of life on Mars, at least life that existed some time ago, was not a totally dead concept.

How could we find out? Two robot spacecraft, named *Viking 1* and *Viking 2*, lifted off from the launch pad at Cape Kennedy in 1975, partly planned with the hope of resolving this question. Each spacecraft included an orbiter and a lander, and when the Vikings arrived in Mars's orbit in 1976, the landers peeled off to leave the orbiters circling the planet and observing, while they parachuted down to the surface, each in a different spot to gain a rabbit's-eye view of the Martian soil. The lander robots were equipped to scoop up soil from the surface and run a series of tests. One of the biggest questions the Viking science team hoped to answer was the one that had been haunting Earthlings since Lowell's time and before: Is there life on Mars? The disappointing answer came back: No. At least not at the places tested, and at least not now.

A mission to study the Martian moon Phobos, launched by the Soviet Union in 1988, met disappointment when the two mission spacecraft failed before reaching Mars, and the same fate met a U.S. project, *Mars Observer,* which was scheduled to arrive in 1993. Several missions since then have been highly successful, however: *Mars Global Surveyor,* launched in 1996, arriving at Mars in 1997, and still going strong in 2003, took tens of thousands of stunning pictures of Martian terrain. It was the first successful mission to Mars in two decades. *Mars Pathfinder,* also launched in 1996, literally bounced onto the surface of Mars—as it was designed to do—on the Fourth of July 1997. Once settled, the Pathfinder capsule opened up and released the world's longest-distance remote-control vehicle ever built. Called *Sojourner,* this little robot rover, no bigger than a microwave oven, rolled across the rocky surface of Mars, inspecting and sampling rocks in its path while the world watched on TV and the Internet. It was a huge success.

Another orbiter, *2001 Mars Odyssey,* launched in 2001, continues to collect data from orbit to help identify the composition of Martian soil, and after two lost missions, NASA designed two robust

As part of the Mars Pathfinder mission (Mars arrival: 1997), this small rover, dubbed *Sojourner*, made its way off the lander (foreground) to the Martian surface and from rock to rock in the region of the landing site, where it sampled, tested, and photographed. The Pathfinder team back on Earth controlled the rover remotely. Similar missions were launched in the summer of 2003. *(Courtesy of NASA)*

robot rovers (Mars Exploration Rover Mission: *Spirit* and *Opportunity*) to travel to Mars. The two rovers arrived safely in 2004 and set out to explore rocks and surface terrain, where they found strong evidence for past presence of water. ESA also launched a mission in 2003, *Mars Express,* which arrived in early 2004. A lander component, *Beagle-2,* was designed to search for evidence of life on Mars, but unfortunately was lost on the Martian surface.

Many questions about Mars remain unanswered. If Mars did once have a denser atmosphere, allowing water to exist in liquid form on its surface, where and why has all the water gone? Is some of it locked in permafrost just beneath the planet's surface? Exactly how much is stored permanently frozen as ice at the planet's north pole? We know definitely that some water still exists there. Planetologists have determined that water ice exists in at least three regions, according to recent reports: beneath Martian soil in the southern hemisphere, at the surface of the northern cap, and on the surface near the fringes of the southern polar cap. The rest of this ice cap is mostly "dry ice," frozen carbon dioxide. Scientists continue to suspect that the water in these three areas is "just the tip of the Martian iceberg," according to Timothy Titus of the U.S. Geological Survey.

Perhaps there was once swiftly running water that carved out the gigantic Martian channels. Some scientists, including planetary geologist Michael Carr and exobiologist Chris McKay of NASA Ames (who studies the possibility of life on other planets), think that possibly a very exotic form of simple life may have existed in the "just maybe" more hospitable Martian past and that we may someday discover some trace, some fossil evidence, of that past. In the same way that good scientists do, the robot Mars explorers—the Vikings, their predecessors, and their successors—have answered many questions, but have also posed many more.

The Asteroids

In various orbits in the solar system, a group of giant, odd-shaped rocks careen through space, most of them orbiting the Sun in a region called the asteroid belt, which is located between the orbits of Mars and Jupiter. You could think of them as "leftovers" from the formation of the solar system; asteroids are the stuff of which planets were made, the building blocks of the solar system, some of which, planetologists think, coalesced billions of years ago to form the planets. Within their composition, asteroids doubtless retain a multitude of 4.5-billion-year-old secrets, a wealth of primordial information for us to discover, if we can only gain access to it.

Some asteroids have moons, as we found out in 1993, when the spacecraft *Galileo* swung by asteroid 243 Ida for a visit on the way to Jupiter. Much to everyone's surprise, the images revealed the presence of a tiny moon (*far right*), now known as Dactyl. Since 1993, other asteroid-moon pairs have also been found. (*Courtesy of NASA/Jet Propulsion Laboratory*)

Smaller groupings of asteroids do lie outside this belt, though, and about 1 percent of all known asteroids have orbits that cross the orbits of one or more planets. Two of these groups, called Apollo and Aten, for instance, cross Earth's orbit. Considerable evidence has built up in recent years to support the premise that a large Earth-crossing asteroid—as large as six to 10 miles across—collides with Earth an average of once every 50 to 100 million years. The last one that smacked into our planet was most likely the cause of the sudden extinction of the dinosaurs, who had dominated Earth for more than 140 million years, only to disappear suddenly about 65 million years ago (see chapter 5). Given the level of evidence discovered in recent years for this scenario, teams of scientists are seriously engaged in an asteroid watch, searching for Earth-crossing asteroids that have not yet been found. Comets can also collide with a planet, to great effect as we saw in July 1994, when comet Shoemaker-Levy 9 smashed into Jupiter (see next section).

There may be as many as 100,000 asteroids that are bright enough for eventual discovery by telescope or spacecraft, but at present only a few thousand have been officially recognized. Of these, the largest currently known is Ceres, with a diameter of about 633 miles. The smallest probably range down to less than a mile in diameter. In 1991 the spacecraft *Galileo* headed for Jupiter and its system of moons; on the way it visited the asteroid Gaspra, which measures about 10 miles long and about seven or eight miles wide, sending back the first close-up photos ever taken of an asteroid. *Galileo* also visited 243 Ida, which turned out to have a moon of its own. Numerous visits to other asteroids and comets have taken place since then.

According to the most recent theory, most asteroids were probably formed when the gravity of the proto-planet Jupiter (early in its formation) prevented the asteroidal material from forming another full-scale planet nearby, leaving the majority of chunks in their present orbit and kicking still others out of the solar system altogether or into their present planet-crossing paths.

Jupiter the Giant

The largest planet in our solar system, Jupiter intrigues planetary scientists. Because it is so large and its dynamics are so similar to the Sun's, it has formed what comes close to being its own mini-solar system, with at least 28 moons orbiting around it. Across the asteroid belt from Mars, Jupiter is the first and largest of the gaseous giant planets. It is so vast, in fact, that it makes up 71 percent of all mass in the solar system, aside from the Sun.

During the 1940s and 1950s, astronomers began to put together our modern view of this celestial giant, built on evidence gleaned from Earth-based observations. German-American astronomer Rupert Wildt became the major instigator of the effort to understand the structure of Jupiter, its dynamics, and its origins. The most striking fact to surface during this pre–Space Age period was that the giant planet was more like the Sun than it was like Earth. The inner planets in the solar system (those inside the asteroid belt and closest to the Sun) are small rocky bodies with few if any satellites, while planets farther from the Sun are for the most part composed of different stuff altogether. With the exception of little-known Pluto, the other planets are gas giants, composed primarily of the simplest elements, hydrogen and helium. Most of these outer planets also have an extensive system of satellites. And, as recent explorations have shown, all four of the gas giants—Saturn, Jupiter, Uranus, and Neptune—also possess systems of rings circling close around the planet. Taking these major differences between the inner and outer planets into account, modern scientists began to understand Jupiter as a planet with a history much different from Earth's.

Created out of the nebular material that formed the solar system some 4.5 billion years ago, Jupiter and the other giant planets grew very rapidly, and their strong gravity helped them hold on to their original matter. The chemical elements that "built" Jupiter were "Sun-like" in nature and remained so. Although Earth and the inner planets were born out of the same nebula, perhaps because they grew more slowly, they couldn't hold on to light gases like hydrogen and helium effectively. So the two groups developed very differently.

But if Jupiter was a body very similar to the Sun and other stars in its composition, why hadn't it burst forth and become a star?

The answer again lies in Jupiter's size. Although large enough to have retained its star-like composition and its family of satellites, it was not large enough to have begun those nuclear reactions deep inside its core that could have triggered a stellar burst. However, Jupiter does put out more energy than it receives from the Sun (unlike the rocky planets)—caused by the tremendous heat generated within by a combination of leftover energy from the

Jupiter, the largest of the planets, has a huge family of more than 30 moons, and is also intriguing in its own right with its stormy and complex atmospheric processes. *(Courtesy of NASA/Jet Propulsion Laboratory)*

planet's formation, its tremendous gravitational contraction, and other processes.

The first interplanetary spacecraft to reach Jupiter was *Pioneer 10*, launched in 1972. On June 13, 1983, all its planetary flybys completed, it became the first object created by humans to leave the solar system. With its twin, *Pioneer 11*, it sent back the best data and photographs we had up to that time. Then, in 1977, the United States launched two Voyager spacecraft that would transform our understanding of the four gas giants with their breathtaking close-ups of the outer solar system's moons, rings, and planets. *Voyager 1* gave us glimpses just of Jupiter and Saturn, passing by Jupiter in 1979 and Saturn in 1980. *Voyager 2* made more ports of call, passing by Jupiter in 1979, Saturn in 1981, Uranus in 1986, and Neptune in 1989. By 2003, *Voyager 1* has already passed beyond the far frontier of our solar system, having exited the outer edges of the solar wind (known as the heliosphere).

The Pioneer and Voyager missions gave scientists their first good look at Jupiter's Great Red Spot and an opportunity to observe the violent atmospheric movements taking place there. To their amazement, they discovered that Jupiter has a system of rings that are much thinner than Saturn's, only about 0.6 of a mile thick and composed of two parts, one 500 miles wide and the other about 3,200 miles wide.

Among the most stunning discoveries made by the Pioneer and Voyager spacecrafts was the existence of a wealth of different environments present among the Galilean moons of Jupiter—the four big inner moons discovered by Galileo in the 17th century. So NASA planned a special mission—the spacecraft *Galileo*, which arrived at the big moon Ganymede in June 1996. One of NASA's most successful missions, *Galileo* made close passes by Jupiter, Io, Europa, Callisto, and Ganymede multiple times for seven years. It discovered even more massive and constantly changing volcanic activity at Io, and possible liquid oceans beneath the icy exteriors of Europa and

The spacecraft *Galileo* spent nearly eight years, from December 1995 to September 2003, studying Jupiter's big Galilean moons, Io, Europa, Ganymede, and Callisto. The spacecraft made 35 orbits of Jupiter, including multiple close flybys of the moons, taking 14,000 pictures. Europa (pictured) is particularly intriguing because scientists think a warm ocean—possibly hospitable to the development of life-forms—may exist beneath its icy surface. *(Courtesy of NASA/Jet Propulsion Laboratory)*

Ganymede. Europa in particular exhibits ropelike marks in the ice of its surface that appear to be refrozen cracks in the ice, where slushy liquid has welled up. Some scientists think that living creatures, possibly microscopic, could exist in the extreme environment of Europa's ocean, especially if it is warmed by tidal forces operating between Europa and Jupiter. Examples of life found on Earth in extreme environments, such as in deep-sea vents or beneath polar ice caps have caused biologists and exobiologists to revise their ideas of what is possible.

Ganymede is the brightest moon in Jupiter's system, possibly composed of rock and ice, and conceivably hosting a liquid ocean. Its surface is punctuated with dark, heavily cratered areas and many parallel lines of mountains and valleys of more recent origin. Callisto, strangely, shows no sign of an active geological history. Its thick, icy crust (possibly up to 150 miles deep) is the most heavily cratered in the solar system. What is the reason for all this diversity?

Galileo concluded its mission, after many extensions, by plunging into the gassy layers of Jupiter in 2003, reporting on its findings as it went. Its mission was a resounding success—and all this despite losing the use of its main antenna, which got stuck and was not used during the entire mission.

Collision Course

Shortly after discovery of a comet in 1993 by Eugene Shoemaker, his wife Carolyn, and another astronomer named David Levy, astronomers realized that it had broken up and was headed straight for Jupiter. What an opportunity! The astronomical community began to marshal all its resources. Mountaintop telescopes were scheduled for use. *Galileo*, on its way to Jupiter, was commandeered, though still pretty far away. The *Hubble Space Telescope* was used. Like a train of freight cars, the comet's fragments slammed into the planet at a speed of more than 130,000 miles per hour over a period of days in July 1994. Scientists studied the effects of the impacts—huge explosions in Jupiter's stratosphere, extreme turbulence, and lingering dark spots that remained long after the collision. No one had ever seen anything like it before, and the event was a grim reminder of the fact that violent collisions still do take place in the solar system, long after the early days of the solar system when they were so common.

Saturn and Its Rocky Rings

Once seen through the eyepiece of even a backyard telescope, the bright jewel of Saturn and its rings in the night sky can never be forgotten. Galileo, who was the first person to see the strange bulges that turned out to be Saturn's rings, was puzzled over what they might be. "The weakness of my understanding, and the fear of being mistaken, have greatly confounded me," he wrote to a friend in 1612. In fact, until *Pioneer 11* and two Voyager spacecrafts sent home close-ups, even our most powerful observatory telescopes did not enable us to unlock the intricacies of their structure.

From Pioneer we learned in 1979 that Saturn is very cold, –279°F and even colder in the rings at –328°F, backing up a theory that the rings were composed mostly of ice. The pictures Pioneer took of Saturn and its largest moon, Titan, were fuzzy, but they set the stage for the crisper, closer views to come a year later from *Voyager 1,* and the following year from *Voyager 2.*

Looking through the Voyagers' remote eyes, scientists saw a planet with much less color than the striking contrasts seen on Jupiter. Since Saturn is colder, it is subject to different dynamics and different chemical reactions. The Voyagers also gave scientists their first close views of turbulence in the belts and zones of Saturn's atmosphere. They measured winds on the planet that reached 1,118 miles per hour, four times faster than those found on Jupiter. Also, the Voyagers verified that the giant multi-ringed planet generates nearly twice as much energy as it receives from the Sun, the equivalent of 100 million large power plants.

Saturn's rings, moreover, held thousands of surprises.

Saturn's rings have fascinated astronomers since their discovery nearly 400 years ago, and they have become more intriguing than ever in the 21st century, now that scientists have discovered the complexity of their dynamics and structure. *(Courtesy of NASA/Jet Propulsion Laboratory)*

Titan, Saturn's biggest moon, hides its surface beneath a thick, cloudy atmosphere. Planetologists think this far-off world may harbor life, if not now, then perhaps sometime in the future, and they hope to find out more about this mysterious moon from the *Cassini/Huygens* spacecraft (depicted at Saturn) and future explorations. *(Courtesy of NASA/Jet Propulsion Laboratory)*

These regions of orbiting rocky, icy material turned out to be much more complex than anyone had ever imagined. There were not three rings, which is what astronomers thought they saw from Earth, but a complex and constantly changing system made up of tens of thousands of interacting ringlets. The ring system is nearly 249,000 miles across and is composed of millions of tiny particles of ice and snow. Shepherding satellites orbiting close to the rings produced kinks and clumps, even "braids" in the structure. Radial alignments of dust looked like spokes radiating out from the planet through the rings.

Among Saturn's nine known satellites, the most interest settled on Titan, known as the "atmospheric," because observations from Earth had shown that the icy world had an atmosphere of methane and that hydrocarbons might also be present. Larger than the planet Mercury, Titan seemed like a possible candidate for having hosted some form of life at some point in the distant past. The news from Voyager was even more interesting. The atmosphere of Titan is thicker than Earth's by one and a half times, and it is mostly nitrogen, with only a small constituent of methane. Before Voyager, Earth was thought to be the only place in the solar system with an atmosphere primarily of nitrogen. In fact, the nitrogen on Titan registered at levels 10 times those of Earth. Unfortunately, chemical reactions in the thick atmosphere created a dense smog-like condition that made the surface of the satellite itself invisible to Voyager's cameras, so much remains unknown about Titan.

What's going on in that "smog" and under it, on the surface? Since nitrogen is usually a clear gas and the atmosphere is mostly nitrogen, what is making the haze? The science fiction mind, of course, can take off from here—but scientists seriously think that the smog could be a kind of organic haze and that the chemical reactions taking place might be similar to reactions that occurred in the Earth's atmosphere billions of years ago. These questions have stirred up such great interest that several nations' space programs, including ESA and NASA, have collaborated on a two-part mission, known as *Cassini/Huygens*, launched in 1997 and scheduled to reach Saturn in 2004. On arrival the *Huygens* probe will drop down through Titan's atmosphere and try to answer some of these questions. *Cassini*, meanwhile, will orbit Saturn for detailed studies of the planet, its rings, and its moons (which number at least 31).

Mysterious Uranus

A far-off greenish Ping-Pong ball in the night sky, Uranus completely escaped detection until 1781, when it was first sighted by William Herschel. Four times the diameter of Earth, Uranus orbits far away in a path that is 1,695,700,000 miles from the Sun at its closest. Before *Voyager*, only five of its moons were known. Also, until 1977, little else was known about it except one major oddity: Its axis is "tipped," sloped at 98 degrees. So, unlike Earth and the other planets, whose equatorial regions point toward the Sun, Uranus spins on its axis almost sideways. It takes Uranus 84 years to complete its orbit around the Sun, and during that time, each pole experiences 42 years of light followed by 42 years of darkness.

In 1977, before Voyager's journey, one other fact came to light by accident. A group of astronomers were observing aboard NASA's *Kuiper Airborne Observatory*, which was a specially equipped high-altitude aircraft that could fly above much of the distorting turbulence of Earth's atmosphere. (It has now been replaced by another airborne observatory, known as *SOFIA,* the Stratospheric Observatory for Infrared Astronomy.) The plan called for observing Uranus as it passed in front of a particular star, a method called occultation, frequently used by astronomers to gain more information about one or the other object. To their amazement, the light from the star behind Uranus dipped slightly before the planet passed in front of it and again afterward. Had they discovered two new satellites on either side of the planet? Further telescope observations confirmed that, no, what they had found was that Uranus had rings!

So one of *Voyager 2*'s prime tasks was to take a close look at the Uranus rings. It turned out that the innermost ring was about 10,000 miles above Uranus's cloud tops and six of the 11 rings (two of which were discovered by *Voyager 2*) were only three to six miles across. The three widest were only about 10 to 30 miles wide. An even bigger surprise was that the rings appeared to consist primarily of large chunks of almost coal-black material, most of them between 23 to 3,000 feet across—much larger than the dust-like particles of Saturn's huge ring system.

Still another curious mystery for the *Voyager 2* scientists was Uranus's strange magnetic field. While most of the other planets in the solar system are closely aligned with their axis of rotation, Uranus's magnetic field is displaced nearly 55 degrees from its rotation axis. As the planet rotates along its axis, its offset magnetic field wobbles in space. Also, the solar wind arriving from the Sun and streaming past the planet draws the far side of the wobbling field into a gently elongated banana shape, an effect never observed anywhere else.

Uranus's atmosphere of hydrogen, nitrogen, carbon, and oxygen was found to have a strange sheen rising from the upper atmosphere—possibly ultraviolet light—and the entire planet was shrouded in a smog-like haze with a surprisingly uniform temperature throughout. Strong, 200-mile-per-hour winds, twice as strong as Earth's jet stream, moved through the upper clouds. But *Voyager 2* could not penetrate the haze.

The moons, however, amazed the science team. Miranda, the innermost moon, gave evidence of tremendous geological activity in its ancient past. It had two different kinds of terrain, one very old and heavily pockmarked with ancient craters, the other young and more complex, obviously the result of major geological changes. Strange racetrack-like patterns and rope-like imprints marred the surface. And, though Miranda is only 300 miles in diameter, a canyon some 50,000 feet deep—10 times deeper than Earth's Grand canyon—carved a path across its face. *Voyager 2* offered quick views as well of the four other largest moons. Ariel had broad, curving valleys and canyons on a young and complex surface. Umbriel was black like Uranus's rings. Titania showed evidence, possibly, of comet impacts in the last 3–4 billion years. Oberon, like Miranda, showed evidence of enormous fault structures, including tall mountains and craters that appeared to have once been flooded with a dark fluid and then frozen over.

The visit was short, but it left the Voyager mission's science team with much thought-provoking data as *Voyager 2* sped away from the Uranian system in January 1986 to head for its next and last stop before speeding toward the edge of the solar system.

Neptune, Outer Giant

Although Neptune, the eighth planet out from the Sun, travels at a distance nearly a billion miles farther away from the Sun than Uranus, it is similar to its distant neighbor in many ways. It is the last, in order of distance from the Sun, of the gas giants, and it appears nearly featureless as seen from Earth-bound telescopes. Its diameter is 3.8 times the size of Earth's while its mass is 17.2 times greater. Neptune's atmosphere is mostly hydrogen with small amounts of helium and methane, and it is probably the methane that gives the planet its bluish cast. Some scientists also believe that the methane, although slight, may affect the planet's balance of heat by absorbing sunlight. Earth-based measurements indicate that Neptune gives off more heat than it absorbs from the Sun. Some scientists think this excess heat may be caused by a release of energy as heavy molecules gradually sink toward the planet's core. Although most planetologists think that Neptune has no solid surface, the density of the planet does suggest that it may have a small rocky interior with a mantle of water, methane, and ammonia.

But in August 1989, when *Voyager 2* swung past Neptune, it changed forever the formerly faceless image of the great blue planet and its satellites. Before *Voyager 2*, only two of Neptune's satellites were known: Triton, which is about the size of Earth's Moon, and Nereid, whose far-flung, eccentric orbit made it impossible for *Voyager 2* to photograph it at high resolution. As early as June 1989, two months before arriving at the planet, *Voyager 2* had already found another satellite, a dark, icy moon larger than Nereid. Then, close by the planet's ring system, it found a total of five more small moons, similar to the shepherding moons *Voyager 2* found near the rings of both Jupiter and Saturn.

Early in *Voyager 2*'s approach to the strange, blue ball of gases that is Neptune, the spacecraft discovered an enormous storm system in its atmosphere, the Great Dark Spot, which extends over an area as large as Earth. It is located at about the same latitude as Jupiter's Great Red Spot, and its size relative to the planet is comparable. Whipped up by winds as fast as 450 miles per hour, the Great Dark Spot looks like a giant pod exploding at one end as it orbits the planet. It is just one of several enormous storm systems topped by higher-altitude clouds that scoot above them, but scientists are puzzled that Neptune could have such turbulent storm dynamics so far from the energy of the Sun.

Yet another major surprise discovered by Voyager was Neptune's rings, which from Earth had appeared to be incomplete arcs. Neptune's great distance from Earth, however, had made identification extremely difficult, and *Voyager 2* established that although the rings are very faint, they do completely encircle the planet as a ring system.

But probably the greatest excitement surrounding *Voyager 2*'s flyby at Neptune centered on Triton, Neptune's largest moon. This mottled pink body appears to be the coldest place in the solar system, at about –400°F. (Both Pluto and Charon, which *Voyager 2* did not visit, appear from ground-based measurements to be warmer though much farther away from the Sun.) Triton also appears to have volcanoes of ice, which may even still be active, blasting frozen nitrogen crystals as big as 15 miles into the thin atmosphere.

A computer-generated montage showing Neptune as it would appear from a spacecraft approaching Neptune's largest moon, Triton. *(Courtesy of NASA/Jet Propulsion Laboratory)*

Neptune was the last stop for *Voyager 2* before heading

for the edge of the solar system and beyond, toward the Milky Way. The small spacecraft and its twin have left behind a great wealth of information and images that continue to stimulate insights as scientists examine and analyze them in hundreds of different ways.

Pluto, the Far Traveler

Looking toward the Sun from Pluto, at an average distance of 3.7 billion miles, a future space traveler would see a small, bright spot in the sky no larger than Jupiter appears to us from Earth. The ninth planet to be discovered, Pluto was once considered the last outpost of our solar system, although portions of Neptune's orbit are more distant. However, neither rates any longer as the most distant known object in the solar system. That honor goes to a small, reddish, planetlike body named Sedna—too small to earn the name *planet*— which was first sighted in 2004 at a distance of 8 billion miles. With its diameter of only around 1,000 miles and a highly eccentric orbit, some scientists have speculated that Pluto may not be a planet at all, but a comet, asteroid, or even an escaped "moon" of Neptune.

Pluto wasn't even discovered until 1930, when Clyde W. Tombaugh located it using the telescope at Lowell Observatory in Arizona—aptly enough, since it was Percival Lowell who predicted Pluto's existence based on disturbances in the orbits of Saturn and Uranus. In 1988 scientists traveling in an airplane at 41,000 feet made direct observations of the atmosphere of Pluto, about which planetologists had previously held suspicions but no proof. There had been considerable controversy over the planet's density. Although we still know little about the planet, it is believed to be composed mostly of water ice with a crust of methane. The discovery of this methane frost on Pluto's surface in 1976 caused planetologists to downgrade their estimate of the planet's size. The methane frost, they reasoned, would make the planet reflect more light from its surface, misleading astronomers into thinking that Pluto was larger than it actually was.

In 1978 Pluto offered yet another surprise when research led to the discovery by James W. Christy and Robert S. Harrington of Charon, Pluto's only moon. With a diameter one-tenth the size of Pluto's, the tiny satellite is the most massive relative to its planet of any in the solar system.

Charon's discovery further helped to give scientists a more reliable estimate of Pluto's mass. As a result, astronomers realized Pluto couldn't be as large as some had speculated; the present estimation of its size is around 1,926 miles in diameter, about one-fourth the size of Earth. In fact, some planetologists think that Pluto's small size calls for a demotion from planet to asteroid, but since asteroids don't generally have either moons or atmospheres, for now Pluto's status seems safe.

How It All Began

The data from all these spacecraft have gone a long way toward filling in the picture of how our solar system may have formed. Planetary geologists and physicists continue to pore over the millions of photos, images, and statistics. Computer modeling helps them test scenarios and measure the results of impacts, temperatures, orbits, angles, and velocities. Most agree that the Sun, Earth, and eight other planets of our solar system were formed a little over 4.5 billion years ago by the contraction of a giant cloud (the primeval nebula) of interstellar gas composed mainly of hydrogen, helium, and dust. No one is sure what the exact trigger was that began this contraction, but some scientists believe that it may have started when shock waves from a nearby supernova, or stellar explosion, rippled through space, upsetting the delicate balance of the loose cloud's original state. Whatever the case, once the process started, the contraction continued under the natural and inevitable force of the gravitational attraction within the cloud itself. Contracting and spinning violently, the cloud became disk-shaped and flattened around its outer edges. Meanwhile, the huge ball of matter that collected in its center contracted into a heavier and heavier mass to become the developing Sun.

As the cloud continued to spin more and more rapidly, its billions of small particles of dust began to collide with greater violence and frequency, concentrating in the plane of the disk. Gradually these grains built up into larger and larger chunks. As these "planetesimals," early ancestors of the planets and their satellites, reached a certain size, they no longer depended only upon accidental collision to expand their mass. Instead they began to build enough mass to use gravity to reach out and attract more and more particles of solid material. These "protoplanets" gradually built up, most of them continuing to rotate and revolve following the direction of the parent nebula from which they were born.

Meanwhile, although the gigantic mass of the slowly developing and contracting Sun had not yet begun to turn on its nuclear furnace, the temperatures in the inner solar system were high enough to keep volatile substances such as water, methane, and ammonia in a gaseous state. Thus, the inner planets formed from such nonvolatile components of the nebula as iron and silicates. But out farther from the embryo Sun, the lower temperatures allowed the volatiles to become incorporated into the formation of the giant outer planets (Jupiter, Saturn, Uranus, and Neptune), at the same time allowing these giants to expand by attracting and gathering large quantities of light elements such as hydrogen and helium from the surrounding nebula.

As the Sun continued to collapse and the density and temperature in the inner core began to rise, it approached a critical temperature of around 10 million Kelvin and began to generate energy by the nuclear fusion of hydrogen. Once it was switched on, the Sun also began to generate a solar wind, a flow of electrically charged particles, which like a giant leaf-blower began driving the remaining gas and dust grains out of the solar system.

Meanwhile, heated by internal radioactivity and the energy generated by the addition of matter, the cores of the protoplanets began to melt, forming the internal structure the planets still have today. Finally, the remaining planetesimals, those too heavy to be swept away by the solar wind, began to blast the developing planets during a great half-billion-year bombardment, the impact scars of which can still be seen on most of the planets today.

What Is It Worth?

Human beings have always wanted to know how things work and why, and that is what "pure science" is all about—finding answers and raising new questions, and then finding new answers and seeing new patterns and the way things fit together. But it has become very expensive to find these answers, and many people rightfully ask, Why do we need to know? How can we justify sending spacecraft to other planets when people die on Earth of diseases that can be cured and of hunger that is unnecessary?

Perhaps the best answer is that throughout the short span of time humans have existed, compared to all species that have ever lived on Earth, what measure of success we have achieved at extending and improving human life has always resulted from our search to know and understand. In this case, the understanding that comes from comparative study of atmospheres, geology, magnetic dynamics, and the rest of the physics and chemistry at play cannot be achieved in any other way. The diversity of types and complexity of facts discovered so far has astounded scientists, raised many questions, and challenged countless assumptions. The most direct and important result of planetary exploration is the new and urgent understanding we have gained of the delicate nature of our own planet—recognizing the uniqueness of its ecosystem in the solar system and the warning parallels we can see as we have explored the other lifeless and inhospitable planets in our solar system.

5
Mission to Planet Earth

AFTER EXPLORING THE BARREN, rocky spheres and giant balls of gas that orbit with us around the Sun, our Earth seems all the more a welcome oasis of a planet, as seen from space, swirling like a blue, green and white marble. Water sloshes across its surface, the Sun's benevolent radiance gently warming its atmosphere, which is rich in nitrogen and oxygen and covers everything like a protective and nurturing blanket. This is the only planet presently known to support life—and Space Age exploration of our solar system has served up a healthy reminder of the fragility of the intricate systems that support living organisms here. In the last half of the century, as geologists, atmospheric scientists, oceanographers, and resource specialists explore the forces at work, they have made use of an ever-expanding range of new tools, from comparative planetology to radiocarbon dating to computer modeling to satellite mapping, tracing the history of our planet and predicting its near and distant future. The combined effort has become a worldwide mission to explore the intricate secrets of our own planet, Earth.

The View from Above

Since the success of the first artificial satellite, *Sputnik I*, in 1957, the Earth itself has been under almost constant observation by satellites orbiting high overhead. Although many of these are used for military information-gathering, commercial purposes and communications, many others have studied the Earth's environment and resources. The first Landsat satellite (*Landsat I*) was launched in

1972, and many others have followed since. Circling the globe in a variety of orbits, satellites have discovered the Earth's Van Allen radiation belts, tracked the movements of fish in the oceans, uncovered ancient lost roads and cities in the deserts, and monitored the growth of vegetation and the spread of pollution. Weather satellites have brought us the reasonably accurate five-day forecast plus invaluable information about the state of our atmosphere, including discovery of a growing hole in the protective ozone layer in the upper stratosphere. Resource-imaging satellites track changes in forests and crops worldwide and locate mineral deposits. And oceanographers have used satellite data to study the dynamics of the ocean and its vast, vital currents.

Earthrise, as seen from the Moon (Courtesy of NASA)

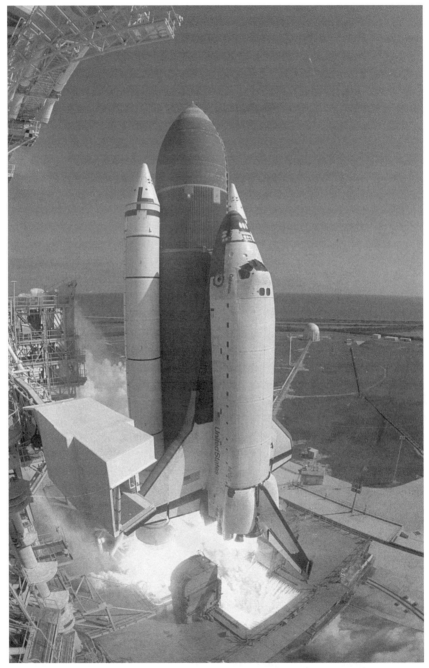

NASA's fleet of space shuttles has launched numerous Earth resource-imaging satellites and countless others for measuring change in Earth's atmosphere, oceans, and crust. *(Courtesy of NASA)*

Literally, the Space Age has both changed the way humankind lives and caused us to see ourselves in the context of the universe around us. But perhaps the most dramatic changes in our view of the Earth since mid-century resulted from a series of bold, new ideas about the Earth's crust, resulting from the use of new tools and methods.

Drifting Continents

This revolution in our understanding of the Earth's crust occurred in the 1950s and 1960s, when geologists developed the idea that the crust of Earth is broken into a number of large plates that move relative to each other. The roots of this idea went back a century earlier, when New York State geologist James Hall (1811–98) noticed that sediments built up along the mountain belts are at least 10 times thicker than in interior regions of the continents. From this observation developed the idea that the crust of continents began as ancient and folded troughs in the Earth's surface that thickened through progressive additions of sediment then hardened and consolidated.

Between 1908 and 1912, German geologist Alfred Lothar Wegener and others came to a recognition that these continents, over long spans of time, tend to rupture, drift apart, and eventually collide. These collisions crumple the sediment buildup in the folded troughs, and that's how mountain belts are formed.

Wegener argued that the way the continental edges fit together like a huge jigsaw puzzle reinforced the concept of continental drift. Further, he pointed out that rock formations along the two sides of the Atlantic—in Brazil and Africa—match each other in age, type, and structure. They also contain fossils of the same land creatures, creatures that could not have made the long swim across the ocean. Not everyone was convinced, though—especially geophysicists.

That's where the recent story takes up. English geologist Sir Edward Crisp Bullard (1907–80) ran computer analyses on the way these two continents pieced together and found a perfect fit. Other ocean edges did not show the same kind of clear evidence, though, especially around the Pacific and Indian oceans. Many geologists think that mountain chains are still in process of creation along the edges of the Pacific Ocean, explaining the existence of parallel ranges, strings of volcanoes, and frequent earthquakes in these regions.

Studies of the ocean floor with echo-measuring devices in the 1920s had enabled scientists to map and model the seafloor with new accuracy, and this led to the discovery that the mid-ocean ridge first found by 19th-century cable layers in the Atlantic extended over 40,000 miles, nearly around the world. But after World War II, marine geophysicists adapted the military's airborne magnetometer to measure variations in magnetic intensity and orientation of the ocean floor. This led American geophysicist James Ransom Heirtzler (1925–   ) to see, from crossing back and forth across the ridge, that the two sides were mirror images of each other.

Further studies, using radioisotope dating of basaltic rocks at the top of the ridge and sediments at intervals down the sides, revealed that the top of the ridge was extremely young in terms of the Earth's history—only about 1 million years old—and the farther away from the ridge on either side, the older the crustal rocks were found to be and the thicker the layer of sediment. The conclusion reached by geophysicists was that the North Atlantic ridge is the spot where new ocean crust is being created, carried up by convection currents as hot lava and immediately cooled on contact with the deep ocean waters. The crustal segments on either side of the ridge move continually apart, about 0.4 inch a year in the North Atlantic and almost two inches annually in the Pacific. These relatively slow rates of movement, powered by thermal convection currents that come from deep in the Earth's mantle, have caused what we call continental drift. This same great gash in the ocean floor connects with the Great Rift Valley that cuts across eastern Africa, where the shifting African and Arabian plates have collided and pulled apart, creating a "floor" bracketed by parallel geological faults. This is a land where intense volcanic activity has played havoc, while upward-shifting segments of rock create jutting shoulders, and sinking areas of the floor create great depressions that have filled with water to become the famous lakes of Africa, such as Lake Turkana. (These areas have also become some of the richest sources of fossils of ancient humans and human-like creatures ever found, which we'll discuss further in chapter 8.)

Scientists at Columbia University completed detailed maps of the ocean floor in the 1960s, when Harry Hess came up with the idea that a new ocean crust is being formed at the rift, while the old crust sinks into deep trenches in the ocean floor. (One such trench is located off the Philippine Islands in the Pacific.) Known as seafloor spreading, Hess's theory was confirmed by measuring the ages of rocks dredged from the ocean bottom.

Geologists have synthesized Hess's ideas about seafloor spreading and theories about continental drift into a single theory, known as integrated plate tectonics (*tectonics* meaning movement of the Earth's crust). The crust of the Earth, according to plate tectonics, is broken into several large plates, some of them consisting of crust that's entirely under water, while others have portions of continental crust. Geologists have found, through analysis of seismic (earthquake) data, that a slow-moving, somewhat fluid layer lies 30 to 80 miles beneath the crust, where its shifts contribute to these movements. The plates move, sometimes bumping into each other, causing the formation of mountains, volcanoes, and fault lines along which earthquakes occur. One of the plates, for example, contains most of the crust lying beneath the Pacific Ocean; another contains the North American continent and the western half of the crust lying under the Atlantic.

Plate tectonics explains such diverse geological phenomena as the existence of mountains (pushed up by plates overlapping or pushing together), the location of volcanoes and earthquakes (caused by tension between plates), and the formation of trenches and rifts on the floor of the ocean (caused by plates pulling apart from each other).

Although some geologists did not accept the theory at first, by the late 1980s there was firm evidence that plates were moving in the predicted patterns. The theory has proved successful in predicting many features of the Earth's surface, and in the 1980s the use of satellites such as *LAGEOS* and laser measurements enabled scientists to measure the slow-motion movements of the plates at about one inch a year.

Dirty Death of the Dinosaurs

Since the 18th century geologists have engaged in heated controversies over the history of the Earth and how it has developed over the millennia. Some highly respected 18th- and 19th-century geologists and comparative zoologists, including biologists George Cuvier and Charles Bonnet, thought the Earth's history must have included periodic catastrophes. But they had little evidence to reinforce their claims, and their point of view was overridden by another theory, known as uniformitarianism, which was later replaced by gradualism.

The evidence has piled up showing that the dinosaur dynasty on Earth ended about 65 million years ago, when an asteroid plowed into a region that we now call the Yucatan Peninsula and the Gulf of Mexico. The impact sent gigantic quantities of dust and smoke up into the atmosphere, where the particles blocked out the sunlight, causing cataclysmic destruction of many life forms on Earth, including the extinction of the dinosaurs. *(© C. Butler / Photo Researchers, Inc.)*

Supported by the work of James Hutton and the well-considered theories and writing of Charles Lyell and Charles Darwin, gradualism held that the geologic processes of Earth and the evolution of its living organisms had taken place over long expanses of time, without sudden changes or breaks with the past. Where fossils and geological strata failed to back up this premise, surely a link was missing from the record.

So when Niles Eldredge and Stephen Jay Gould (1941–2002) came up with the idea of "punctuated equilibria" in 1972, they knew it was bound to be a controversial idea. In fact, it inspired one of the decade's most passionate debates about the evolutionary process.

Eldredge, who became chairman and curator of the Department of Invertebrates (creatures without backbones) of the American Museum of Natural History in the 1980s, had made a study of trilobite fossils throughout the northeastern United States. Like shrimp and crabs, trilobites—now long extinct—wore their skeletons on the outside and shed them as they grew. So, conceivably, you could find as many as 20 fossilized trilobite skeletons shed by one trilobite over its lifetime, making trilobite fossils a lot easier to find than, say, dinosaur fossils. The tall, thin, bearded young man in glasses scoured upstate New York and Ohio, as well as an area along the Ausable River in Ontario. He found good examples, many of which were around 350 million years old. But he found little evidence that any significant change had taken place in trilobites during long periods of time, as measured by where he found them in the geological strata. Because trilobites have more visible fossil details than most invertebrates—eyes, tail, and body ridges—Eldredge was able to make detailed comparisons, using a microscope to measure the distance between the eyes, the height of the eyes, and the length of the tail. He compared his findings with similar fossils from Germany and the northern areas of Africa.

Then he noticed, as T. H. Huxley and a few others had in the previous century, that the fossil record seemed to show "bursts" of

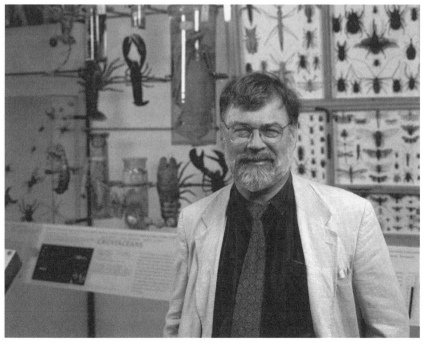

Niles Eldredge *(Courtesy American Museum of Natural History)*

Stephen Jay Gould *(Courtesy American Museum of Natural History)*

change, or diversification into new species, punctuating long periods of stability. When Huxley had brought this idea up to his friend Charles Darwin, the author of evolutionary theory, Darwin, who saw evolution as a gradual, steady process, had replied that the fossil record was too sketchy to support speculation. But Eldredge's work on trilobites was extensive, and his discovery of relatively short periods of rapid evolution supported Huxley's 100-year-old arguments.

When Eldredge consulted his colleague, Stephen Jay Gould, who was a professor of paleontology at Harvard University and curator of its Museum of Comparative Zoology, he found enthusiastic agreement. Gould had investigated variation and evolution in Bahamian land snails, which had been around as long as trilobites, and he supported Eldredge's idea that it was time to acknowledge the tale of episodic pattern told by the rocks and fossils. The two of them developed the idea together and published a joint paper describing the evolutionary pattern that Gould dubbed "punctuated equilibria" (often known by the nickname "punk eek"). Gradualism, they argued, was never supported by the evidence offered by fossils and rocks. Instead, change took place in relatively short time frames (lasting perhaps as long as 100,000 years—but that is, as Gould said, a blink of an eye in geological time). And change is interspersed with extended periods of changelessness. Not everyone agreed with this revolutionary idea, but it set the stage for a chance geological discovery published in 1980 by geophysicist Walter Alvarez that suddenly brought catastrophism back to the forefront of scientific thought.

Alvarez was working at a site in Italy, investigating ancient layers of sedimentation to test the rates at which they were laid down. He asked his father, Luis Walter Alvarez (1911–88), a Nobel laureate in physics, to help analyze some of the clay cores for the presence of certain metals, including iridium. The senior Alvarez had colleagues at the Lawrence Berkeley Laboratory who had access to the equipment necessary to check the clay for heavy metals, and he persuaded them to run some tests of the Italian clay. To everyone's complete surprise, one clay layer showed levels 25 times higher than those just above and below it. It so happened that the high-iridium layer was the very layer that had been laid down 65 million years ago, at the end of the Cretaceous age, just before the beginning of the Tertiary age, at what is known as the Cretaceous-Tertiary boundary, often referred to by geologists as the K-T boundary. The question was, why? Moreover, when samples of the K-T boundary from all over the world were examined, they showed the same high levels of iridium!

Iridium is a rare element on Earth, but it is contained in abundance in asteroids and comets. So the Alvarezes and their colleagues came up with a highly controversial idea: The iridium deposits were caused when a large body crashed into the Earth—an asteroid or comet perhaps as large as six or more miles across. Such an impact, they reasoned, could explain not only the high content of iridium and other unusual metals they found, but also the "Great Dying" that took place at the end of the Cretaceous age—extinction of the dinosaurs and most other life that had dominated the Triassic, Cretaceous, and Jurassic ages. When the asteroid hit, they figured, it would have sent huge clouds of dust laden with iridium and other metals common in asteroids billowing up into the atmosphere, blotting out the radiation from the Sun for as long as five years. The lack of sunlight would have cooled the Earth and stopped photosynthesis and killed most plant life on Earth, which in turn would have brought an end to most animal life—some estimates run as high as 75% or more. Eventually, the iridium filtered out of the atmosphere to form the layer of rock at the K-T boundary.

The idea caught on in the popular press, and *Time* magazine carried a cover story headlined, "Did Comets Kill the Dinosaurs?" Here was an explanation for the extinction of dinosaurs that had actual evidence to back it up. But the theory was both bold and controversial, and not everyone agreed.

Yet, some took the idea even further. The well-known mass extinction at the K-T boundary was not the only one in Earth's history. When two investigators, David M. Raup and J. John Sepkoski, Jr. (1948–99), looked at other mass extinctions of the type that occurred at the K-T boundary, they noticed a regular pattern, with similar extinctions occurring about once every 26 to 28 million years. They could not think of any factor on Earth that would be likely to cause that kind of cyclical "great dyings." But what about factors from beyond Earth? The most prominent idea was that something periodically disturbs the cloud of comets—known as the Oort cloud—located at the edge of the solar system, and when this happens, about 1 billion of the comets fall toward the Sun, and a few of them would almost certainly strike the Earth, causing such catastrophes as mass extinctions.

What could cause such a violent disturbance of the solar system's equilibrium? One theory centers on the idea that our Sun has a twin, a companion star called Nemesis, that periodically comes close enough to the Oort Cloud at the edge of our little system of nine planets to throw comets or asteroids into a tailspin. The search for Nemesis continues, but the mystery is still open for new ideas and investigation.

Although much of the new catastrophism is still in dispute, the idea that started it all, the impact of an object at the K-T time boundary, has gradually gained acceptance by most geologists and paleontologists. Whether or not the rest of the theory holds, whether or not Nemesis exists, apparently something did strike the Earth at the point in the Earth's history that we now see as the K-T time boundary and caused the mass extinctions. The exact reason is still open to investigation.

Investigations of these ideas, including computer modeling of atmospheric reactions to such a cataclysmic event, also spurred exploration, initiated by astronomer Carl Sagan and Stanford ecologist Paul Ehrlich, of what would happen to the Earth in the event of the most dread of all human-created catastrophes, nuclear war. And so, the concept of nuclear winter became another spinoff of the Alvarezes' theory about the dirty death of the dinosaurs caused by cooling of the Earth by soot and dust clouds in the sky.

Hole in the Ozone

The last half of the 20th century has seen a dramatic change in our view of Earth as bountiful and indestructible—a change brought about in part by the perspective we've gained by looking at Earth from space. One observation is the disappearance of large quantities of ozone from the stratosphere.

Ozone has been an essential part of Earth's ecology for a billion of years or more. Early in the planet's history, once plants began to contribute oxygen to the atmosphere, ozone also began to form through the interaction of solar energy and oxygen. As a result, an ozone (O_3) layer formed—a vast shield centered about 20 miles above the planet that protects terrestrial life from ultraviolet radiation that can be harmful, even lethal. Because ozone has begun to disappear, without its protection humans face increases in skin cancer, and all life-forms may be seriously affected. In addition, due to related chemical reactions, the planet faces a general warming trend that may result in the melting of polar ice caps and widespread changes in agriculture and the balance of Earth's ecology.

Scientists first began to notice that ozone was disappearing from Earth's upper atmosphere in the 1970s, but in 1985 the drama came to a sudden unexpected head. From data reported by the *Nimbus 7* weather satellite, scientists discovered that, since 1973 a gap in the ozone layer develops high in the skies over Antarctica during the Southern Hemisphere's spring, each September and October.

In 1986 a similar, though smaller, hole was discovered over the Arctic by balloons first launched from Alert, a Canadian town near the North Pole. The scientists for Canada's Department of Environment whose instruments were carried by the balloons found a vast crater above the North Pole, a sort of "drain hole" for ozone of the Northern Hemisphere.

As far back as 1974, F. Sherwood Rowland and Mario Molina warned that chlorofluorocarbons (also called freons or CFCs), commonly used as spray propellants and in refrigeration and Styrofoam packaging, might cause a depletion of the ozone layer. By mid-1988 it became clear from investigations that one of the major culprits responsible for the disappearance of ozone in the upper atmosphere was definitely CFCs. In a complicated chemical process, when these chemicals reach the upper atmosphere, their components combine with ozone to form other substances. Hence the disappearance of ozone. Rowland and Molina received the 1995 Nobel Prize in chemistry for their work in the formation and decomposition of ozone.

In the 1990s the use of CFCs finally began to show a reduction. Following worldwide environmental pacts involving most of the nations of the world, several fast food chains have yielded to pressure to eliminate Styrofoam packaging, fewer CFCs are used in sprays, and refrigeration is coming into use that does not use the "killer" types of freon. But some scientists urge continued and immediate action. As atmospheric chemist Joe Pinto puts it, "We can't go up there with vacuum cleaners, or pump up more ozone."

Earth's Greenhouse Effect

One of the most thought-provoking products of the new Space Age picture we have of Venus—once thought to be a Garden of Eden—is our recognition that Venus doubtless did, like Earth, at one time have great oceans of water. Now those oceans are long-since boiled away by the searing heat of Venus's oven-like atmosphere, and Venus has become a blast furnace in which no creature could possibly live. Could Earth's oceans and atmosphere travel the same route?

On Earth, growing levels of carbon dioxide wastes spewing into the atmosphere from automobiles and factories, combined with CFCs that have damaged the protective ozone layer in the atmosphere, have caused a noticeable overall rise in temperature. Wholesale destruction of rain forests has also disturbed the balance of carbon dioxide and oxygen in the same atmosphere. (Botanist Wayte Thomas of the New York Botanical Garden estimated in 1993 that humans have chopped down all but 2 percent of the Atlantic coastal forest of Brazil since the Portuguese explorers first landed there some 500 years ago.)

Some atmospheric scientists have estimated that, if we continue to expel carbon dioxide into the atmosphere at the present rate, the atmospheric carbon dioxide level will double by sometime in the middle of the next century. Recent computer models indicate that in about 140 years, the current levels will quadruple, producing a weakening of the conveyor-belt system of ocean currents that transports heat around the globe. This would create major changes in the ocean circulation, reducing the mixing between the deep ocean and surface waters and limiting the exchange in which nutrients from the deep ocean are brought to the surface and oxygen from the surface is carried to the deep regions. The atmosphere would gradually warm more and more to a temperature equal to what the Earth experienced during the Cretaceous period, when dinosaurs lived and both polar ice caps melted, 65 million years ago. The process, they add, would not be reversible at the level of increase, although if the carbon dioxide level only doubles, the ocean currents will gradually recover over the following centuries.

Although some disagreement exists about these statistics, the message seems clear: Recognize and change the effects we produce on our atmosphere, or suffer enormous consequences in our environment in the coming century.

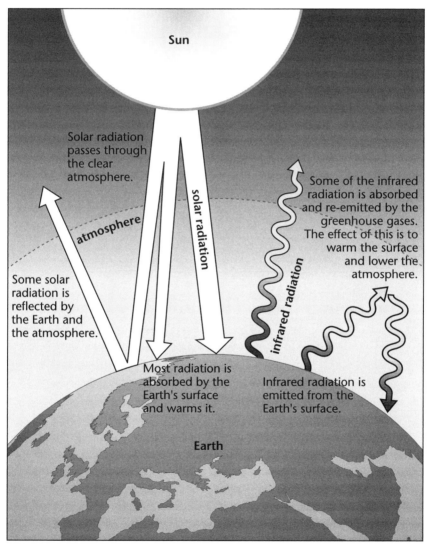

Some atmospheric scientists, ecologists, and others are concerned that Earth's "greenhouse gases," such as carbon dioxide, are increasing global warming beyond desirable limits.

With a growing recognition worldwide of the fragility of our planet, a new call has gone out to the international community to negotiate the successful management of planet Earth. The lessons learned from the Alvarezes, Sagan, and Ehrlich tell us what happens when the Earth's atmosphere becomes dirtied, by whatever means. A look at the conditions on Venus sends up a warning flare about the dangers of a runaway greenhouse effect. Mounting incidence of skin cancer, especially in Australia and in equatorial and temperate zones, signals the urgency of controlling the causes of the hole in the ozone layer. And the fragility of species and their habitats pleads for thoughtful reflection about the natural surroundings we live in and the balance our planet requires. Whether we are capable of becoming good managers, time will tell. But one thing we can be sure of: We can only manage our environment well if we can find out and understand all the ways in which the parts interact with each other—from the most fundamental and basic constituents. That theme has marked the efforts of physical scientists in the past half-century, and it has infused the work of the life scientists as well.

PART II

The Life Sciences, 1946 to the Present

6

The Architects of Life
Proteins, DNA, and RNA

BEFORE THE DAWN OF THE 20TH CENTURY, the central role played by one complicated molecule in the shape of all living things was one of nature's best-kept secrets. Who could imagine that a molecule known as deoxyribonucleic acid (DNA) was the great architect of life? Or that ribonucleic acid might act as its messenger? The detective route to the discovery was twisted and steep. For one thing, the discovery of these roles required progress in three separate areas: cytology (the study of cells through a microscope), genetics, and chemistry.

Like the particle physicists in the physical sciences, life scientists came into the second half of the 20th century with a quest to explore the smallest, most basic building blocks in their field, in this case the essence of living things—proteins, DNA, and RNA—at the most fundamental level. Out of this quest a new field was born, a joining of biochemistry and physics in the new molecular biology. It is a field that few a hundred years before could even have imagined—an examination of processes of life at the molecular level that no one had known existed before the beginning of the century, when Gregor Mendel's work in genetics was rediscovered and biologists began to examine the role of chromosomes in heredity.

Friedrich Miescher (1844–95) had observed the presence of nucleic acids in cell nuclei in 1869, and in the 1880s Walther Flemming (1843–1905) had discovered chromosomes (long, thin structures he spied during cell division); yet, at first, no one realized that any connection with heredity existed. Not until Thomas Hunt Morgan began breeding experiments with fruit flies in 1907 (skeptically, at first) did the study of heredity and its tiny, powerful mechanisms begin to take off. By 1911 his laboratory at Columbia University succeeded in showing that the chromosome carried the agents of heredity.

Meanwhile, in chemistry, in 1909 Phoebus Aaron Theodor Levene (1869–1940) became the first to find that nucleic acids contain a sugar, ribose. And 20 years later he found that other nucleic acids contain another sugar, deoxyribose, establishing that there are two types of nucleic acids, ribonucleic acid (RNA) and deoxyribonucleic acid (DNA). That started the ball rolling on, exploring the chemical nature of these substances.

Yet no one suspected that DNA was connected with heredity. For, while chromosomes contained DNA, they also contained proteins, which seemed much more complex. So proteins seemed like the best candidate for the job of carrying hereditary material—that is, until 1944, when Oswald Avery and a team of other researchers discovered that DNA, not proteins, contain the genetic material of life.

But by 1946 it had become clear that all life-forms employ two categories of chemicals: one that stores information and a second that acts, based upon that information, to duplicate the organism. It had even become clear that enzymes carried out the instructions and DNA held the blueprints, which it also passed on in a nearly exact duplicate to the next generation. What no one yet knew was what structure DNA could possibly have that could enable all this to take place.

The Double Helix

Jim Watson was a tall, lanky young man, bright and ambitious from the time he was a child. In fact, he was on a "whiz kid" radio program called *Quiz Kids* when he was 12. Watson graduated from high school at 15 and had two bachelor's degrees (in philosophy and science) from the University of Chicago within four years. From his teen years, he had decided that he would do something that would make him "famous in science." As a stroke of luck, he attended graduate school at Indiana University, where he studied under the distinguished geneticist Hermann J. Muller and worked with Salvador E. Luria and Max Delbrück, who had become experts in the study of bacteriophages (viruses that attached bacteria). After Indiana,

Watson went to Copenhagen for postgraduate studies. By sheer chance, he met Maurice Wilkins, who was working on X-ray crystallography of DNA at King's College in London. The idea of doing crystallography—a method of chemical and physical analysis—on DNA, an organic substance, was startling and attracted Watson's attention. Just a few days later, the word was out that at Caltech, Linus Pauling, who was the king of chemistry in those days, had worked out a three-dimensional model of the structure of proteins: a helix. The basic shape of a

Linus Pauling *(Courtesy of the National Library of Medicine)*

helix is like a spring or the spiral on a spiral notebook (although Pauling's model did not look much like that).

That's when James Watson decided to go to London to learn more about DNA. He wound up, instead, looking for a position at the Cavendish Laboratory at Cambridge, and that's where he met physicist Francis Crick. Crick, who was 12 years older than Watson, was working for Max Perutz on the use of X-ray crystallography to determine the structure of hemoglobin, and his physics background brought new insight to this area.

Watson immediately liked the way Crick thought, and the two men seemed to have an amazing rapport. When they talked, they finished each other's sentences, and they found the same things fascinating. Through a bit of finagling (Watson's fellowship was supposed to be for study in Copenhagen), Watson went to work with Crick in 1951. They were not technically supposed to work on the structure of DNA, however. That was supposed to be Wilkins's territory, and the Cavendish Laboratory did not want to tread on his toes. So they did their work on the side, on their own time.

A few things were already known about DNA. From X-ray crystallography photos that Wilkins's colleague, Rosalind Franklin, had taken, it looked as if DNA formed a helix, too, as proteins did. Also, it was known that DNA consisted of a long chain of nucleotides, and that the chain contained alternating sugar and phosphate groups. A nitrogen base extended off each sugar. Wilkins's work had also shown that (here was a surprise) the molecule was constant in width throughout its entire length.

What Crick and Watson set themselves to find out was how the component atoms were arranged so that they would give a regular structure to the molecule, allow it to be chemically stable, and permit it to copy itself faithfully. That is, how could all that fit together? How many helixes were there? Exactly what arrangement did the nitrogen bases have? Did they stick out, making the spiral bristle?

Watson attended a lecture given by Franklin, in which she discussed her preliminary results. Franklin, who had studied X-ray diffraction techniques in Paris, worked with clarity and precision, testing to compare the effect of varying degrees of humidity on her results. She saw that her photographs consistently showed that the molecule had a helical form, but she wanted to test more thoroughly before assuming that the molecule took a helical shape under all

Francis Crick (left) and James Watson enjoying a stroll along the Backs River in Cambridge, England in about 1952 *(Cold Spring Harbor Laboratory Archives)*

conditions. And, even though Franklin produced ever clearer photographs showing the diffractions, the details of the complex structure remained hard to detect. However, she did describe in detail what she saw and mentioned that she believed that the sugar and phosphate groups, the backbone of the helix, were on the outside, with the nitrogen bases tucked inside. All this, she said, was very speculative. Watson listened attentively but did not take notes, relying on his unusually excellent memory.

Back in Cambridge, with the data Watson brought back in his head from Franklin's lecture, he and Crick were

Rosalind Franklin *(Cold Spring Harbor Laboratory Archives)*

optimistic that they were not far from building a model. How many possible ways could the thing go to together? They started building. But Watson, for once, had not remembered the data correctly. For one thing, he did not remember the figure Franklin had given for the amount of water attached to DNA—about eight molecules of water for each nucleotide in DNA, according to Franklin's estimate. Watson thought she had said about eight water molecules to each segment of the DNA molecule—a far lower amount of water. What's more, he did not remember Franklin's remark about the position of the nitrogen bases. He and Crick came up with a model composed of three polynucleotide chains with sugar-phosphate backbone on the inside and the nitrogen bases on the outside. The arrangement corresponded with the data that Watson had brought back from London, and they were confident that they had solved the problem—just 24 hours after they started working on it.

The next day, they invited Wilkins and Franklin, along with a few other colleagues, to come take a look at their model. Franklin's remarks were deflating. Franklin immediately saw the error caused by using the incorrect data and was blunt about it. A molecule designed the way they had built it could not hold a fraction of the water it actually held.

Watson and Crick were thoroughly demoralized and embarrassed.

But they could not stop thinking about DNA. And they kept hearing news of Linus Pauling. They knew that Pauling was probably working on the same project, but they also heard enough to know that he was probably on the wrong track.

Several major problems still remained unresolved: How many helixes were wound together in a molecule? Were the nitrogen bases on the inside or the outside? Rosalind Franklin had said she thought they were inside, but if so, how were they arranged? Today a researcher would punch some equations into a personal computer and come up with some what-if models. In the 1950s it was not so easy. So Crick asked a friend, John Griffith, who was a mathematician, to work out how many ways four nitrogen bases might be attracted to each other. Griffith found that electrical forces dictated just two combinations: adenine to thymine and cytosine to guanine.

The second piece of the base-pairing puzzle emerged from a casual conversation that Crick and Watson had over lunch with biochemist Erwin Chargaff from Columbia University. Chargaff mentioned that the "1:1 ratio," about which he had published three years earlier, might be of interest to anyone looking into the structure of DNA. Watson and Crick, unfortunately, knew nothing at all about the 1:1 ratio and, embarrassed, had to confess ignorance. Chargaff was referring to his discovery, in testing several different biological substances, that equal amounts (a 1:1 ratio) of adenine and thymine occurred, as well as equal amounts of cytosine and guanine. That is, regardless of the species—whether the DNA was from a fish or mammal or reptile—the ratio would be the same.

Crick did not take long to recognize that Chargaff's 1:1 ratio, together with Griffith's mathematical calculations, were signposts. The nitrogen bases in DNA must pair with each other in a specific way: adenine with thymine, and cytosine with guanine.

But Crick and Watson were still blocked from making real progress. They were not in touch with the cutting-edge data that was being produced in this field—because Rosalind Franklin and Maurice Wilkins, two of the key researchers, were not in communication with them. (In fact, Wilkins and Franklin had a very poor working relationship with each other and barely spoke, even though they were supposed to be working together.) Crick and Watson were not officially working on DNA, of course, and their approach to the problem—building models and then trying to match them to the data—seemed like putting the cart before the horse to Franklin and many others.

Then bombshell news arrived. Linus Pauling had come up with a structure for DNA. Linus Pauling's son, Peter, was doing research at Cambridge at the time and had become friendly with Watson, a fellow American. So when Peter received a copy of his father's paper on the structure of DNA in January 1953, he passed it to his friend. Crick and Watson thumbed nervously through the pages. Had Pauling gotten there first?

But no. Pauling had postulated a three-helix model, with the nitrogen bases on the outside, not the inside. This arrangement, Crick and Watson had become convinced, was not correct. He had also made other errors in this paper that surprised the younger scientists.

They still had a chance. Watson decided to make a move, using the excuse of business in London to make an appointment to meet with Maurice Wilkins. The decision—and a sort of seamy serendipity—would provide the key that the two eager young scientists needed. As it turned out, when Jim Watson arrived at King's College, Wilkins was busy, so Watson stopped by to see Rosalind Franklin first. He showed her Pauling's paper, and Franklin was furious, although the reasons were unclear. Watson assumed it was because she did not think the DNA molecule could exist in the form of a helix. But it is not likely this was the reason, since Franklin, as will become apparent, already knew that at least one form of DNA had a helical structure. Watson tried to show the parallels between Pauling's model and Crick and Watson's first, failed model. This could have irked her, seeming like an attempt to convince her she had been wrong. And she could have been angry that Watson, who was not supposed to be working on DNA, had a copy of Pauling's paper, while she, who *was* working on DNA, had not been sent one by her colleagues in California.

In any case, Wilkins entered the room just in time, according to Watson, who claims he feared Franklin would have attacked him physically at any moment—a rather ludicrous fear, which the six-foot young man confided in Wilkins after they left her office. Wilkins, who had gotten off on the wrong foot with Franklin from the time she arrived at King's, seemed to open up at this new understanding that Watson now

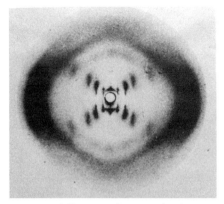

An X-ray diffraction photograph of a DNA molecule, form B, taken by Rosalind Franklin in late 1952 *(Ray Gosling, Cold Spring Harbor Laboratory Archives)*

had, having faced Franklin's ire as Wilkins had done on more than one occasion.

Unfortunately, this example shows how scientific discovery, like every other human endeavor, can be either waylaid or aided by the fits and starts of human jealousy and miscommunication. Now, months after the discovery was made, Wilkins finally told Watson that one of Franklin's most telling breakthroughs was that she had found two forms of DNA, which she called form A and form B. Unlike form A, which she had never thought could be definitively pronounced a helix based on her photographs, this new form B clearly had a helical form.

Watson was excited. Could he see a photograph of form B, he wanted to know. As it turned out, Wilkins had been making copies secretly of all Rosalind Franklin's photos—afraid as he was that when she left in a few months for another institution, she would take with her all the work she had done at King's, leaving him with nothing. No doubt, since he had allowed such bad feelings to develop between them, he did not have the courage to ask for copies. In any case, that's how he happened to have a copy of Franklin's now famous photo No. 51, which clearly showed the structure of form B.

"The instant I saw the picture my mouth fell open and my pulse began to race," Watson later wrote in *The Double Helix,* his autobiographical account of this period. "It was unbelievably simpler than those obtained previously ('A' form). Moreover, the black cross of reflections which dominate the picture could arise only from a helical structure."

Finally, Crick and Watson had the clues they needed. Based on Rosalind Franklin's photo No. 51, they decided to reconsider the double helix. And after five long weeks of trial and error, they arrived at the new model.

The DNA molecule they proposed consisted of two helixes wound around each other, something like a spiral staircase, with the steps made of paired chemical groups of atoms. The nitrogen bases paired with each other, turned inward from two parallel helixes. Then, during replication, the two sides of the DNA helix would break apart before the chromosomes split, leaving the nitrogen bases free to pair up again. Each strand of the double helix was a model, or template, for the other. In cell division each DNA double helix would separate into two strands, and each strand would build up its complementary strand on itself. By matching up the nitrogen bases the same way they were before (no other way possible), the DNA molecule could replicate accurately.

The Watson–Crick model of DNA made so much sense that it was accepted almost at once. They had done it! The new model of DNA enabled people to visualize how it could work to guide the construction of other molecules. The basic principle of how one species can reproduce its own kind was at last discovered. It was April 1953.

Watson, Crick, and Wilkins received the Nobel Prize in physiology or medicine in 1962. (Franklin died of cancer in 1958, before the prize was awarded, and since Nobel Prizes are never given posthumously, she did not receive a share of the recognition.) Pauling, who had received a Nobel Prize for his work on chemical bonds in 1954, received the Nobel Peace Prize in 1962 for his opposition to atmospheric nuclear-weapons testing (making him the second person in history, after Marie Curie, to win two Nobel Prizes).

Few discoveries in science have had both the immediate and far-reaching impact of Crick and Watson's discovery of the structure of DNA. Not only did their double-helix model provide the structure of DNA, but it also predicted a mechanism (using strand separation) by which genetic information could be duplicated

Watson and Crick's model of the DNA molecule *(Cold Spring Harbor Laboratory Archives)*

Sugar-
phosphate
backbone

Hydrogen bonds

Cytosine	Guanine
Adenine	Thymine

**Deoxyribonucleic acid
(DNA)**

The structure of DNA

faithfully. By 1958 M. Messelson and F. Stahl at Caltech had carried out an experiment showing that DNA does, in fact, replicate itself by separating the two strands, which serve as templates for creating the complementary sister strands. Moreover, Watson and Crick's model offered the key to understanding how genetic information could be stored in the chemical molecule called DNA.

The RNA Story

But Crick and Watson's triumph was not the end of the story. Now that the structure was known, new questions arose: How did the DNA convey its instructions to the proteins in the cell? And how were the proteins synthesized? What mechanisms took place?

Using an electron microscope in the 1950s, George Palade initiated a study of microsomes, small bodies in the cytoplasm of a cell. By 1956 he had shown that they were rich in RNA and identified a group of these bodies, which became known as *ribosomes*. The ribosomes, it quickly became apparent, were key to the mechanism of information transfer.

In 1956 Mahlon Bush Hoagland (1921–   ) discovered relatively small molecules of RNA in the cytoplasm. There seemed to be several different types. Hoagland showed that each type was able to combine with a particular amino acid. The RNA molecule was capable of combining with a particular spot on a ribosome. Amino acids lined up on the other side, so that the RNA molecules hooked up to both and transferred the information from the ribosomes to the proteins (amino acids). Hoagland called the small ribonucleic acids *transfer* RNAs.

But how did the RNA know how to hook up? Transfer RNA was located outside the nucleus in the cytoplasm of the cell, while DNA was deep within the cell's nucleus. A closer look revealed that, in fact, there was also RNA in the nucleus. Two French researchers at the Pasteur Institute in Paris, Jacques-Lucien Monod [moh-NOH] (1910–76) and François Jacob [zhah-KOB] (1920–   ), proposed that the DNA molecule transfers the information it holds to an RNA molecule in the nucleus that had used a DNA strand as a model in its formation. These RNA molecules carried the information (message) out into the cytoplasm and were therefore called *messenger* RNA.

Each transfer RNA molecule had a three-nucleotide combination at one end that fit similar combinations at exchange centers on the messenger RNA. So the messenger RNA would settle on the ribosome surface, and the transfer RNA molecules would line up, matching the trinucleotides up to the messenger RNAs on one side and matching up to the amino acids, combined in the correct order, on the other side.

So information was transferred from DNA in the chromosomes to the messenger RNA, which then journeyed out of the nucleus to the ribosomes in the cytoplasms to give the information to the transfer RNA molecules. These in turn transferred the information to the amino acids and formed the protein. Three adjacent nucleotides (a trinucleotide) along the DNA molecule plus the messenger RNA molecule plus the transfer RNA molecule made a particular amino acid. The question was: which one?

Genetic Code

So, as the 1960s began, the outstanding problem in molecular biology was the genetic code. How could researchers predict which trinucleotide corresponded with the manufacture of which amino acid?

Without understanding this process, one could not understand how information passed from DNA to proteins.

The stage for exploring the genetic code was set in 1955, by Spanish-born American biochemist Severo Ochoa (1905–93), who isolated the enzyme that enabled one strand of DNA to form a second strand from a bacterium. This enzyme, he discovered, could catalyze the formation of RNA-like substance from individual nucleotides. (American biochemist Arthur Kornberg shortly did the same for DNA, and Ochoa and Kornberg received the Nobel Prize in physiology or medicine in 1959.)

And that's where American biochemist Warren Nirenberg (1927–) came in. Making use of synthetic RNA to serve in the role of messenger RNA, he began to sleuth out the answer. Nirenberg's breakthrough came in 1961. He formed a synthetic RNA, formulated according to Ochoa's methods, that had only one type of nucleotide, uridylic acid, so that its structure was . . . UUUUUU . . . the only possible nucleotide triplet in it was UUU. So when it formed a protein that contained the amino acid phenylalanine, he knew that he had worked out the first item in his "dictionary." Uridylic acid formed phenylalanine.

Indian-American chemist Har Gobind Khorana, meanwhile, was working along similar lines. He introduced new techniques for comparing DNA of known structure with the RNA it would produce and showing that the separate nucleotide triplets, the "letters" of the code, did not overlap. Independently of Nirenberg, he also worked out almost the entire genetic code. He and Nirenberg shared the 1968 Nobel Prize in physiology or medicine with Robert Holley, who also worked in this area.

Khorana later headed a research team that in 1970 succeeded in synthesizing a gene-like molecule from scratch. That is, he did not use an already existing gene as a template but began with nucleotides and put them together in the right order, a feat that ultimately would enable researchers to create "designer" genes.

Overall, the first decades after World War II witnessed progress by giant leaps in our understanding of the fundamentals of heredity. *DNA* and *RNA* became household worlds. And knowledge of the very essence of life seemed just around the corner.

7

The Origins
and Borderlines of Life
From Soup to Viruses and Designer Genes

AS CRICK AND WATSON AND THEIR colleagues delved into the structure of life's architectural process, other life scientists explored an ever-widening pool of questions surrounding the nature of life, how it got started, and how it operates. Using the new tools of molecular biology and microbiology, investigators came up with more new and astounding insights in these areas.

Many of these lines of inquiry led to consequences and break-throughs for complex organisms—most notably for medicine and our understanding of the human body, how it works, and how it fits in with the environment around it. The past half-century has seen extraordinary interdisciplinary advances that have virtually revolu-tionized medicine, including CAT scan and MRI imaging, open-heart surgery, and organ transplants—most of which are beyond the scope of this book. The study of viruses and bacteria, as well as the body's immune system, resulted in successful vaccines against polio in the 1950s and made possible an ever-escalating, if still unsuccessful, battle against the continuing AIDS epidemic that began in the 1980s.

Breakthroughs in genetic engineering began to provide tools to adapt agricultural products, address genetic disorders more effec-tively, and control inheritance of specific traits in organisms through cloning—meanwhile raising many challenging ethical and public policy issues.

The Primordial Soup

While cosmologists and particle physicists struggled with questions surrounding the birth of the universe and its earliest years, life scientists have grappled with similar questions about living things. Perhaps the most overarching questions of all have been: What is life and where did life come from? These questions have intrigued humans for as long as we have any record. The answers are not that easy to figure out—in fact today, some scientists doubt that it can be done at all.

The problem is, as NASA life scientist Sherwood Chang once remarked, "the record is mute. Geologists and atmospheric chemists will tell you there is no evidence one way or the other" about what the Earth was like when life first appeared or how life may have begun. The mystery constitutes one of the greatest scientific detective cases of all time—one that, so far, remains unsolved. With very little hard evidence to go on, dozens of basic questions need to be answered, including: What were conditions like on Earth before life began? What elements were present? What processes acted on them? What were the original building blocks of life?

For centuries scientists had been trying to figure out whether living things could spring spontaneously out of inorganic substances. Aristotle was sure that they did, and for centuries afterward, scientists tried to prove one way or the other that spontaneous generation could or could not take place. In the 19th century, it seemed, Louis Pasteur had finally provided a definitive answer: It could not. By correcting flaws in previous experiments that had seemed to prove otherwise, Pasteur had shown that a completely sterile, inorganic solution would not produce any signs of life, even with all the needed requirements of life (such as hospitable temperature, presence of oxygen, and so on). His trick was to use a special, swan-necked flask that kept out contaminants such as plants or mold spores, while allowing normal atmospheric conditions. But maybe Pasteur's results were not definitive for all time.

An early breakthrough that produced some of the chemicals required for the origin of life was first explored experimentally in the early 1950s by a young graduate student named Stanley Lloyd Miller, who was working on his Ph.D. at the University of Chicago under the guidance of H. C. Urey (1893–1981), a noted American chemist who had received the Nobel Prize in chemistry in 1934 for his discovery of heavy hydrogen (deuterium). In recent years Urey had become interested in geochemistry, the formation of planets, and atmospheric conditions in the early years of Earth's history. He also began to wonder about Pasteur's definitive proof that spontaneous generation could not happen. What if, Urey and Miller began thinking, instead of waiting just four days, Pasteur had waited the billions of years that Earth had waited for the first life to appear? And what if, instead of the modern mix of nitrogen and oxygen, he had used the primordial atmosphere that existed in the first few billion years of our planets' existence? And what if, instead of a flask full of solution, he had had an ocean full of inorganic molecules?

For one thing, Urey was reasonably sure that Earth's primordial atmosphere was quite different from today's atmosphere. He estimated it was most likely made up almost entirely of hydrogen-containing gases such as methane (CH_4), ammonia (NH_3), and water vapor (H_2O). So, under Urey's direction, about the time that Crick and Watson were struggling to work out the arrangement of the double helix, Miller set up a landmark experiment in the history of biology,

Stanley Lloyd Miller examines the apparatus he used in his 1953 experiment (© Bettmann/Corbis)

one aimed at simulating the imagined early-Earth scenario. He postulated a time when great clouds of gases rolled across the turbulent surface of the planet and lightning flashed across the skies—when gas molecules of methane, hydrogen, ammonia, and water were jolted into combinations by ultraviolet radiation from the Sun (since this was before the formation of the ozone layer)—a time when inorganic building-block molecules rained down into the Earth's shallow oceans. There, Urey and Miller imagined, these pre-organic building blocks bumped into each other and eventually combined into longer, more complex, organic molecules, such as amino acids, proteins, and nucleotides. Ultimately, in this imagined sequence of events, these molecules would grow more and more complex until they developed into a nucleic acid capable of replicating itself.

In a small-scale version of this scenario, Miller created an "atmosphere" of hydrogen, with components of ammonia and methane, floating over a flask of carefully sterilized and purified water. Into this primordial "soup" of gas and liquid, he introduced an electric charge to simulate ultraviolet (UV) radiation. Later in Earth's history, plants would begin photosynthesis and produce oxygen, which in turn would contribute to the formation of an ozone layer in the upper stratosphere, protecting the regions below from the Sun's UV rays. But in the beginning, Miller and Urey reasoned, there must have been plenty of UV radiation to jump-start the biologic process in this way. Also, for now, there would be no free oxygen, but plenty of hydrogen. Miller ran his experiment for a week, and at the end of that time he tested his water solution. He found, to his great excitement, that, in addition to simple substances, he had produced two of the simplest amino acids, plus some indication that a few more complicated ones were in the process of forming.

When he made longer trials, more amino acids formed; other researchers tried the experiment and found they could repeat it. The amazing thing was that the kind of organic molecules that formed in Miller's apparatus were the same kind that are found in living organisms. Miller had not created living creatures, but he had set in motion a process that seemed to be pointed in that direction. Maybe the development of life was not so unusual after all, but a natural consequence of the way the universe is constructed. In the late 1960s this line of thinking gained even more credibility when more and more complicated molecules were discovered in gas clouds in outer space.

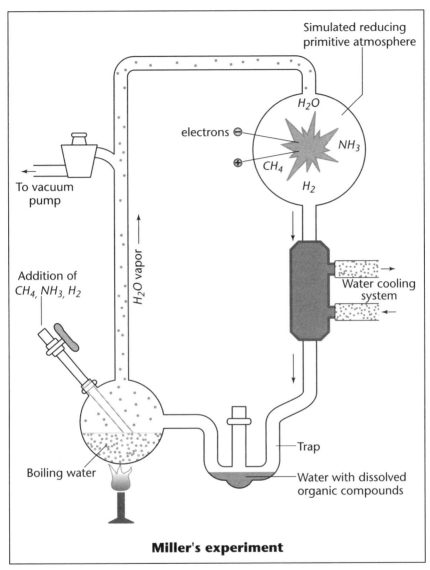

Miller's experiment

A diagram of Miller's experiment, conducted in 1953 at the University of Chicago. Miller wanted to test whether organic compounds would form if he simulated atmospheric conditions that may have existed on Earth long ago and then stimulated the gases electrically, as perhaps lightning may have done. Above the flask of water on the right he created an atmosphere of hydrogen (H_2), methane (CH_4), and ammonia (NH_3), and then subjected his "soup" to electrical discharges. After operating his experiment for a week, Miller noticed that the water in the flask and in the trap below it had turned orange-red. Tests showed that the water contained amazingly high concentrations of amino acids. The experiment has been repeated successfully many times, producing all 20 protein-forming amino acids.

The evidence reinforcing these ideas built up even further when, in 1970, Ceylon-born biochemist Cyril Ponnamperuma found traces of five amino acids in a meteorite that had landed in Australia on September 28, 1969. After careful analysis, he and his team of investigators found glycine, alanine, glutamic acid, valine, and proline—the first extraterrestrial constituents of life ever to be found. Ponnamperuma was able to show that the meteorite could not have picked up these amino acids through contamination by its contact with Earth. Clearly, they were synthesized by non-chemical process like those that took place in Miller's experiment.

In the Beginning . . . Clay?

Not everyone completely agrees that some version of Miller's primordial soup is the answer to the age-old question. An interesting concept put forth by one group of scientists is the idea that life might conceivably have sprung directly from clay.

Apparently lifeless and inert, clay appears to be the direct opposite of everything we normally associate with living creatures. But the mineral crystals of clay offer some advantages for beginning life that most of us would overlook. For one thing, as biologist Sherwood Chang once pointed out in an interview, in the early days of Earth's history (some one and a half billion years ago or more), the environment would obviously have been dominated by inorganic things. Among those, seawater was certainly present in great abundance. But so was clay.

According to the clay-life scenario, the beginning went something like this: In the early formational days, the basic elements were all present in fair abundance: hydrogen molecules, nitrogen, carbon. Of the ingredients required for organic life, only oxygen was missing. Rocks weathered, shifted, and shattered, formed soils, and compacted into new sediments, making new rocks and mineral clays. At the molecular level, these clays had (and still have) some special properties. They possessed a highly organized molecular structure, loaded with intrinsic defects that could provide sites for chemical reactions as well as a method for storing and passing on information and energy.

As the environment changed, with alternate wetting and drying, freezing and thawing, and the movement of wind, water, and earth, those clays that could persist and evolve advantageously were the ones to "survive." Graham Cairns-Smith, of the University of Glasgow, Scotland—originally delineated this theory in 1982 in his book *Genetic Takeover and the Mineral Origins of Life.* He postulated that these clays might have developed by adaptive structural evolution or a sort of primordial "natural selection." The clay-life theory contended that these clays might have been primordial life-forms in themselves and, at the same time, a sort of template for living organisms before any living organism existed. These templates, Cairns-Smith suggested, could replicate using a kind of mineral genetic system based on defect structures in crystal formations. He also postulated that the templates could pass on these defects (mutations, in a way) to daughter generations in classic evolutionary style.

Gradually, organic molecules formed based on the mineral molecules, using the clays as a scaffolding. The organic molecules developed an organic genetic system that was more effective and efficient than its mineral predecessor and finally replaced the original mineral formations in a kind of "genetic takeover." In the same way that scaffolding is no longer needed once a cathedral is built and no wooden abacus beads are ever found in electronic calculators, we see no evidence of this "low-tech" life form in today's "higher-tech" organic systems.

Still other theories abound about the origins of life. One of the most favored, supported by biologist Carl Sagan, contends that the carbon required for the formation of organic molecules came from bombardment of our planet by extraterrestrial asteroids containing carbon. As Ponnamperuma and many others since have discovered, carbon-based molecules have been identified in many meteorites—lending credence to this idea, which is referred to as panspermia, the idea that the seeds of life are found throughout the universe.

But whichever of these scenarios may be closest to the truth, the work done in this field is both exciting and thought-provoking, challenging many long-held assumptions about the line of separation between organic and inorganic and about the nature of organic life and its evolution.

Life Processes: Growth Factors

While Miller, Urey, Cairns-Smith, and others were working on how life may have begun, the work continued on the nature and the structure of that basic building-block of nature, the cell, as well as other aspects of the body and what makes it work. Great strides had been made in the first half of the 20th century, and, thanks to improved staining techniques and microscopes, much of the fine structure of the cell had been identified. Now progress began to be made on many questions about fundamental life processes. One example is the Nobel Prize–winning work done by Rita Levi-Montalcini on growth factors, which she and others discovered were responsible for growth in embryonic cells.

Rita Levi-Montalcini grew up with a passion for physiology. She and her twin sister, Paola, were born April 22, 1909, in the city of Turin, Italy, where, despite her father's objections, she attended medical school; her sister became a famous artist, and the two remained close friends throughout their lives. (Levi-Montalcini never mar-

Teaching Evolution

The science of how life began still stands on highly hypothetical ground, but the process that produced the vast diversity of life on Earth is no longer considered hypothetical. The theory of evolution—introduced by Charles Darwin in the 19th century—by now has been well documented. Yet the war against the scientific theory of evolution waged by religious fundamentalists continued throughout the latter half of the 20th century. At the end of the 20th century, as the millennium approached, the "antievolutionists" developed a new tactic in the battlefront, which they called "intelligent design" (ID). It was based on a much-used argument that, simply put, many complex structures found in nature, such as the human eye, could not have come about by chance, in piecemeal fashion described by evolutionary theory. Such wonders must have been designed by an omniscient God. The favorite simile is that just as such a complex device as a watch implies a watchmaker, so the many complexities of nature imply the existence, and active involvement of, a creator.

While the modern proponents of intelligent design generally use more sophisticated arguments based upon the complexities in molecular biology and information theory, for most scientists this position rehashes the same old story, countered and answered many times in the past by a clear understanding of evolutionary theory. Many scientists also point out that a great many of nature's products, rather than exhibiting evidence ried—her hyphenated name is a tribute to her mother, whose name was Montalcini.)

Levi-Montalcini completed her medical studies during WWII, but had to go into hiding almost immediately after receiving her degree to avoid being sent to a concentration camp by German Nazis. Although journals in her field were hard to come by during the war years, she had the opportunity to read a paper by physiologist Viktor Hamburger describing research that intrigued her, and she developed an idea for an experiment she could do on chicken embryos while hidden in her bedroom. Aided by her brother Gino, who built the equipment she needed, Levi-Montalcini examined the earliest stages of embryo development, when cells begin to differentiate, with particular attention to nerve cells. As it turned out, these

of intelligent design, appear to have been put together in pretty sloppy ways. For example, why would an intelligent designer put nipples on a man's breast, give sightless eyes to cave-dwelling fish, or exhibit hundreds of other apparently foolish, wasteful, and ill-conceived "designs"? Although many of nature's productions are beautiful, they often appear to have been hacked together rather than designed, settling for a "what works" result rather than an economical and elegant form.

Meanwhile, proponents of "intelligent design" continue to press to be included in classroom curricula for science. They demand an equal standing with the teaching of evolution in science classes, and yet ID is clearly not a science, but only an argument against the well-established scientific theory of evolution. While the ID proponents carefully avoid the word *God* in their arguments—thus avoiding constitutional and legal pitfalls—their deliberately vague intelligent designer or creator remains a supernatural construct and not a scientific one, and given our current scientific knowledge, it is also a superfluous and unnecessary construct. Further, ID proponents offer no scientific explanation for the existence of such a "designer" or how such a designer or creator actually achieves the material transition from design to actuality.

For most scientists seeking natural explanations for the wondrous works of nature, "intelligent design," like the so-called creation science before it, may have a place in philosophy or theology classes, but it has no place in science, or in the schoolrooms in which science is taught.

Rita Levi-Montalcini at work in her lab at Washington University in St. Louis *(Photo by Herb Weitman, Courtesy of Washington University, St. Louis)*

were the first steps toward solution of a problem that ultimately would win her the Nobel Prize. After the war, Levi-Montalcini went to St. Louis, Missouri, where Hamburger was continuing his research. For many years she lived part of the year in St. Louis and part of the year in Rome. She became well traveled and prominent in her field, respected for her experimental studies of the nerve growth factor (NGF), a substance that promotes the growth of nerve cells in the peripheral nervous system. Levi-Montalcini was elected to the U.S. National Academy of Sciences in 1968, and in 1986 she shared the Nobel Prize in physiology or medicine with Stanley Cohen, a student of hers. His award was for his discovery of epidermal growth factors, while hers was for her discovery of the nerve growth factor.

While Levi-Montalcini, Cohen, and other life scientists continued to explore life processes, chemistry, and physiology, a group of biologists turned to a fascinating—and health-threatening—near-creature at the borderline of life, which posed a challenge to understanding that intrigued researchers for many reasons.

Viruses: At the Threshold of Life

At the very boundary between living and nonliving, populating a world somehow in-between, is the virus, a bundle of molecules that, like living things, can duplicate itself. But, unlike living things, this parasite can only reproduce inside a living host cell, from which it must borrow essential contributions. The smallest viruses, called viroids, carry only 240 bits of information on their chromosomes, compared to the human body's 3 billion. But simple as they are, viroids can cause serious plant diseases in the course of their life cycle, which requires duplicating themselves inside the cells of plants. Viruses come in a vast variety of types, and different viruses have different effects on their hosts, exacting a wide range of tolls.

Viruses and the diseases they cause in humans have played an enormous part in human history, with many viral diseases, such as smallpox, traceable as many as 2,000 years back. But only since the 1880s and 1890s have we known about viruses as the special entities they are. Today we can confidently say that we have eradicated smallpox, with no cases reported (aside from accidents in laboratories) since 1977. But human immunodeficiency virus (HIV), the cause of the current AIDS epidemic, is another matter. So far, it is well beyond our ability to control or understand. Obviously, medical concerns provide an urgent motivation for studying these tiny creatures on the borderline of life.

Viruses, for example, may give us a new understanding of cancer, its causes, and, potentially, its prevention. Viruses sometimes can cause cancer by confusing the host cell—distorting its functions and signals. By identifying these distorted functions and signals, we have come to a new, molecular understanding of what happens in cancer, pointing the way to new treatment and approaches. In a revolutionary program conducted in Taiwan, 63,500 newborn babies received vaccinations against infection with the hepatitis B virus, resulting in prevention of 85 percent of potential HBV infections, according to a 10-year follow-up published in September 1996. Scientists predict that this preventative step could stop as many as 8,300 cases of liver cancer in these babies, before it ever gets a chance to get started.

But viruses also provide a sample of how an organism may work at the very simplest level, and so they give researchers a window for understanding more complex living things.

As German-American microbiologist Max Delbrück (1906–81) wrote in 1949, "Any living cell carries with it the experience of a billion years of experimentation by its ancestors." (Delbrück and microbiologists Alfred Day Hershey [1908–97] and Salvador E. Luria [1912–91] won the 1969 Nobel Prize in physiology or medicine for their work on the genetic structure of the virus.) As Delbrück implied, by observing at these levels, we have learned a great deal, and we continue to do so as we ask and answer such questions as, What are

Microbiologist Alfred D. Hershey (1908–97), shown in this photograph, shared the Nobel Prize for physiology or medicine with Salvatore E. Luria (1912–91) and Max Delbrück (1906–81) for work on the replication mechanisms and genetic structure of the virus. *(Courtesy of the National Library of Medicine)*

viruses? Are they alive? What do they look like? Are there many different kinds of viruses? Does each virus cause one specific disease? How do viruses cause diseases? How do viruses duplicate themselves? What have we learned about viruses that can be applied to humans?

By the 1930s scientists had agreed to use the term *virus* to refer to any agent that could pass through a filter that would ordinarily retain bacteria; today the definition has been refined to refer only to submicroscopic agents (less than 0.3 micron). All viruses require a host cell in order to duplicate themselves, and this parasite behavior often causes the death or alteration of the host cells—which is why most viruses cause diseases.

Also in the 1930s two events contributed to an expanding understanding of the virus and its nature. First, in 1935, Wendell Stanley showed that a virus can take on a crystalline form. Second, German electrical engineer Ernst August Friedrich Ruska (1906–88) introduced a new tool, the electron microscope, which uses electron beams instead of visible light. The instrument's powerful focus permitted the resolution to increase initially by 400 times and was rapidly improved. (Somewhat late, Ruska received the 1986 Nobel Prize in physics for his work.) By the late 1940s and 1950s, the magnifications were improved to 100,000 times, and objects as small as .001 micrometer in diameter could be resolved. From 1959 to 1961 Finnish cytologist Alvar P. Wilska and French cytologist Gaston DuPouy worked out ways to set the parts of the virus in relief and use an electron microscope on living viruses. Now electron micrographs enabled scientists to see the microscopic world of viruses, whereas before they could only guess.

Researchers found that viruses have a nucleic acid core containing genetic information that is protected on the outside by a protein coat and, in some, a fatty envelope around that. The shell is in the shape of a geodesic dome with 20 equilateral triangular faces. Some viruses use DNA to carry their genetic code (as nonviral living organisms do), and others use RNA.

As for the question whether viruses are alive, the debate continues. They share many characteristics with living cells, and they use the same genetic code as living things—they could not successfully live off the cells if they did not. They function according to a plan and can program their own replication within the confines of a cell. Like other living things, viruses evolve and respond to changes in their environment. Do these characteristics describe the simplest of living things? Or do they describe an extremely complex set of molecules—a handful of chemicals?

Retroviruses

Retroviruses were encountered initially around 1908 in chickens, where they were discovered to cause leukemia, but no one at first suspected their strange life cycle. The retrovirus's chromosome, it turns out, consists of RNA, not DNA. Originally known as an RNA virus, the retrovirus produces a DNA copy, or provirus, which in turn is transcribed into viral RNA. (This is backward, hence *retro*.) In 1970 Howard Temin and David Baltimore independently announced the discovery of an enzyme in the virus particle itself—the reverse transcriptase—that copies RNA to DNA (the opposite of the transcription that takes place in most cells). This process was key to the way certain viruses replicate. It also provided a new tool that allowed molecular biologists to copy any RNA species to DNA. This would become a key step in the 1970s revolution of gene cloning and genetic engineering. Lessons from the study of retroviruses have also formed a cornerstone of our modern understanding of cancer.

The retrovirus attaches itself to a specific receptor on the surface of the host cell and then penetrates into the cytoplasm of the host cell. There, this sneaky invader shirks off its protective coating, and then, through reverse transcription, turns its RNA into a double strand of DNA. This double-stranded DNA moves into the nucleus and is integrated into the host cell's set of chromosomes (or genome), where the DNA creates a DNA copy (called a provirus), which in turn is transcribed into viral RNA. Now the virus itself is inherited by the offspring of the host cell. When, during the cell's

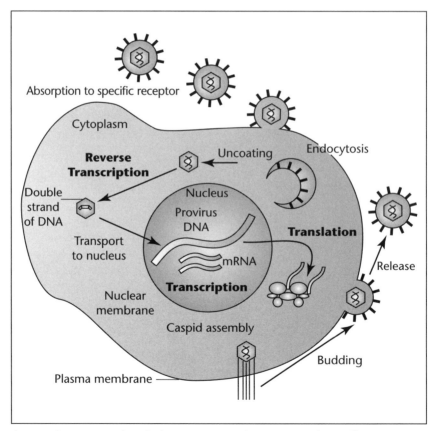

The complex processes by which a retrovirus replicates using a host cell

normal replication process, the RNA is transported out of the nucleus and onto the cell ribosomes to be translated into proteins, certain enzymes associate with two copies of the viral RNA in the cytoplasm and move to the plasma membrane surrounding the cell. There the budding process takes place: The virus particle surrounds itself with an envelope borrowed from the plasma membrane of the infected cell, is released from the surface of the cell, and travels off to look for a new host cell and begin the cycle again.

Some retroviruses do not kill the host cell, which goes on carrying the provirus in its DNA structure and multiplying it as it replicates. Other retroviruses cause changes in the host cell that result in tumors. A third type, of which HIV is a member, kills the host cell by means that remain unclear.

While other retroviruses have usually not been impossible to control, HIV remains the greatest challenge to face researchers in the past quarter of a century. It has turned out to be a subtle, determined, and mean adversary.

Stealthy and Insidious: The Story of AIDS

In the late 1970s physicians in New York and San Francisco began to encounter some unusual cases of fungal infections and a rare cancer called Kaposi's sarcoma. By 1980–81, at the Centers for Disease Control (CDC) in Atlanta, Georgia, which distributes experimental drugs for cases of rare diseases, a technician named Sandra Ford began to notice suddenly high numbers of cases of *Pneumocystis carinii*, a rare form of pneumonia that usually struck only those with greatly weakened immune systems, most often as a side effect of chemotherapy for cancer. But these cases were otherwise healthy men. So the CDC began looking further and found that some 500 cases of a mysterious disease had been reported—a lethal affliction that knocked out the victim's immune system. About four-fifths of these first-known cases were homosexual and bisexual men, and in the beginning the disease was named the Gay-Related Immune Disorder, but the name was soon changed to Acquired Immune Deficiency Syndrome, or AIDS. In the early 1980s this now widely known disease was relatively obscure. But by the end of 1982, more than 800 cases had been reported in 30 states.

Then in August 1985 the news broke that popular film star Rock Hudson had AIDS, and he died of the disease shortly thereafter. Now

An electron micrograph of the Human Immunodeficiency Virus (HIV), the infectious agent that causes acquired immunodeficiency syndrome (AIDS) *(Courtesy of the Centers for Disease Control, Atlanta, Georgia)*

AIDS suddenly burst upon general public awareness as a very serious problem with a rapidly increasing number of victims. It also soon became clear that the disease was not confined to the male homosexual population. The disease had been active in the general population in Africa and Asia since the late 1970s, and studies estimate that between 5 percent and 20 percent of the entire sexually active adult population in some areas of Africa were infected by 1992. Also by 1992 AIDS had become the leading cause of death among women of reproductive age (between the ages of 20 and 40) in the major cities of North and South America, Western Europe, and areas of Africa south of the Sahara Desert. What's more, studies indicate that between 24 percent and 33 percent of the children born to women infected with HIV will develop AIDS.

The questions were now, finally, recognized as urgent. What caused AIDS? How was it transmitted? How could it be cured, or even controlled? By this time it was clear that AIDS was an infectious disease, and it soon became recognized that a virus known as the HIV-1 virus was the probable cause (discovered separately in 1983 by Luc Montagnier at the Pasteur Institute in France and by U.S. National Institutes of Health researcher Robert Gallo). The virus spreads virtually exclusively by infected blood or sperm— although researchers also found HIV in several other body fluids, including saliva, tears, urine, breast milk, cerebrospinal fluid, and certain cervical and vaginal secretions. Initially, HIV was sometimes transmitted by blood transfusions and, in some cases, in clotting factors used to treat hemophilia (a hereditary disease typified by excessive bleeding). One of the first defense moves was to begin test-ing the blood supply and the clotting-factors supply for the HIV-1 virus, and, as a result, that source of infection was virtually elimi-nated by 1985.

In January 1983 came the first reports of cases in the United States among heterosexual victims who were partners of intra-venous drug users. The disease can be transmitted by very little infected blood—in fact, health officials discovered that when drug users pass a used needle from one person to another, an infected drop of blood on the needle is all it takes to transmit AIDS. Intra-venous drug users rapidly became recognized as a major group at risk for the disease.

AIDS attacks the host's immune system, and that's how it kills. The immune system is the part of the body that defends against disease and infection by fighting off viruses, bacteria, and other invaders. HIV attaches to a specific receptor on the host cell's sur-face, climbs inside the cell, replicates there, and kills the cell. HIV's favorite receptor is an important member of the human body's immune system known as the CD4 T cell. The CD4 T cells recog-nize foreign attackers in the bloodstream and help other cells in the system make antibodies. They also help a third type of cell develop into killer T cells. So the loss of CD4 T cells has a devas-tating effect on two arms of the immune system, affecting both the production of antibodies to fight off attacking viruses and the creation of killer T cells.

Death is not immediate—and in fact seven to nine years or more can pass between infection with the virus and development of AIDS. During this time a victim can be a carrier without know-ing it. By the early 1990s one estimate set the figure between 1 mil-lion and 1.5 million people in the United States infected with the virus. Once AIDS develops, the progress of the disease can move slowly, but the end result is always the same: repeated bouts with opportunistic illnesses that take advantage of the weakened immune system and, finally, death. Between 1981 and 1991 some 190,000 cases of AIDS were reported in the United States; 120,000 people had died from it. Worldwide, the number of people infected with HIV had reached 34.7 million by 2000. In sub-Saharan Africa one in four adults was infected. The World Health Organization reports that 21.8 million people died of AIDS between 1981 and the end of 2000.

What makes the HIV-1 virus uncommonly deadly is the way it disguises itself as a part of the body and then disables the T cells, a key part of the immune system. Finding a cure becomes particularly elusive, since the HIV virus readily transforms itself to resist the toxins of any drug. Then the new, mutated virus goes on about destroying and replicating in a new form, unaffected by the drug and unrecognized by the body's immune system.

Several drugs have been found that effectively slow the progress of the disease, including azidothymidine (AZT) and dideoxyinosine (ddI), although they have many toxic side effects. Hopes are constantly raised that a cure may be just around the corner, but the job is tough. The HIV virus changes its form more than 1,000 times faster than most influenza viruses, and trying to develop either a

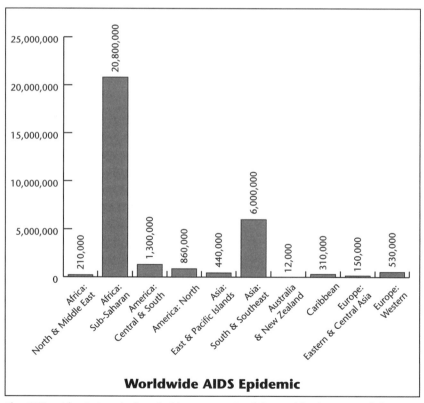

Worldwide AIDS Epidemic

The AIDS epidemic is out of control in some parts of the world. *(Courtesy of the Centers for Disease Control, Atlanta, Georgia)*

vaccine or a cure to defeat it is, as some scientists put it, "like trying to hit a moving target." In addition, most cures for disease try to bolster the body's own immune system to win the battle. But in this case the immune system is the very system under attack. One such hope arose, however, in February 1993, when researchers studying HIV in the laboratory found that some combinations of drugs—especially a particular three-way combination—produced a hopeful effect on the virus. Although the virus was able to mutate, as usual, to avoid the toxic effects of the drugs, the new version of the virus was sometimes unable to replicate. This meant that, once the particular virus individual had lived its lifespan, it would die without offspring. Eventually, if this worked over the long term and consistently, the virus would completely die out in its host and the war would be won. But by October it became apparent that this threefold strategy does not always work. Sometimes HIV that is resistant to multiple drugs and can continue to survive and replicate does evolve. In fact, in tests by other researchers, the strategy did not work; the mutated HIV now seemed able to survive and continue its normal life cycle. So the three-drug attack does not necessarily lead to a disabled virus. Neither has any vaccine turned up, despite efforts to find one, and the prospects do not look bright. As one researcher cautions, because of the nature of this virus, a vaccine could backfire, mistaking the immune system itself for the virus it had been sent out to destroy. And so there is still no magic bullet for AIDS.

As a result, AIDS remains a great frustration. In this, the century of science and its triumphs, we have come to expect the kind of security produced by sulfa drugs, penicillin, and an army of immunization—resulting in longer and more productive lives than ever in history. Can we find a way to outwit this deadly killer, this tiny adversary with its extraordinary evolutionary ability to adapt? Only time will tell.

Meanwhile, our best defense against AIDS has become education. If we can succeed in preventing HIV from traveling from host to host, eventually it will die out. The key to this plan is to make everyone aware of the high risks attached to sexual relations without protection ("unsafe sex") and intravenous drug use (especially, sharing needles). These are two of the three most likely ways to contract AIDS. (The third method by which the HIV virus is most commonly transmitted is from mother to child during pregnancy.) Once infected with HIV, as far as the research shows, the host ultimately develops AIDS and dies from it. But everyone (except the child born of an infected mother) can protect himself or herself, just by avoiding risky behavior.

For the many thousands of afflicted individuals, the hope for a cure continues. For the many thousands more who may otherwise develop the disease in coming years, the cry for a vaccine and a cure has not stopped. The search goes on.

Birth of Genetic Engineering

While HIV continues to elude understanding, spectacular advances in other areas have taken place. At mid-century the breakthroughs made by Crick and Watson at the molecular level coincided roughly with investigations that other biologists conducted on a special, fascinating class of viruses that attacked bacteria. Known as bacteriophages ("bacteria eaters"), or just phages, this group of viruses had an unusual characteristic that led ultimately to the discovery of ways to transfer genetic material from one organism to another. The combination of new understanding of these mechanisms and new technology led to one of the most stunning scientific advances of the century: genetic engineering.

Some of the first steps, though, were in the study of bacteria, not their parasites. Joshua Lederberg started down this path in 1952, when he noticed that bacteria exchange genetic material by conjugating, or joining together in pairs, in a process much like sexual intercourse in more complex organisms. Lederberg also observed that there were two groups, which he named M and F. The group he called F all possessed a body he named a *plasmid*, which the F bacterium passed on to the M bacterium. The plasmid, it turned out, consisted of genetic material, as William Hayes discovered the following year. By this time it had been clear for several years that the genetic code was carried by DNA; the plasmid, it seemed, was a ring of DNA, floating separately from the main DNA in the chromosome of the bacterium.

This discovery brought immediate help for solving a growing problem in the medical field. Sulfa drugs and antibiotics developed in the 1930s and 1940s had been in use for several years, so that many bacteria had begun to develop resistance to them—and unstoppable epidemics had begun to threaten again, especially in hospitals. In

1959 a group of Japanese scientists discovered that the gene for resistance was carried by the plasmid, of which one bacterium could have several copies, which were then passed on from one bacterium to another. A few drug-resistant bacteria introduced into a colony resulted in an entire colony of drug-resistant bacteria in short order.

As early as 1946, meanwhile, Max Delbrück and Alfred D. Hershey, working independently on bacteriophages, found that genes from different phages could combine with each other spontaneously. Swiss microbiologist Werner Arber took a look at this strange mutation process in detail, and he made what would turn out to be a stunning discovery. Bacteria had an effective method for fighting off the enemy bacteriophage virus: They used an enzyme, which became known as a "restriction enzyme," to split the phage DNA and restrict the phage's growth. The phage became inactive, and the bacterium went on about its business.

By 1968 Arber had located the restriction enzyme and found that it was designed to locate only those DNA molecules that contained a certain sequence of nucleotides that was characteristic of the enemy bacteriophage.

Arber watched what happened. The split phage genes fought back by recombining after they were split. Once split, he found, the split ends of the DNA are "sticky." That is, if the bacteria's restriction enzyme was not present to prevent recombination, different genes that had been split at the same location would recombine when placed together. The birth of recombinant DNA—that is, DNA that has been artificially prepared by combining DNA fragments taken from different species—was close at hand.

On the heels of this discovery, in 1969, Jonathan Beckwith and coworkers succeeded for the first time in isolating a single gene, the bacterial gene for a part of the metabolism of sugar. Now the stage was set for genetic engineering.

By the early 1970s American microbiologists Daniel Nathans and Hamilton Smith picked up the baton and began to develop various restriction enzymes that break DNA at specific sites. In 1970 Smith discovered an enzyme that broke a molecule of DNA at one particular site. Nathans worked on this process further and found ways to create tailor-made nucleic acid fragments, of a sort, and study their properties and ability to pass on genetic information. Now investigators were truly on the road to work with recombinant DNA that would make it possible to take nucleic acids apart and put them

Barbara McClintock and
the Case of the Shifting Gene

Understanding genes has never been easy. When botanist Barbara McClintock presented a paper at a Cold Spring Harbor Symposium for Quantitative Biology in 1951, few people really understood what she was talking about. A highly independent researcher, she was saying, based on her careful studies of generation upon generation of genes in corn, that some genes shift easily and frequently from place to place on chromosomes.

"Transposition," as McClintock's observations came to be called, or "jumping genes," clashed with the copious work on the genetics of fruit flies (*Drosophila melanogaster*) that Thomas Hunt Morgan and his team accomplished in the early decades of the century.

When McClintock began her work in this area in 1944, she had just been elected to the National Academy of Sciences and had taken office as president of the Genetics Society of America, the first woman to hold that position. She recognized that she was cutting against the grain with her theory, but, from the beginning, she sensed that the evidence led in the direction she was testing. She persevered, even though for two years she was in limbo, not knowing whether the line she was pursuing would pay off or be a blind lead. She later remarked, though, to Evelyn Witkin, a colleague at Cold Spring Harbor Laboratory:

> It never occurred to me that there was going to be any stumbling block. Not that I had the answer, but [I had] the joy of going at it. When you have that joy, you do the right experiments. You let the material tell you where to go, and it tells you at every step what the next has to be because you're integrating with an overall brand new pattern in mind. You're not following an old one; you are convinced of a new one, and you let everything you do focus on that. You can't help it, because it all integrates. There were no difficulties.

McClintock was far too rigorous a scientist to rely on the reading of tea leaves. But, like most productive scientists, she played hunches—which

together in other forms. Smith and Nathans shared the 1978 Nobel Prize in physiology or medicine for their landmark discoveries.

In 1973 Stanley H. Cohen and Herbert W. Boyer combined the two techniques—the ability to locate restriction enzymes in plasmids and in reality were based on many years of close observation and a fine ability to read patterns. The phenomenon she found was a complex process of regulation and control that, at the time, was unlike anything yet observed. Prompted by a control mechanism, a chromosome could break, dissociate, and rejoin differently—all in systematic, observable ways. She arrived at this conclusion by observing changes in color patterns in kernels of Indian corn and correlating them with changes she observed in the chromosome structure.

Only recently has McClintock's work on transposition become recognized as a fundamental and revolutionary concept of gene functioning. For many years, like Gregor Mendel's work on genetics, her work on transposition was ignored; she was ahead of her time. However, McClintock turned out to be right—and when other investigators began to find evidence that genes did sometimes move around, they remembered that she had said it first.

In 1983, at the age of 81, Barbara McClintock received the Nobel Prize in physiology or medicine. She died in Huntington, New York, near Cold Spring Harbor, in September 1992. James Watson has described McClintock as one of the three most important figures in the field of genetics.

Barbara McClintock at a Cold Spring Harbor seminar in 1951 (*Cold Spring Harbor Laboratory Archives*)

the isolation of specific genes—to introduce an extraordinary breakthrough that would become known as genetic engineering. They cut a chunk out of a plasmid found in the bacterium *Escherichia coli* and inserted a gene from a different bacterium into the gap. Then they put the plasmid back into *E. coli,* where the bacteria made copies as usual and transferred them to other bacteria. It was an amazing and powerful trick. Other scientists jumped in within months to repeat it with other species, inserting genes from fruit flies and frogs into *E. coli.*

Genetic Markers and the Human Genome

Some diseases are not caused by a parasitic virus or bacterium, but are genetic—that is, passed on from generation to generation. In fact, some 3,000 diseases are known to be caused by specific genes. Huntington's disease, caused by a single gene, is one example; cystic fibrosis, caused by a combination of two genes, is another. It would be enormously helpful if we could isolate the specific genes that caused specific diseases, but this turns out to be a tall order, since one human being's characteristics are produced by some 2 billion genes. (The full complement of genes that produce an individual human is known as the human genome.)

But it is not impossible. DNA can be divided into lengths, using the restriction enzymes produced by bacteria. And techniques have been developed for sorting these short pieces of DNA by length, followed by a technique known as Southern blotting (named after inventor Edward A. Southern) for picking out particular pieces of DNA from the sorted lengths.

In a family in which some members have inherited a particular disease, if you can compare lengths of DNA from each member of the family, and if you know which members of the family have the disease, then it is often possible to identify a particular piece of DNA that appears similar in the affected family members. This piece of DNA becomes a marker for the gene that causes the disease. Ultimately, scientists can use this marker to find the chromosome (one of 23 pairs) on which the gene is located. Using these methods in 1983, Kay Davies and Robert Williamson found the first marker for a genetic disease, Duchenne muscular dystrophy.

In 1988 the U.S. National Academy of Sciences called for a major national effort to map all the genes in the human genome, and the undertaking soon became international in scope. Completed in April 2003, this effort has already proved to be one of the greatest endeavors in the life sciences in the modern era.

But not everyone thought this was a good idea. In July 1974 Paul Berg and other biologists held a meeting backed by the U.S. National Academy of Sciences to draw up guidelines for careful regulation of genetic engineering. The tension has continued since that time between those who want to explore genetic engineering further and those who worry about undesirable consequences and want to control it.

But by the 1980s genetic engineers succeeded in producing several proteins needed by those who were sick, such as human growth hormone, human insulin, interleukin 2, and a blood clot dissolver. They also came up with a vaccine for hepatitis B and improved tissue matching capabilities for transplants. Most of these enterprises used tanks for production in carefully controlled environments, and opposition to this type of genetic engineering has lessened. Additionally, genetic engineering has succeeded in locating gene markers for such genetic disorders as Huntington's disease or Duchenne muscular dystrophy.

In 1952 a new area of inquiry opened up when an extraordinarily delicate operation was successfully carried out by American biologists Robert William Briggs and Thomas J. King in which they removed the nucleus of a cell, which contains all the genetic material of the organism, and substituted it with another. It was the birth of a procedure known as nuclear transplantation.

Fifteen years later, in 1967, British biologist John P. Gurdon successfully cloned a vertebrate, a feat never before accomplished. From a cell in the intestine of a South African clawed tree frog, he removed the nucleus and transferred it to an unfertilized ovum (egg cell) of the same species. From that beginning a new, completely normal, individual developed—a clone of the original.

From Gurdon's breakthrough, coupled with others at the gene and chromosome level in the 1970s, would come a new comprehension of how living things function at the most fundamental levels.

As scientists have learned more about genes and DNA, new and varied prospects have arisen for controlling some of the outcomes of inheritance. The desire to control inherited traits is certainly not new—wheat farmers, horse trainers, and pigeon fanciers, to name just a few, have directed the characteristics of strains of plants and animals for centuries through crossbreeding. Now, however, issues surrounding intervention at the genetic level—genetic engineering of all types—has become a controversial subject. Genetic engineering

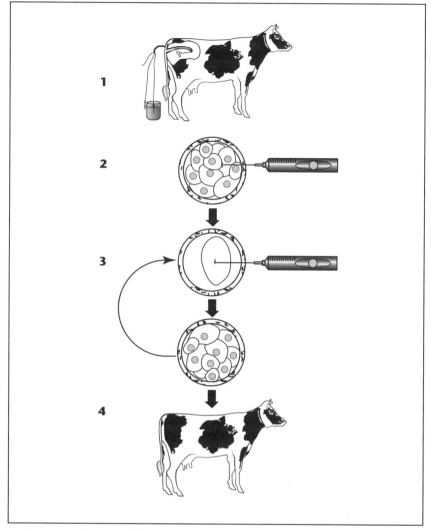

Nuclear Transplantation (1) Removal of an embryo from a donor cow (or from in vitro fertilization). (2) Removal of individual cells from the donor embryo. (3) Injection of each cell from the embryo into an egg cell from which the nucleus has been removed. (4) The egg cell grows with its new nucleus, becoming a multicelled embryo and then is either re-entered into the cloning process (upward arrow) or placed in the cow's uterus to develop and be born. *(Adapted from Office of Technology Assessment, adapted from R. S. Prather and N. L. First, "Cloning Embryos by Nuclear Transfer,"* Genetic Engineering in Animals, W. Hansell and B. K. Weir (eds.), *Journal of Reproduction and Fertility Ltd., Cambridge, U.K., 1990, pp. 125–134)*

(GE) in foods has caused consumers to ask questions about their safety, as well as environmental concerns about the unwanted spread of GE seeds. The issue has become a political football, with African countries refusing inexpensive GE food for fear of losing the important European market for their agricultural produce on the presumption of contamination to their crops from imported GE seeds.

With the completion of the Human Genome Project (see sidebar), another avenue for genetic engineering—stem cell research and gene therapy—had a much more complete knowledge base to draw from. The idea behind gene therapy is to treat or cure some of the 4,000 recognized genetic disorders. For many sufferers, the outcome without therapy would be lifelong suffering and often death at a young age. Though not currently approved as a medical therapy to treat disease, gene therapy is undergoing the required clinical trials and tests for safety and efficacy, and scientists are optimistic that it will prove to be a powerful new tool in the treatment of genetically transmitted disease.

Ethical considerations enter in, however, where stem cell research is required, since stem cells (cells taken from an embryo before differentiation has begun) are the most easily adapted for genetic engineering purposes, and the embryo is sacrificed in the process. Though smaller than the period on a printed page, even such a young embryo is considered a human life by some groups and therefore they consider that a human life is lost when stem cell research is done. Ethics are also called into play where nuclear transplant technology is used; the nuclear material is inserted into an ovum, or egg, from which the nucleus has been removed—therefore involving what some groups consider the destruction of a potential life.

That is one reason that a sheep named Dolly made such big news when she was born in 1997.

Life and Death of a Famous Ewe

In February 1997 researchers at Roslin Institute near the city of Edinburgh, Scotland, made a big impact when they made an announcement that a sheep named Dolly had been born the previous summer and was enjoying life in good health. But this young female sheep was special. She was a clone of her mother, a six-year-old adult sheep—the first mammal successfully cloned from adult cells—not stem cells. Scientists had tried many times to clone mammals using adult cells, without success, and many people assumed it could not be done. Dolly had just proved them wrong.

Cloning admittedly steps outside the expected processes for reproduction. Although Dolly looked completely normal, she did not come from a normal egg and no sperm was involved. Dolly was a copy of her mother only, who supplied the DNA. Dolly had no father. The Frankensteinian flavor of this event made some people uneasy, but many people took heart that perhaps cloning was not only feasible but safe and did not involve use of embryonic stem cells, having possible implications for human use of the technique. Dolly appeared to be a completely normal sheep in every way—not stitched or bolted together. By 1998 she conceived normally with a Welsh mountain ram and gave birth to Bonnie, a normal, 6.7-pound lamb.

Sadly, Dolly died at the age of six on February 14, 2003, after coming down with a respiratory illness. Scientists think that her early death was caused by rapid aging—since she started life with adult cells in which the aging process had been going on for several years. Still, the researchers at Roslin Institute in Scotland, led by embryologist Ian Wilmut, had done the impossible. That is, they did what everyone up until that moment had thought was impossible. Other researchers had tried, and they all had failed.

So, as of 1997, suddenly genetic engineering and its ethical issues took center stage in the news. With the birth of Dolly, many "what-if" ques-

Dolly, the world's first sheep to be successfully cloned using adult cells. Dolly is shown here with her first lamb, Bonnie, which was conceived and born naturally and was completely normal. Unfortunately, Dolly, born in 1996, lived a short life of only six years. *(Roslin Institute)*

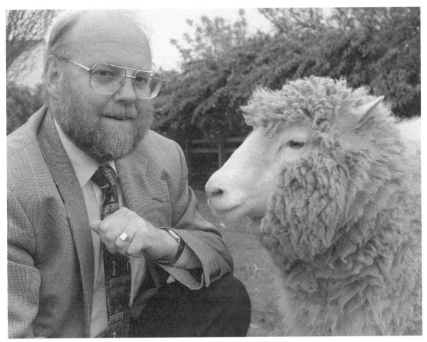

Ian Wilmut and Dolly (*Roslin Institute*)

tions swiftly became much more real. Today opinions are still many and varied—not just about cloning, its pros and cons and the future, but also about the entire field of genetic engineering. Controversies swirl around all of genetic engineering's many faces. People are concerned about the use of genetic engineering with plants, food, viruses, endangered species, and medical therapies for humans. Dolly dramatically brought these questions and controversies into focus in the public eye for the first time.

Public policy began to develop rapidly in response. U.S. president Bill Clinton immediately called for a law making the cloning of humans illegal in the United States. Many countries worldwide have also banned human cloning. As scientific knowledge and skills in manipulating genes have advanced, the issues have become more and more complex. In 1998, 19 European countries signed the first binding international treaty to ban the cloning of human beings. On August 9, 2001, U.S. president George W. Bush announced his decision to limit availability of federal funds for research using human stem cells.

Polly, the first sheep to be cloned by nuclear transfer technology bearing a human gene. With her are her sisters. (Roslin Institute)

In the meantime Ian Wilmut's team at Roslin Institute and other research facilities continue to explore the uses of cloning in animals. The same year as the announcement of Dolly, Roslin announced the birth of Polly, the first sheep cloned by nuclear transfer technology bearing a human gene. However, Polly was cloned using fibroblast cells from a sheep fetus—not an adult. Polly was one of five lambs produced by the technique, and two of the five lambs had the human gene, which could theoretically be used therapeutically to address a human genetic disorder. For example, the gene might induce production of proteins in the ewe's milk that would aid clotting of blood in hemophiliacs.

Genetic engineering enjoys an uneasy peace with both the public and science. Many people hesitate about such experiments as releasing genetically engineered bacteria into the environment, and even an apparently innocent product such as genetically engineered tomatoes seems to have a negative public image. But, responsibly used, genetic engineering can be a powerful tool for managing our lives and our health, and it is, without question, one of the most important discoveries of the century.

8

Where Did Humans Come From?
The Search Continues

THE GREAT RIFT VALLEY THAT SLASHES across seven countries from the southern tip of Turkey to Mozambique looks like a rough-edged scar across the arid face of most of eastern Africa. Barren, hot, and forbidding, lashed by eroding winds, this badlands region of jutting shoulders of rock and exposed ancient geological layers has become a giant treasure chest for those who seek to know the history of humankind. For here, near several ancient lake beds, skeletons that are hundreds of thousands to millions of years old have been found. Thanks to the sifting along fault lines, these skeletons are lifted up from where they were buried beneath eons of rock and sediment deposits and are exposed by the erosion of constant winds. Eventually, a passing paleontologist, by training always ready to notice the odd fragment or telling shape or color, picks it up and catalogs it—and the search is on for the rest of the skeleton, for other skeletons, and, possibly, for tools and other evidence of a way of life.

The work in this land is not easy. And the piecing together of the history of hominids—a term used to describe us and our two-legged, upright-walking ancestors—requires keen eyes, patient and careful hands, often several teams of scientists from varied disciplines, and, above all, thick skin and a lot of charm. Paleontology is among the most controversial of sciences. Because paleontologists draw conclusions, necessarily, from fragments of bones and often scanty evidence, fellow scientists tend to look down on their theories, which non-paleontologists think say too much based on too little data. Even, or perhaps especially, among themselves, pale-ontologists find agreement hard to come by. What's more, their business is the exploration of one of the touchiest, most emotional of subjects: exploring data that indicates human beings and apes share the same ancient ancestors.

When Charles Darwin first put forth this idea, the bishop of Worcester's wife is said to have remarked, "Let us hope it is not true, but if it is, let us pray that it will not become generally known." And that is the unqualified opinion still held by many people. As a con-sequence, funding is hard to come by in this orphan profession, although one institution and one family have gone a long way toward capturing the public interest and enthusiasm: the National Geographic Society and the Leakey family of Kenya.

The Famous Leakey Luck

Louis Seymour Bazett Leakey (1903–72) was born in Kenya, where his British-born parents had gone as missionaries, and to him, Kenya was always his home. A maverick, highly independent, tall, intuitive man with a twinkling eye, he did more than anyone before him to bring the hunt for the hominid story to public attention in a positive light. He was also enormously controversial. But Leakey and his wife, archaeologist and paleoanthropologist Mary Nicol Leakey, together transformed the entire picture of human prehistory.

Mary Leakey (1913–96) was the one who actually ran most of the sites, setting up systems that became the standard of the profes-sion, and she made many of the finds. Systematic, careful, and atten-tive to detail, she contributed the perfect complement to Louis's impulsive, swashbuckling, hunch-playing approach. "If we'd been the same kind of person," she has asserted, "we wouldn't have accomplished as much." A trained artist, Mary also illustrated most of Louis's publications.

One morning, in 1959, Mary was walking the dogs at a site in the Olduvai Gorge in northern Tanzania, where she and Louis had been working (Louis was back in camp with a fever). Her ever-watchful, trained eyes lit on something striking, in an exposed cross-section about 20 feet down from the top layer. A closer look revealed a bit of exposed bone, which at first didn't appear to be hominid. But when she brushed away the soil and could see the teeth, she became excited. "I was tremendously excited by my discovery and quickly went back to camp to fetch Louis," she later wrote. Louis was not quite as excited as Mary. To him, it looked like an *Australopithecus* skull, and he was looking for fossils in the *Homo* species.

Australopithecus africanus was a name first coined by Raymond Dart in 1924 to describe the fossils he had found in South Africa that together became known as the "Taung baby." *Australopithecus* means "southern ape," but most researchers had concluded, based in part on further discoveries by Robert Broom in South Africa, that *Australopithecus* was not an ape, but a two-legged, upright-walking hominid. Leakey, however, had always maintained that the *Homo* species had been around a very long time and that Broom and Dart's australopithecines were not old enough to be ancestral to humans, a point on which few paleontologists agreed with him at the time.

The original type specimen of *Australopithecus africanus,* based on fossils discovered in a lime quarry near Taung in South Africa *(© J. Reader/Photo Researchers, Inc.)*

But even Leakey became excited as they examined the site further. They had found what is referred to in paleoanthropology as a living floor, where, thousands of years before, a group of hominids had camped. It was older and less disturbed, and contained more evidence, than any living floor discovered up until that time.

Located about 300 miles west of the Indian Ocean, near Lake Victoria in Tanzania, the Olduvai Gorge cuts 300 feet deep or more, slashing across an ancient lake basin, now dry and dusty. The layers of deposits exposed along its walls cover a time span of 1.96 million years—from the early Pleistocene epoch. And as it cuts through what used to be the shoreline of the ancient lake, the gorge exposes campsites, layer upon layer of them, of ancient hominids where they used to live along the edge of the lake. As the lake had risen and fallen in the past, hominids had camped by its shores, and then moved away, leaving their debris, which was covered by water and sediment and sometimes, by luck, a layer of volcanic ash from a nearby erupting volcano. Although the organic remains rotted away, the bones and stones used as tools were protected from the erosion of sun and wind and were preserved.

At this site, bones of animals consumed by the hominids remained nearby, many of them broken so diners could extract the

Tools of Science: How Old *Is* It?

How do you tell how old a fossil is, since there's no date stamped on the back? In the past few decades, several different dating techniques, most of them highly sophisticated, have been developed. Many of them rely on the fact that radioactive isotopes have a predictable half-life, and the first person to come up with such a method was an American chemist named Willard Frank Libby (1908–80), who invented the method known as carbon 14 dating in 1947.

The carbon 14 isotope, discovered in 1940, has a surprisingly long half-life (the time it takes for half a radioactive substance to decay) of 5,700 years, and Libby saw how this fact could be put to use for dating. Cosmic rays convert some of the nitrogen 14 in the Earth's atmosphere into carbon 14, and the chemical process works in such a way that a certain amount of carbon 14 is therefore always present in the atmosphere. Since plants absorb carbon dioxide during photosynthesis, Libby figured, the molecules in all plant tissues would naturally contain a percentage of carbon 14 that occurs naturally in the atmosphere—a very small percentage, but it's always there. Since carbon 14 is radioactive, it's possible to measure the beta particles it emits with great precision.

Once a plant dies, though, and photosynthesis stops, the plant no longer continues to absorb carbon dioxide, or carbon 14, and the carbon 14 that was present at the moment the plant died continues to break down without being replaced. Libby figured out that, by measuring the concentration of carbon 14 in a once-living plant, one could figure out how long the plant had been dead. The accuracy of the method was amazing, and it could be used on samples of wood, parchment, cloth—anything that was made from a plant—to date objects up to 50,000 years old (70,000 years with special techniques). Because animals eat plants (or eat other animals that eat plants), the carbon 14 dating method can be extended to marrow. And the area was strewn with stone tools—all this surrounding the skull that Mary had found. What's more, the volcanic layers of rock make it possible to use a new type of dating technique, potassium-argon dating, which was used for the first time on Mary's find. "Zinjanthropus," as Louis named it, was 1.75 million years old. The presence of the tools meant, by definition, that this was an early human. This was the oldest hominid discovery yet made that

fossilized bones as well. In the study of fossils, this is one of the few dating techniques that makes use of the fossil itself.

We now know that carbon 14 concentrations in the atmosphere vary, depending upon the level of cosmic ray radiation, so that carbon 14 dating has to be calibrated against some known standard, such as annual growth rings in trees.

Because carbon 14 dating is limited in range, some method was needed for use when dating very ancient hominid fossils. Potassium-argon dating, discovered in 1961, is useful for dating rock from volcanic areas such as the Great Rift Valley of East Africa. This advantage in dating in a volcanic area is one of the reasons the Great Rift Valley's fossils are so much easier to date than those found in the cave areas farther south.

When a volcano erupts, it spews forth molten lava, which includes minerals containing potassium. A tiny proportion of all potassium consists of its radioisotope, potassium 40, which decays at a known rate to form the gas argon. In molten lava from a volcano, as the lava cools, crystals form, and the argon formed by the potassium 40 decay becomes trapped inside the crystals. By measuring the relative proportions of potassium 40 and argon in the crystals, it's possible to find out how long ago the lava cooled. There are also ways of checking to see if argon has been lost from the crystals.

In an area like the Great Rift Valley, layers composed of lava flows are typically interspersed with sediment, where the fossils are found, and a series of dates can be calculated at a series of intervals throughout the formation.

These and other dating techniques—such as thermoluminescence dating, fission-track dating, faunal dating (based on the stage of evolution of types of animal fossils found in the same layer), and measurements of remnant magnetic orientation—have added to the researcher's bag of tricks for dating very old fossils.

was associated with tools, and the find radically changed scientific views about the timescale of human evolution. Most scientists had not thought australopithecines were capable of making tools—and Louis Leakey didn't want to accept their presence in the direct line of human history. Yet there it was.

In keeping with his views, Leakey created a new genus, *Zinjanthropus*, meaning "man from East Africa" (*Zinj* is the ancient name for East Africa, and *anthropus* means "man"). The full name of this specimen became *Zinjanthropus boisei*, after a benefactor, Charles Boise, who had made it possible for the Leakeys to work the site. (Leakey was a tireless fund-raiser and later took the Zinj skull with him to the United States and used it to persuade the National Geographic Society to back him.) "Nutcracker Man," as he was also sometimes called, had a distinctive ridge on the top of his head, where large muscles attached to move its powerful jaws and huge grinding molars (the reason for the name). Leakey eventually lost the nomenclature battle, however, and the specimen was later reclassified as *Australopithecus boisei*.

Meanwhile, as the Leakeys had been working at their sites in the Olduvai in Africa, just a few years before Mary's discovery of Zinj, a furor had taken place in the sedate halls of the British Museum in London: A scandal was afoot in the world of paleonanthropology.

Piltdown Man Revisited

For British paleontologists and anthropologists in 1911, the discovery of the Piltdown skull had been one of the most exhilarating, though baffling, of all the hominid fossils discovered up to that date. Found in a gravel pit near a place called Piltdown Common in Sussex, England, by workmen building a road, the skull first came to the attention of a lawyer named Charles Dawson. Thinking that it surely must be a fossil, he took it to Arthur Smith Woodward, a paleontologist at the British Museum. Woodward was struck by the fact that, unlike the Neanderthal, a 30,000- to 40,000-year-old fossil discovered in Germany in 1857, this skull did not have prominent browridges and looked much more like modern humans. Intrigued, he went with Dawson to the site to see if they could find additional parts to the skeleton. After searching for several days, Dawson found a jawbone not far from where Woodward was also looking. The jawbone had the same brownish color as the rest of the skull and seemed to be part of the same skeleton. But, while the skull looked strikingly like modern human skulls, the jawbone looked ape-like. Yet the teeth were not ape-like, but were ground down from chewing, like human teeth.

Tremendous controversy ensued, as investigators tried to explain some of Piltdown's strange characteristics. Based on the sketchy evidence of two fragmentary pieces—the face was missing and so were some of the hinge pieces for the jaws—Woodward put together a reconstructed skull that

A reconstruction of the Piltdown skull *(The Natural History Museum, London)*

modeled the shape of the head and size of the brain capacity to fit with the ape-like jaw. Meanwhile, Sir Arthur Keith, a renowned anthropologist, preferred to emphasize the large brain capacity and apparently more human-like structure of the cranium—a clearly more desirable heritage than Neanderthal—and fitted the jaw to look less ape-like. This, surely, was the link between apes and humans.

In fact, Keith liked the idea of a large-brained ancestor so much that, when Raymond Dart made his australopithecine find in Africa in 1924, Keith strongly questioned that it could be part of the line— having, as it did, a small brain and a humanlike jaw, just the opposite of Keith's reconstruction of Piltdown. And Keith was a well qualified opponent in these matters. He once invited doubters to smash a known skull, whereupon he reconstructed it perfectly from just a few fragments.

Not until the early 1950s, however, did the truth become certain about Piltdown, when Kenneth Oakley of the British Museum came up with a new method for measuring whether ancient bones were the same age (a method that is highly useful for any paleontological dig). When Oakley tested the jaw and skull of Piltdown with his radioactive fluorine test, he discovered that the skull was many thousands of years older than the jaw. Unless, as one wry scientist put it, "the man died but his jaw lingered on a few thousand years," the two fragments could not have belonged to the same individual.

Closer examinations showed more. The jaw, it turned out, belonged to an orangutan and had been doctored, the teeth filed to look human and broken at the hinge to obscure its identity. Both fragments had been painted with brown stain and planted together in the gravel pit.

In November 1953 Kenneth Oakley announced his findings, and immediately the headlines blared: PILTDOWN APE-MAN A FAKE—FOSSIL HOAX MAKES MONKEYS OUT OF SCIENTISTS.

No one knows for sure who the culprit may have been who pulled off the hoax. Dawson may have been a good candidate: He had always been fascinated by fossils and Piltdown did put his name in the science history books. Arthur Conan Doyle, the creator of Sherlock Holmes, is another possible suspect: He lived nearby and had a rascally liking for taunting scientists. But no one knows for sure. What is certain is that a prominent group of British scientists believed it was real—maybe because they were tired of seeing France and Germany get all the credit (at that time) as the cradle of early humanity, or maybe in some cases because the large brain echoed their own belief that the brain was the distinguishing trait that had spelled success for modern humanity.

It's easy from our vantage point to be amazed that such eminent and erudite scientists would fall for such a (now) obvious hoax. But hindsight, as Isaac Asimov once wrote on this subject, is cheap. Little was known in 1911 about the evolution of hominids—and none of the sophisticated dating and testing techniques now available were at the disposal of these investigators. Piltdown stands as an excellent lesson in how easy it is to be fooled by one's own bias and assumptions. We too often see what we want to see—and if we want to find truth we have to look much further than that.

The immediate effect for paleoanthropology was disgrace. One member of Parliament suggested dismantling the British Museum. Sir Arthur Keith died in 1955, embarrassed, an otherwise fine career badly marred. The entire scientific validity of the profession was called into question as people wondered how so much could be surmised accurately from so little.

But science is designed to be self-correcting, to learn from mistakes. Before World War II, most anthropologists thought that a large brain was one of the prime distinguishing characteristics of hominids. Human vanity and the Piltdown hoax had gone a long way toward reinforcing this idea. Now that Piltdown man was discredited, more anthropologists paid attention to the mounting evidence that the small-brained australopithecines had walked erect. And the definition of the hominid now became focused less on the size of the brain than on the shape of the legs and pelvis. Not everyone has agreed on this premise, though, and cranial capacity still held some sway, as well as the use of tools.

"Handy Human"

In 1961, only shortly after publication of the news of the "Nutcracker Man," which had fit so badly with Louis Leakey's view of human prehistory, his son Jonathan found a fragmentary skull at Olduvai Gorge that appeared to be an "advanced" hominid. Experts were able to place the date at 1.75 million years old by potassium-argon dating, and tools found in the area seemed to suggest the ability to use hands skillfully. So the fossil remains were named *Homo habilis,* or "Handy Man."

"This was the first evidence," the Leakeys' son Richard wrote, "that early members of the human lineage were contemporaries of the australopithecines, not descendants as was generally believed."

But debate rose up over whether this was really a distinct species or another australopithecine. Other fragments were found in the area that the Leakeys included as part of the same specimen, but some critics contested some of their identifications and assumptions.

In 1972 Bernard Ngeneo, who was working with Richard Leakey, found a similar skull, known as "1470," at East Turkana in Kenya. More pieces of this skull turned up, and Richard's wife, Maeve, and a team of anatomists pieced it together. Richard Leakey believes that this skull, with its fairly large cranial capacity and dated age of 1.89 million years old, is the oldest fossil of a true human ancestor (with australopithecines and other hominid fossils as side branches).

Meanwhile, more australopithecine evidence was building up elsewhere.

Lucy

On November 30, 1974, anthropologist Donald Johanson (1943–   ) made one of the most exciting fossil discoveries ever made. He and his colleagues working at Hadar, in the Afar region of Ethiopia, had unearthed the most complete skeleton from 3.5 million years ago ever found. Judging from the shape of the pelvis, the field team made the assumption that the specimen is of a woman, and they named her Lucy. Although it is not absolutely certain she is a woman (there are no male pelvises around for comparison), the name stuck. The scientific name given "her" is *Australopithecus afarensis,* meaning "southern ape from Afar." (Even though none of these fossils is from the south, the first australopithecine was discovered in South Africa. Some people would also debate whether "ape" is the right description, but the name has stuck.)

Lucy was small of stature—standing only four feet tall—and had a small brain, reinforcing the concept that "walking tall" preceded enlarged brain capacity. The idea that a fossil woman had been found gave Johanson's discovery wide public appeal. As usual, however, there ensued many debates: about the age of the fossil (maybe it's only 3 million years old), over whether or not a fossil found by Mary Leakey

A reconstructed model of an adult *Australopithecus afarensis* couple, based on the discovery in South Africa of fossils of "Lucy," who probably lived about 3 million years ago *(American Museum of Natural History)*

Mary Leakey uncovering fossil remains of early humans in July 1959 in Olduvai Gorge, Tanzania *(© Des Bartlett/Photo Researchers, Inc.)*

1,000 miles away was the same species (Johanson claimed it was, while she claimed it wasn't), and about the fossil's place in hominid history.

At the beginning of the 1980s, considerable confusion reigned and, while the finds of the 1980s were exciting, they did nothing, really, to clear it up.

Turkana Boy

One day, in August 1984, while working near Lake Turkana in Kenya, Kamoya Kimeu was retracing his steps to look at a rhinoceros skull he had passed by the previous day. Kimeu was the foreman of a group of experts working with Richard Leakey, who had become the director of the Kenya Museum, and Alan Walker of the Johns Hopkins Medical School. Sharp eyes and the ability to recognize odd and telling shapes, colors, or textures are among the great skills required for this kind of work, along with the patience to retrace, relook, and rethink everything.

Something odd caught Kimeu's eye: a small skull fragment. The next day the whole crew went back, and by dusk they had found it: additional scraps of a *Homo erectus* skull. They sieved and sorted and glued broken pieces together for a few more days. But large sections were still missing. They decided to give it one more day. The next day, by sheer luck, a stroke of a tiny dental pick disturbed soil and stones by the root of a thorn tree and the missing facial bones appeared. The team pressed on. By the time they were finished they had found the most complete skeleton of *Homo erectus* to date, and the first recovered of such great antiquity: 1.6 million years old. It was the skeleton of a boy, around 12 years of age, who stood about five feet four inches tall—surprisingly large for his age.

The Black Skull

Harking back to Mary Leakey's 1959 "Nutcracker Man," in 1985 Alan Walker discovered another australopithecine with huge jaws and pronounced ridges or crests. The "Black Skull"—so called because of the color of the fossil—was found near Lake Turkana in Kenya and has been dated between 2.5 and 2.6 million years old. Sometimes referred to as "hyperrobust," this older robust specimen was classified as *Australopithecus robustus*. It had the smallest brain capacity seen to date in a hominid skull, although it is not the earliest hominid ever found. Its bony ridge or crest is the most prominent ever found. Judging from the great grinding molars (four to five times as large as those of modern humans), the huge jaw muscles that attached to the crest apparently were used for chewing tough plant stalks or for cracking seeds or pits. The head and face were thrust farther forward than in other australopithecines, as well.

The fact that the Black Skull is three-quarters of a million years older than *A. boisei* suggests that robust australopithecines were a long-lived and successful branch of the hominid family. And, in fact, by 1989 Richard Leakey had put distance between himself and his original ideas about lineage, coming to the conclusion that, based on evidence, it's too early yet to tell much about the exact evolution of man.

Unsolved Mysteries and Later Finds

The fossil record, though still sketchy, has become clearer on one point in the last few decades: Australopithecines have to be recognized as a subfamily that shared important characteristics. They were habitually erect, bipedal beings with human-like teeth and relatively small brains. They used tools. And they were good candidates for the role of ancestors for humankind. By the end of the 20th century, it was also becoming increasingly clear that the so-called family tree of humanity was beginning to look a lot less like a tree with clearly defined branches and subbranches, and more like a thick and tangled bush. A continuing spate of new fossil discoveries and the

Hot Debate

One of the hottest questions for debate among anthropologists as the 21st century turned was whether modern humans evolved solely in Africa and then moved outward, or whether they evolved concurrently in several places around the world. If they migrated out of Africa, when did the migration begin? What directions did they move in, and did they interbreed with or replace archaic species? The two leading hypotheses, the "Out of Africa" argument and the multiregional argument, in many ways symbolize two of modern anthropology's major approaches to the problems of human evolution and lineage—what someone has called the "stones and bones" school (archaeologists and paleoanthropologists), and the "white coats," population geneticists and molecular biologists. Currently, the argument seems tipped to favor the geneticists' and molecular biologists' hypothesis that modern humans originated in Africa, spreading from there to various parts of the world in several "waves" of migration that gradually replaced other species. According to S. Blair Hedges, a molecular biologist at Pennsylvania State University, "Genetic evidence tells us that *Homo sapiens* are of recent origin and arose in Africa." In a *National Geographic News* article in 2003, Hedges went on to explain that "African populations have the most ancient alleles (gene pairs that code for specific traits) and the greatest genetic diversity, which means that they're the oldest. Our species probably had arisen by 150,000 years ago, with a population of perhaps 10,000 individuals." According to the geneticists, there is no genetic evidence that supports the idea of interbreeding, and, in fact, a few DNA studies argue strongly against it.

re-examination of some older finds in the light of new theories and technologies had revealed that australopithecines were not one homogenous species but seven distinct species living between 5 million years ago and 3.9 million years ago. The seven species (see chart) are currently identified as *Australopithecus anamensis, Australopithecus afarensis, Australopithecus bahrelghazali, Australopithecus aethiopicus, Australopithicus africanus, Australopithecuus robustus,* and *Australopithecus boisei.* It should be noted, though, that not all experts agree that there are seven distinct species; some question the inclusion of one of more of the seven, and some argue for still others to be added to the seven. Most experts generally accept, however, that the australopithecines all belong to the subfamily hominea, a group that includes humans, and that one species (experts disagree on which one) of the australopithicenes is the ancestor of modern humans.

To complicate matters even more there is no consensus among the experts about the evolutionary relationship among the various australopithecines. What has been generally agreed upon is that, about 2.5 million years ago, the evolutionary line leading to modern humans diverged from subsequent australopithecine species and that about 1 million years ago the most recent of the australopithecine species, for unknown reasons, went extinct.

The discoveries in East Africa and the recognition that the earliest humans and australopithecines occupied the same territory at the same time have raised many questions. Could australopithecines and humans have intermarried? Did humans eradicate the australopithecines? What happened? At the very least, we can be sure that the known australopithecines and humans shared a common ancestor.

Many experts think we can reasonably postulate that *Homo* was present in East Africa by at least 2 million years ago, developing in parallel with at least one line (*A. boisei*) of australopithecines. These two hominid lines apparently lived at the same time for at least a million years, after which the australopithecine lineage apparently disappears forever. At the same time, the *Homo habilis* line was emerging into a later form, *Homo erectus,* which, in turn, developed into *Homo sapiens* (modern humans).

It seems increasingly likely that the family tree branched out about 6 million years ago, after which several types of apes, humans, human-apes, and near-humans all coexisted for a long time. Some experts think that as many as 15 species of humans have existed over time, and some even suggest that up to 10 million years ago, 10 different species of humans existed at the same time. We still can't be sure from the evidence whether they lived together peaceably or as enemies—and we may never know the answer to this question. We also can't be sure, as the record now stands, which are our direct ancestors and which are just distant cousins.

There is a lot more of the story to come, and there is sure to be a lot more controversy along the way, as the search for more clues to the human and pre-human past continues.

PART III

Science and Society, 1946 to the Present

9

Hot and Cold on Science

THE SPECTERS OF THE TERRIBLE destruction suffered in Hiroshima and Nagasaki had cast their shadows over the world. There had always been those to whom science appeared a threat. In the 1950s, though, the threat suddenly became more real, more immediate, and more disastrous—not just to those who already found fault with science but to the world as a whole. Suddenly, a new kind of plague had appeared almost overnight, changing the world forever. As Hiroshima had all too horribly demonstrated, death and destruction on a scale never seen before could come all too suddenly, all too swiftly, with the sound of an airplane, the wail of a siren, the push of a button. The war against fascism had been won, but the celebration of peace was short. After Hiroshima and Nagasaki, the word *peace* had lost some of its assurance. A new line had been drawn between peace and war, an uneasy line called the "cold war," in which the two superpowers and one-time reluctant allies, the United States and the USSR, stood like two giants on opposite sides of a great battlefield, each holding the power to destroy the other, each aware that retaliation would be instant and fatal. In the process, they could easily destroy the whole world. No one was left out of this demon's path.

Had the scientists at Los Alamos changed the face of the world forever? Death and destruction could come to nations more swiftly, more ruthlessly, than ever before—all this the entire populace clearly understood. Towns and cities could disappear from the face of the world in an instant. Millions of human beings could be incinerated in the blink of an eye, replaced by a mushroom-shaped cloud.

"I have become Shiva, the destroyer of worlds," Robert Oppenheimer reportedly remarked when the test bomb at Trinity was detonated. The brilliant and conscience-tortured scientist most instrumental for the creation of the world's first atomic bomb was not bragging. He had come to the aid of his country and the free world. He had done what he clearly thought had to be done. And he would spend the rest of his life in an agony of guilt for his part in the destruction that resulted. Now the United States and the USSR raced each other to build bigger and more destructive bombs. Under the guidance of physicist Edward Teller, the United States built the world's first hydrogen bomb (H bomb), powered by nuclear fusion of the heavy isotopes of hydrogen and tested on an isolated atoll in the Pacific Ocean on November 1, 1952. It was the equivalent of several million tons of TNT, a thousand times more deadly than the atomic bomb that destroyed Hiroshima. "The bomb" became a part of the world lexicon. School children were given instructions on how to protect themselves in case "the bomb" was dropped during school hours. The instructions, of course, had little value other than psychological reassurance, a reassurance that did more for the parents than for the frightened children. Families built "bomb shelters" in their backyards while intellectuals waxed philosophically about the ethics of such shelters. Do you let your neighbors in? What do you do if they try to break in? Do you really want to come out and try to live in a destroyed world? The questions, like the shelters themselves, were of little value. Only the most innocent believed the shelters would do any good anyway.

Reflecting, and perhaps contributing to, the fears of the public during the cold war years, the motion picture industry offered a steady diet of science fiction thrillers. Hideous, overgrown monsters created by the mysterious effects of atomic radiation (according to the screenwriters) rampaged across the screens in movie theaters and drive-ins. "Science Runs Wild!" the advertisements shouted. "There are some things man is not meant to know!" If "mad scientists" were not directly or indirectly creating either monsters or some other form of trouble for the world, they were portrayed as incredibly naïve, bumbling, or cumbersome, as the military or other stalwart heroes battled and defeated the deadly and hideous things created in Hollywood by the scores.

Deadly and hideous things they were. The "mad scientists" of the popular imagination of the 1930s and 1940s created Frankenstein-

The photo shows a mockup of *Sputnik I,* launched by the Soviet Union on October 4, 1957. It was the first human-made object ever to reach Earth's orbit and was the first step for humans beyond Earth's atmosphere. *(Courtesy of NASA)*

like monsters that only terrorized villages, while the giant ants, spiders, and "atomic men" created by the villains of 1950s movies threatened to destroy Earth itself and everything on it. Straining under the tensions of the cold war, threatened constantly with the possibility of total annihilation, and frustrated by the apparent inability of the individual to control his or her own fate in a world dictated by politicians, militarists, and scientists, people found that the fantasies of the movie screen offered at least some resolution, whether played out to victory or defeat.

While the mood of the world and its distrust of science was reflected in science fiction movies in the early years of the cold war, a startlingly science-fiction-like event in 1957 brought a 180° turnabout in public attitude. A tiny beeping object suddenly appeared, a new twinkling star on the evening horizon, orbiting high above the Earth's surface. Its name was *Sputnik I*, launched by the USSR. Though allies with the United States, England, and France during the war, the Soviet Union was a dictatorship, ruled with an iron hand, guilty of genocide of its people and frequent false imprisonment. This new show of strength was frightening, and for the Western world it cast a new focus on science; for the United States, it made scientific expertise into an important component of national prestige. In the struggle to win a cold war competition for international respect, Americans developed a heightened appreciation for intelligence, technology, and scientific accomplishment.

In many ways the face of the world began to shift in October 1957. Soon, for the first time, human beings would view their own planet from the silence of space. One of the two great giants had opened up another front in the cold war. The USSR had been the first to put an artificial satellite into orbit around Earth, but U.S. rocket builders were not far behind. The United States, the USSR, and England had played "Capture the Scientist" with the German scientists as prizes as World War II ground to an end in 1945. The designers of the deadly German V2 rockets were at the top of the most-wanted list. Head German rocket scientist Wernher von Braun sensed the value of his team of rocket builders to both the USSR and the United States. He and much of his team envisioned a better life in the United States, and von Braun led a large contingent from his team in a mass surrender to U.S. forces. Others surrendered to the USSR. Both groups were exported from Germany in relative secret, and the result was an influx of rocket-building expertise on both sides of the USSR's so-called Iron Curtain.

The immediate name of the game was guided missiles built to carry instruments of mass destruction swiftly to the enemy. Von Braun, though, along with key members of his team, had long dreamed bigger dreams. Since his childhood Von Braun had dreamed of sending men and rockets not to enemy territory but to space. The authorities of both America and the USSR had also turned their eyes toward space, not just for its promising potential for the military but also as propaganda. Which of the two giants would be the first to demonstrate their superior power and knowledge by breaking through the barriers of science and technology to make the grand leap into space?

With *Sputnik I* the USSR had won the lead in the so-called space race. A humbled America, after experiencing a couple of disastrous and highly public failures, finally managed to put its own satellite into orbit. Suddenly, it seemed, all eyes were turned toward space, and once again toward science. Schoolrooms in both the USSR and America sharpened their science instruction. "Science fairs," exhibiting and promoting the science projects of young minds, grew in popularity and prestige. Despite the ever-present specter of "the bomb," the world now saw science as a hero. The public and the news media wrote about "our scientists" and "their scientists," and in both the superpowers, everyone knew that "our scientists" were the best scientists. Sensing the tremendous propaganda value in taking a bold and dramatic stance, the president of the United States, John F. Kennedy, announced on May 5, 1961, the nation's intentions to put a man on the Moon and bring "him safely back to Earth." As the cold war continued, the space race heated up, and from 1969 to 1972, the glory days of the U.S. space program, 12 different American astronauts walked on the face of the Moon during six missions.

Beaten in the high-profile contest to put humans on the Moon, the USSR claimed indifference to the American flights, opting instead to concentrate its resources on long-duration space flights by its cosmonauts, flights that gave the USSR space program valuable information for longer flights and longer stays in space. It was information that would be needed if permanent space stations in orbit were to be occupied full time by humans, stations that could be used for either civilian or military use. Now that the old communist dictatorship is gone and the USSR no longer exists, it is knowledge that is shared today between Russian and U.S. space programs as they build and staff the *International Space Station* and other cooperative efforts.

The *Hubble Space Telescope* (*HST*) opened up vast vistas of new knowledge about the universe. In this picture, taken in December 1993 during the first servicing mission, astronauts are busy performing maintenance and repairs on *HST* while the telescope is docked on the orbiting space shuttle *Endeavour*. *(Courtesy of NASA)*

Although driven initially by the engines of national pride, propaganda, and the secret needs of the military, the space programs of both America and the USSR also opened up a new era for science. The Apollo program, carrying American astronauts to the Moon and back, died a quiet death from public indifference as the "novelty" wore thin. Also, NASA shifted emphasis toward reusable space shuttles, siphoning off funds and attentions. Yet many other purely scientific missions expanded the reach of science far beyond the makeshift science played at by the moon walkers. Space programs with names like Pioneer, Explorer, and Voyager sent crewless space vehicles packed with scientific instruments to study not only the planets of the solar system but planetary moons as well. Robotic "eyes" and electronic sensors sent astounding pictures and information back to expectant scientists on Earth. Small robotic "landers" not only landed on but also crawled slowly over the surface of Mars, revealing many of the "red" planet's secrets and opening up new mysteries and questions. The much-anticipated "eye in orbit," the *Hubble Space Telescope,* has turned its instruments toward distant galaxies and the dark depths of the universe, answering old questions and opening up new ones about the birth, life, and possible death of the universe itself.

As the 20th century came to an end and the 21st began, science seemed on the verge of a new golden age, not only for astronomers

"Star nurseries" are believed to be located in clumps of gas such as those located in great pillars of gas and dust like this one, which forms part of the Eagle Nebula (M16). *(J. Hester and P. Scowen, Arizona State University/NASA)*

and astrophysicists, but also for particle physicists unraveling the depths of the atom and the strange world of quarks, and for biologists and geneticists probing the secrets of genetics and the engineering and understanding of life itself.

Strangely, though, as the 20th century wound down, the uneasy relationship between science and society once again took a turn for the worse. As science learned more and more about life and the universe, it seemed to many people to become too powerful, too knowing, too esoteric in its language and instruments, too solitary and aloof in its relations with the commonplace world to be trusted. Frustrated by the apparently ever-increasing complexity of the world and unable to find solace in either traditional religion or science, many people began not only to turn away from science but also to turn toward its old traditional foes, mysticism and superstition. While many people enjoy and appreciate many benefits of science—from instantaneous worldwide communication to fast delivery service, and from easily laundered clothes to stunning pictures of the objects of the universe—few have discovered the joys of science as a process, or of that most fundamental aspect of science, its method and approach to problem solving and discovery. Perhaps as the 21st century unfolds, that will change.

10

Science, Postmodernism, and the "New Age"

GIVEN THE DEEP INROADS INTO nature's mysteries that science has continued to make in the past 50 years, it is ironic that a major conference was held in the United States in 1995 to discuss ways to defend science against the increasing defection of large segments of the educated public who were turning away from it and embracing many bizarre beliefs in anti-science and pseudoscience.

According to a report in *The New York Times*, "Some 200 worried scientists, doctors, philosophers, educators, and thinkers from around the country convened for a three-day meeting at the New York Academy of Sciences to exchange views and plot strategy. Held under the rubric 'The Flight from Science and Reason,' the meeting was organized as a call to arms." As the *Times* explained it, "Defenders of scientific methodology were urged to counterattack against faith-healing, astrology, religious fundamentalism and paranormal charlatanism."

Reading the newspaper that day must have seemed to some readers like a bizarre taste of time travel, as if the world had somehow slipped back in time a hundred years or more. On the surface, it was surely the world of the 20th century. By 2001 science and technology had transformed the trappings of everyday life far beyond the imaginings of ordinary citizens of the 1800s or early 1900s. Automobiles jammed the busy city streets shaded by towering skyscrapers. High above the buildings, jet aircraft whisked passengers from airport to airport, city to city, country to country. Inside those same buildings,

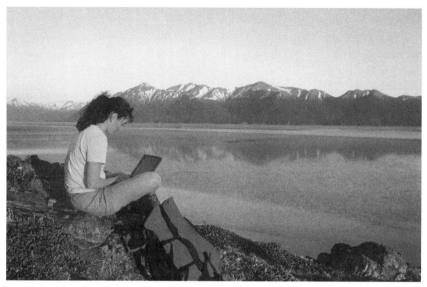

Despite negative opinions about science and scientists, 21st century citizens commonly embrace the handy technology of cell phones, notebook PCs, MP3s, DVDs, and PDAs. Even a hiker enjoying the natural beauty of a mountaintop scene may bring along a Global Positioning System (GPS) receiver, cell phone, electronic organizer—and even a laptop—technologies that would not exist without science and scientists. (© Michael De Young/CORBIS)

office workers and apartment dwellers talked to customers or friends on their cordless telephones or cell phones, watched the latest news on their television sets, sent e-mails everywhere in the world from their notebook computers or PDAs, and immediately accessed newspapers and magazines published electronically thousands of miles away. Humans had walked on the Moon and split the atom, sent robot probes to explore the planets, and extended the all-too-brief human life span by a couple dozen more precious years.

What then was so worrisome to the 200 scientists, doctors, philosophers, and educators who attended the New York conference, as well as hundreds more who did not attend but who shared similar deep concerns?

According to a 1990 Gallup poll, 49 percent of Americans believed in ESP, 21 percent believed in reincarnation, 17 percent believed that they had been in contact with someone who had died, 25 percent believed in ghosts, 14 percent believed in haunted houses, 55 percent believed in the actual existence of the devil, 14 percent had recently consulted a psychic or a fortune-teller, 25 percent believed in astrology, 46 percent believed in psychic or spiritual healing, and 27 percent believed that extraterrestrial beings had visited Earth in the past. A more recent poll taken in 2001 showed increases in the paranormal beliefs of Americans, especially in spiritual healing, increased to 54 percent; communication with the dead, increased to 28 percent; and belief in haunted houses, increased to 42 percent. It was also estimated that Americans spent billions of dollars a year on medicinal herbs, acupuncture, homeopathic medicine, and various other physical and psychological products and services of the so-called alternative health movement.

Clearly, as the 21st century approached, many well-educated people were either very uneasy about science or had become actively antagonistic toward it. It was not only the attacks on science that troubled many scientists and thinkers around the world, but attacks

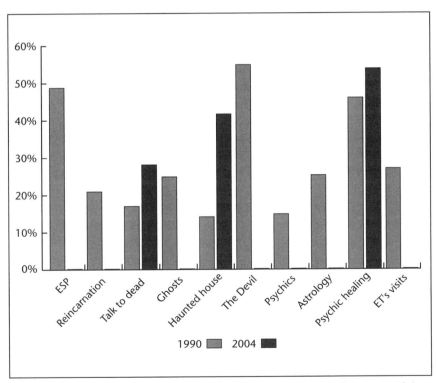

A poll taken in 2001 reflected increased belief among Americans in three areas of the paranormal: psychic healing, communication with the dead, and haunted houses.

on scientific methodology itself and the very validity of such concepts as "objective reality," "reason," and "truth."

"There is a growing danger, many said," *The New York Times*
continued in its report on the conference, "that the fabric of reason
is being ripped asunder. . . . Moreover . . . the same cognitive disease afflicting science in the United States and many other countries
could even eventually unravel democracy, which depends on the
capacity of citizens to reach rational estimates."

There was some argument over whether the situation was really
that serious—after all, hardly anyone seriously considered abandoning science or throwing it on the scrap heap of discarded ideas.
However, most of those attending the New York conference agreed
that there was deep cause for concern. While it might have been too
strong a statement to say that the "fabric of reason" was being
"ripped asunder," little doubt existed in any educated person's mind
that a diverse array of cultural forces certainly had placed science
under attack.

Just what was this "cognitive disease" mentioned in the newspaper report? Although its symptoms were obvious, its causes were
varied. Most observers, though, generally put two major suspects at
the top of the list: the popular social phenomena known as the "New
Age" that swept over much of the Western world in the latter half of
the 20th century, and "postmodernism," a largely academic philosophy that held sway in many colleges and universities during the
same period.

Although its exact description often fluctuates according to who
is describing it, the academic concept of postmodernism hit its
stride in the latter half of the 20th century. Flowering primarily in
the social science and humanities departments of many colleges and
universities, postmodernism was a reaction to the philosophy of
"modernism" and its faith in science and rational thinking, which
had emerged out of the Enlightenment in the 18th century. Although
it came in many varieties and bore varying labels, at its core postmodernism claimed that it was impossible for humans, using their
imperfect sensory cues, to know truly the reality of the world. Therefore, all statements that we can make about the world, either in literature or in science, are at best only narratives, or stories, that we
tell about that world, based upon the ways that our culture and language have taught us to see and describe it. What we may think that
we know about the world, then, is based on the assumptions of our

own or other cultures about the nature of "truth" and "reality." So the universe as human beings perceive it—in the only way they can perceive it—is only a vast conglomerate of narratives, each dependent on the biases and prejudices of the culture it sprang from. Since there is no one single "universally valid" truth (because every claim to "truth" must have its roots in the meanings and interpretations of the particular culture from which it sprang), then we have no way of establishing the primacy of one "truth" over the other. The most that we can do is to recognize each and every narrative as true in its own terms and give special priority to no single one, including the narrative known as science. Thus, to the extreme postmodern view, astrology is as legitimate a science as astronomy, Native American origin myths as valid an explanation as those offered by modern "Western science," and speaking with the ghosts of the dead as real as speaking on a telephone.

Small wonder that the scientists at the New York conference were concerned. With little critical examination, many students were adopting the postmodern attitudes as they passed through colleges and universities and moved out into the everyday world. While postmodernism may have made for interesting discussions in a classroom, as one critical observer caustically noted, it was at best "intellectual bubble-gum . . . of absolutely no use in functioning in the real world." While the description may have been too harsh—in some areas of the social sciences and the humanities its cautious use could act as a check against hubris and chauvinism—the attitude when pushed to extremes tended to anesthetize critical faculties. The intellectual worldview of postmodernism plus the social trendiness of the New Age produced a philosophical mix that alarmed not only scientists but also many other thinkers of the late 20th century who still believed in humankind's rational abilities to understand the world.

While the postmodernists claimed there could be no such thing as universal truth, the followers of the New Age insisted that there was indeed one universal truth, but that it could not be discovered by rational thought. Instead, the only path to truth was by abandoning the rational and adopting the spiritual.

As with postmodernism, exact definitions are difficult, but the "New Age" movement could loosely be defined as a broad and diverse affiliation of individuals and groups who believe in the transformation of the individual and society through spiritual awareness. Although for the most part antagonistic to traditional religions, New Age adherents as a general rule believe that the universe is not without meaning and purpose and that everything in it is somehow connected spiritually with everything else. The "New Age" would see the end of social, political, and spiritual chaos and usher in a new era of social, political, and spiritual harmony. At least that was the philosophical umbrella and quasi-official position of many New Age followers.

Although tracing the history of such a diversified and amorphous movement is haphazard at best (many New Age beliefs such as faith healing, reincarnation, and the personal acquisition of special spiritual and psychic "powers" trace back centuries), most observers mark its most significant roots in the counterculture movement of the 1960s. The youth-oriented counterculture of the 1960s, dubbed by the media as "hippies" and "flower children," identified as their rallying point the astrological period known as "The Age of Aquarius." According to the popular superstition of astrological lore, the sign of Aquarius represents peace and harmony. So, as the calendar turned toward the new Aquarian period, many people believed the world was about to undergo a tremendous spiritual reawakening—an awakening that would bring about peace and harmony, first to individuals, and then through their individual actions to the world. "This is the dawning of the Age of Aquarius" ran the words of one of the most popular songs of the period. Although the counterculture movement of the 1960s self-destructed in a haze of drugs and media hype, many of its followers moved back into society and assumed traditional social roles while they continued to hold on to many of the movement's beliefs and to support many of its messages.

The heavy borrowing and adaptation of Eastern religions had been a strong factor in the counterculture of the 1960s. This interest joined in the 1970s with a trend known as "transpersonal psychology" to elevate the individual's spiritual health to prime importance, laying further groundwork for the "New Age." By the 1980s, with many of the '60s counterculture participants and one-time social "drop-outs" now earning wages and holding responsible positions in society, most of the pieces were in place for the New Age phenomena to erupt upon Western society.

And erupt it did. In 1980 *The Aquarian Conspiracy,* a book by Marilyn Ferguson, argued that the world was moving toward a new era of spiritual harmony as more and more people discovered their personal spirituality through the use of "channeling" (contact with spirits, that is, individuals who are no longer living—an updated form of the 19th century's spiritualist movement), crystals, consciousness raising, and various other activities. The book surprised many people by becoming a best-seller. It was the first of hundreds of similar popular works that would crowd the shelves of bookstores throughout the 1980s and 1990s. *Out on a Limb,* a memoir by film star Shirley MacLaine that was published in 1983, was reported to have sold more than 3 million copies. Follow-up books by MacLaine detailed her personal involvement in the New Age movement and her strong adherence to beliefs ranging from channeling, reincarnation, ESP, and visitors from outer space to herbal medicine, astral projection, astrology, and faith healing. She also recounted belief in human auras, ghosts, the magical power of crystals, and half a dozen other ideas once labeled "occult," "paranormal," or "metaphysical," which now found their place under the more "respectable" label of "New Age."

MacLaine followed *Out on a Limb* with a television adaptation (in which she starred) and then followed up the film with another book about the making of the movie. Clearly the New Age was becoming big business! Within a few years after the publication of *The Aquarian Conspiracy,* books by Ferguson, MacLaine, and other New Age writers began to occupy larger and more prominent sections of bookstores, usually taking up much more space than the sections set aside for books on science. Perhaps appropriately enough, they displaced or, perhaps more correctly, absorbed what had once been called the "occult" sections of those same stores.

Informational and "inspirational" seminars given by MacLaine and others drew large crowds (at $300 an auditorium seat in MacLaine's case). More than a few major business corporations invited New Age "motivational" speakers to address their employees or hold seminars.

Writing in *The Aquarian Conspiracy,* Ferguson had called the New Age "a leaderless but powerful network . . . working to bring radical changes in the United States. Its members have broken with certain elements of Western thought, and they may even have broken continuity with history."

By the year 2002, two of the most popular cable television shows in the United States, *Crossing Over with John Edward* and *Beyond with James Van Praagh,* involved a pair of charismatic hosts "communicating" with the dead relatives of audience members. These New Age mediums were featured in national magazines, wrote bestselling books, and were interviewed on network television and radio talk shows. On a lesser scale, newspaper and magazine advertisements, television commercials, and "infomercials" promoted everything from "psychic hotlines" to courses in "psychic healing" and the wonders of meditation, herbal medicine, and acupuncture. "Holistic seminars" and weekend "psychic fairs" played to hundreds of visitors. Many legitimate nursing and medical schools began teaching "therapeutic touch," a method of healing that only required a practitioner to feel the "aura" of their patient and cure his or her ills by manipulating this nonexistent energy field without ever having to touch the patient's body.

A few scandals may have cut down on some of the sweeping gains made by con artists making fraudulent claims. In 2002 the Federal Trade Commission (FTC) charged "Miss Cleo" with false advertising and deceptive billing and collection practices in her psychic hotline business offering "free readings" that ended up costing customers exorbitant phone charges. However, the resulting infamy may only have generated sympathy and served as PR for the accused.

Although leaderless, the New Age was not without its gurus, and, far from breaking the continuity of history, for many critical observers the movement had merely picked up the strands of a long history of occult and metaphysical beliefs and repackaged them for modern consumption. Like "therapeutic touch," much of the foundation of New Age beliefs involved forces and universal energies unknown to science, yet alleged to be present in every living creature and permeating all existence. It was these forces that were released in meditation, used in healing, called forth for ESP, and drawn out of or magnified and focused by crystals and pyramids.

To many critics the New Age was not really new, but the same old superstitions and quackery poured into bright new shining bottles. What was different was the extent to which New Age ideas had penetrated and become acceptable to large educated segments of the public. The most irrational of ideas, once spoken of hesitantly or only with a small group of like thinkers, were now enthusiastically received conversation topics in restaurants, airport lounges, and on television talk shows. Practices once labeled "occult" (meaning "hidden") were now far from hidden—they were everyday commodities in the late-20th-century marketplace of ideas.

While much of the New York conference focused on postmodernism and its direct attacks upon science and scientific methodology, in some ways the New Age presented an even greater threat by its apparent omnipresence in all strata of society. The average couple shopping in the trendy new shopping mall may never have heard the words "postmodernism" or "deconstructionism" (one of the methods of postmodernism) or any of the other "isms" so commonly heard in the academic community. Still, they might drop in at a health food store and check out the wide variety of herbs promising to help everything from aching muscles to failing memory and loss of mental concentration. A few shops away, they could examine shoes with magnetic inserts that promised to aid their weary feet, stop in at a book store and buy a book by the newest popular television "channeler," or drop in at a video shop and choose between renting a video or DVD promising the "true and amazing" story of UFO abductees or psychic pets or one offering instruction on developing personal powers of extrasensory perception.

Some argued that it was the very success of science that had turned so many people away from it. As science stripped away more and more illusions and superstitions of the world, it appeared to many to be leaving little to those who felt the need for more meaning and direction in the universe and in their individual lives. Technology, while making life easier for millions, also left many feeling lost and insignificant in the midst of the hustle and bustle of the modern world.

Modern medicine, for all of its successes, became an impersonalized institution to many. They felt abandoned as the soothing hand of the family doctor gave way to the distant and often economy-conscious bureaucracy of HMOs. As medicine became big business, many people began to feel the loss of personal involvement with their doctors and health care providers, and with this, the loss of personal control over their own health care needs. So-called alternative medicine, one of the central tenets of the New Age, allowed them, it seemed, to once more feel the calming and assured hand of the healer, and to take personal control of their own health.

Traditional religion had also lost its attraction to many people in the late 20th century. While fundamentalist and charismatic churches found themselves gaining converts, large sections of the public no longer identified themselves as members of Protestant, Catholic, Jewish, or other traditional religious groups. Polls showed that the vast majority of the Western world still proclaimed themselves as "believing in God" and "religious," but an increasing number, particularly of those who identified themselves as a part of the "young professional middle class," declared no traditional religious affiliation.

The whys and wherefores were discussed at length, but, to most concerned people, the immediate problem was that science and rational thinking were under serious attack, directly and indirectly, not just on a local scale, but throughout wide sections of society.

What was to be done about it? One determined voice at the New York conference belonged to Barry Gross, a professor of philosophy at the City University of New York. A frequent writer in defense of science and rational thinking, Gross pulled no punches in his belief that scientists and those who supported critical thinking and the scientific method ought to take a dramatic stand. Speaking before the conference, Gross argued that defenders of science must fight against the "anti-science brigade" and "inoculate the rest of the population against them." Echoing strongly the views of many of the conference participants, Gross argued, "Scientists will have to devote some of the energy to systematic confrontation with the enemies of science."

Carl Sagan, visionary who fought for science and rational thinking *(Copyright ©1980 by Carl Sagan Productions, Inc.)*

Mario Bunge, a professor of philosophy and head of the Foundation and Philosophy Unit at McGill University at Montreal, took direct aim at some university departments caught up in the postmodern movement when he said, "some professors are hired, promoted, or given power for teaching that reason is worthless, empirical evidence unnecessary, objective truth nonexistent, basic science a tool of either capitalists or male domination . . . people who reject all the knowledge painstakingly acquired over the past 5 million years."

Many other scientists, educators, writers, and philosophers had already begun taking their stands. The Committee for the Scientific Investigation of Claims of the Paranormal (CSICOP) was founded in 1976 by a small group of eminent scientists and others and spearheaded by Paul Kurtz, then professor of philosophy at State University of New York at Buffalo. By the late 1990s CSICOP had grown into an active and outspoken organization with more than 100 national and international affiliates. In addition to publishing a monthly magazine called *The Skeptical Inquirer* and sponsoring an ongoing series of scientific investigations of pseudoscientific and paranormal claims, CSICOP had also become an outspoken foe of postmodern and New Age thinking. Its well-attended seminars featuring many of the world's top scientists, educators, writers, and other thinkers acted as a valuable exchange and focal point for a growing list of activists determined to fight what they considered society's dangerous fascination with the irrational and the anti-rational. In addition, a growing number of world-class scientists, including Nobel Prize winners, usually too preoccupied with their work to engage in social politics, had also begun to speak out against the attacks on science and reason by the beginning of the 21st century.

To the victor would go the future. Would the world continue to value rational thinking, science, and all the hard-earned progress made by aspiring humankind since the Enlightenment and before? Or would the "New Age" of the 21st century be an era of gradual descent back into darkness and superstition?

And could the complex world of the 21st century survive that descent, or did the greatest hope for humankind lay in its continual striving forward—using all of its intellectual and rational faculties to face and understand the challenges of nature and the sometimes bewildering nature of man?

To science, the answer was clear. But winning back the support it needed from society remained a vexing problem as the clock struck the dawn of a new era.

Conclusion
Voyaging Ever Further

LOOKING BACK OVER THE LATTER HALF of the 20th century and the start of the 21st, one can easily see that scientists made giant leaps—breakthrough discoveries, completing enormous databases of knowledge, and filling in information gaps, ever moving into new and exciting territory. We have begun the 21st century with much to draw upon—and many questions, new questions, raised by the expanded knowledge gained so far. Doing science in the last five decades has, more than ever, become a voyage into strange realms made all the more strange and exciting because they are the very essence of the universe in which we live. Understanding these new realms—the worlds of subatomic particle physics and the Standard Model, of the big bang and the inflationary universe, of solar systems both near and far, of the planet Earth, of DNA and RNA, of viruses and retroviruses, of genetic engineering, and more—provides a window that allows us to see beyond ourselves and our own interests, to become more informed citizens of the universe, and to live as a more harmonious part of it. From this understanding we also learn to appreciate the enormous value of knowledge uncovered by scientists through the ages, to learn from it, and always to question, because using this power—the power to use our minds—is the greatest gift we can give, both to ourselves and to the world; it is the very essence of being human.

In a real sense the future of the world lies in the future of science. We depend upon knowledge to make informed decisions, and we need the fruits of science to gain that knowledge. We as citizens hold the reins. Because much (though not all) science now requires both coordinated teamwork and expensive equipment, science needs support from governments and industry in order to pursue the many big questions that still remain unanswered. The direction provided by us as citizens, taxpayers, stockholders, and consumers will decide the future.

In the opening decade of the 21st century and beyond, many hard choices need to be made. Informed decisions about the use of scientific knowledge, moreover, require a sophisticated understanding of consequences and ethics. We stand at a juncture of time that is more exhilarating than any other in its possibilities. Whether or not we choose to do science ourselves, we all have become participants together in a great, and most human, enterprise.

CHRONOLOGY

1945

▶ May: World War II ends for Europe when Germany surrenders; Germany and Austria are divided by Allies into four zones
▶ August: Japan surrenders, ending World War II in the Pacific, after atomic bombs are dropped on Hiroshima and Nagasaki, causing widespread death, destruction, and injury
▶ The United Nations is created
▶ German rocket pioneer Wernher von Braun immigrates to the United States, where he continues his work, which lays the groundwork for establishment of the U.S. space program in the late 1950s

1946

▶ The term *lepton* is introduced by Abraham Pais and C. Moller, referring to lightweight subatomic particles not affected by the strong nuclear force

1947

▶ Hungarian-British physicist Dennis Gabor develops the basic concept of holography (though it is not truly practical until after the invention of the laser)
▶ Willard Frank Libby develops technique of radiocarbon dating
▶ The two-meson theory is rediscovered by R. Marshak and Hans Bethe, and, independently, by S. Sakata and T. Inoue; they realize that the meson in cosmic rays (now called a muon) is not the same as the one predicted by Yukawa (now called a pion)

▸ Cecil Frank Powell and his team in England isolate the pion (pi meson, predicted in 1935 by Hideki Yukawa of Japan, who is credited with its discovery)
▸ The transistor is invented by a team of scientists at Bell Laboratories in the United States
▸ Under the leadership of nationalist Mohandas Gandhi, independence is won by India from British colonial rule

1948

▸ Mohandas Gandhi is assassinated in January
▸ Richard Feynman, independently of Julian Seymour Schwinger and Shin'ichiro Tomonaga, develops renormalizable quantum electrodynamics (QED); Tomonaga is actually first, with his work completed in 1943 during World War II, but his work does not become known outside Japan until later
▸ George Gamow, Ralph Alpher, and Robert Herman develop the big bang theory of the origin of the universe
▸ Dedication of the 200-inch telescope on Palomar Mountain near Pasadena, California

1949

▸ Soviet Union tests atomic bomb; by 1951 backyard bomb shelters are being sold in the United States
▸ North Atlantic Treaty Organization (NATO) is formed to control Soviet aggression
▸ The People's Republic of China is established after the triumph of Communist leader Mao Zedong in civil war in China

1950

▸ Korean War begins

1951

▸ Ten million U.S. homes have TVs
▸ UNIVAC, the first commercial computer, is accepted by the U.S. Bureau of the Census
▸ The field ion microscope is invented; it is the first instrument that can picture individual atoms
▸ First experimental breeder reactor built, in Idaho

1952

◗ H-bomb (hydrogen fusion bomb), vastly more powerful than the atomic fission bomb, is tested by the United States in the Marshall Islands

◗ American physicist Charles H. Townes invents the maser

◗ U.S. Atomic Energy Commission builds the first breeder reactor, which produces plutonium at the same time it produces energy

◗ First accident at a nuclear reactor, Chalk River, Canada, where the nuclear core explodes due to a technician's error

◗ Contraception pill developed

1953

◗ Francis Crick and James Watson discover the double-helix structure of the DNA molecule

◗ Murray Gell-Mann proposes the strangeness property of some subatomic particles

◗ Physicist Donald Glaser invents bubble chamber to detect subnuclear particles

◗ Piltdown man discovered to be a hoax, 41 years after the discovery of the fossils

◗ Korean War ends; North and South Korea remain divided

1954

◗ Polio vaccine developed by Jonas Salk; with the help of another vaccine developed by Albert Sabin, reduces the number of polio cases in the United States by 96% by 1961

◗ CERN (originally, the Conseil Européen pour la Recherche Nucléaire, now known as the European Organization for Nuclear Research) is founded, located near Geneva, Switzerland

◗ Luis Walter Alvarez constructs a liquid hydrogen bubble chamber in which he can see tracks caused by subatomic particles

◗ Chen Ning (Frank) Yang and Robert Mills develop a gauge symmetrical field theory, a major step toward viewing the universe in terms of underlying symmetries that were broken in early cosmic evolution

◗ Walter Baade and Rudolph Minkowski identify the radio source Cygnus A with distant galaxy

◗ In the case *Brown vs. Board of Education*, U.S. Supreme Court rules that segregated schools (separate schools for white and black students) are unconstitutional

▶ Joseph McCarthy, U.S. senator from Wisconsin, conducts hearings many call a "witch hunt," trying to uncover the existence of communist infiltration in American government and life
▶ Nuclear submarine U.S.S. *Nautilus* is launched
▶ First frozen TV dinners introduced

1955

▶ Albert Einstein dies
▶ Rosa Parks, an African-American woman in Montgomery, Alabama, refuses to give up her seat on a bus to a white man, as required by local law; she is arrested, and African Americans boycott Montgomery buses in protest for more than a year
▶ McDonald's and Disneyland open

1956

▶ Yang and Tsung Dao Lee theorize that parity is not conserved in weak interactions—i.e., that the weak force does not function symmetrically. Experiments conducted by Chien Shiung Wu and collaborators the same year confirm their prediction
▶ Neutrinos are observed for the first time (originally predicted by Wolfgang Pauli in 1930)
▶ Hungarian uprising suppressed by Soviet troops

1957

▶ October: Soviet Union launches *Sputnik,* the first artificial Earth satellite
▶ Schwinger proposes that the electromagnetic and weak forces are aspects of a single variety of interaction
▶ The Civil Rights Act is passed in the United States, and the Civil Rights Commission is formed to monitor civil rights issues; federal troops in Little Rock, Arkansas, enforce school desegregation ordered by the Supreme Court

1958

▶ Jan Hendrik Oort and colleagues use radio telescopes to map the spiral arms of the Milky Way galaxy
▶ *Explorer I,* the first U.S. satellite, is launched into orbit

1959

- Antarctic Treaty is signed among 12 nations who agree to set aside political claims for 34 years and use the continent as a giant scientific lab
- Revolution in Cuba; Fidel Castro ousts the current dictator, seeks support from the Soviet Union, and forms communist government, causing a break in U.S.–Cuba relations
- Soviet Union sends probes to the Moon

1960

- First quasars, the most luminous objects in the universe, are discovered by Allan Sandage and Thomas Matthews
- American physicist Theodore H. Maiman demonstrates the first successful laser
- Luis Walter Alvarez announces his discovery of resonances, very short-lived particles
- U.S. U-2 spy plane is shot down over Soviet Union
- Sixteen African nations gain independence

1961

- Murray Gell-Mann and others develop what Gell-Mann calls the Eightfold Way to classify heavy subatomic particles
- Robert Hofstadter discovers that protons and neutrons have a structure
- Yuri Gagarin (Soviet Union) becomes first person to orbit Earth
- Berlin Wall is erected, dividing East and West Berlin, to prevent travel by East Germans into West Berlin

1962

- A group headed by G. Danby at Brookhaven, New York, discovers there are two types of neutrinos, one associated with the electrons and a second associated with the muon (a third is now believed to exist, known as the tau neutrino)
- The term *hadron* is introduced by L. G. Okun to represent the group of particles affected by the strong nuclear force (such as protons, neutrons, pions, and kaons)
- United States launches communications satellite *Telstar*

▶ Cuban missile crisis
▶ John Glenn becomes first U.S. astronaut to orbit Earth

1963

▶ Maarten Schmidt finds red shift in the spectral lines of quasar, indicating that quasars are the most distant class of objects in the universe
▶ Vaccine against measles perfected
▶ U.S. president John F. Kennedy is assassinated on November 22 in Dallas. Accused assassin Lee Harvey Oswald is shot and killed two days later by nightclub owner Jack Ruby

1964

▶ Murray Gell-Mann and George Zweig introduce the concept of quarks
▶ Discovery of the omega-minus particle at Brookhaven National laboratory confirms Gell-Mann's prediction of the "Eightfold Way"
▶ A fourth quark species, charm, is introduced by Sheldon Glashow and James D. Bjorken

1965

▶ African-American leader Malcolm X is assassinated on February 21
▶ Stanford Linear Accelerator Center (SLAC) starts up in California

1967

▶ Chia Lin and Frank Shu show that the spiral arms of galaxies may be created by density waves propagating across the galactic disk
▶ Jocelyn Bell and Anthony Hewish discover pulsars, leading to verification of the existence of extremely dense "neutron stars"

1968

▶ Although he helped build the Soviet hydrogen bomb, Andrei Sakharov speaks out in favor of nuclear arms reduction in the Soviet Union and writes an essay called *Progress, Coexistence and Intellectual Freedom,* which is published in London, an act for which he is barred from secret work and persecuted most of the rest of his life
▶ Experiments at the Stanford Linear Accelerator Center support the theory that hadrons are made of quarks

- U.S. civil rights leader Martin Luther King, Jr., is assassinated
- U.S. presidential candidate Robert F. Kennedy is assassinated
- Liberal democratic-socialist government of Czechoslovakia is crushed by Soviet troops

1969

- Fermilab is founded in Batavia, Illinois
- English biochemist Dorothy Hodgkin works out the structure for vitamin B_{12} using an electronic computer, for which she receives the 1964 Nobel Prize in chemistry
- Jonathan Beckwith and coworkers isolate a single gene for the first time
- U.S. astronauts land on the Moon

1970

- Howard M. Temin and David Baltimore discover in viruses an enzyme called reverse transcriptase, which causes RNA to be transcribed onto DNA, a key step in the development of genetic engineering
- Har Gobind Khorana of the University of Wisconsin leads a team that completely synthesizes a gene for the first time, assembling it directly from its component chemicals

1972

- Murray Gell-Mann presents the beginnings of quantum chromo-dynamics (QCD), linking quarks and color forces and three flavors of quarks

1973

- U.S. astronauts dock with space station *Skylab,* a laboratory for solar observation
- A calf is produced from a frozen embryo for the first time
- Stanley H. Cohen and Herbert W. Boyer establish genetic engineering when they show that DNA molecules can be cut with restriction enzymes, joined together with other enzymes and reproduced by introducing them into the chromosome of the bacterium *Escherichia coli*

▸ Watergate scandal, involving unethical campaign practices, surrounds Richard Nixon's presidency
▸ Vietnam War ends

1974

▸ Paul Berg leads a meeting of 139 scientists, sponsored by the U.S. National Academy of Sciences and 18 other nations, in which they express concern about the future of genetic engineering
▸ Richard Nixon resigns as president; Vice president Gerald Ford is sworn in as president and shortly thereafter pardons Nixon

1975

▸ In an unusual gesture of cooperation, U.S. and Soviet spacecrafts dock in space in the Apollo-Soyuz project, and their crews meet and exchange greetings

1976

▸ U.S. spacecrafts *Viking I* and *Viking II* make soft landings on the surface of Mars to test for the presence of life, gather other data, and send back photos
▸ First development of a functional synthetic gene, complete with regulatory mechanisms, by Har Gobind Khorana and colleagues
▸ Susumu Tonegawa shows that antibodies are formed by combination by groups of genes that move close to each other on a chromosome
▸ Supersonic travel introduced when the *Concorde,* a British-French enterprise, makes its first flight at two times the speed of sound, 1,500 mph

1977

▸ U.S. Department of Energy is created
▸ A baby mammoth is founded in the Soviet Union; it has been frozen for 40,000 years
▸ *Star Wars* movie premieres

1978

▸ Scientists succeed in finding the complete genetic structure of the virus SV40
▸ United States reestablishes relations with China

1979

▶ Hostage crisis begins in Iran when 66 U.S. citizens are seized from the U.S. embassy and held hostage, most of them not released until January 20, 1981, after extensive attempts to obtain their release

▶ Nuclear reactor at Three Mile Island in Pennsylvania comes close to having a core meltdown

▶ Revolution in Nicaragua deposes dictator Anastasio Somoza Debayle and establishes the Sandinista National Liberation Federation in power; eight years of civil war follow between SNLF under Daniel Ortega and U.S.-funded "contra" guerrilla forces

▶ Revolution in Iran establishes religious extremist Ayatollah Ruhollah Khomeini as leader

▶ Soviet troops are sent to Afghanistan to quell an uprising; many Western nations boycott the Olympic Games in Moscow to protest the move

1980

▶ First publication of a photo of an individual atom, taken at the University of Heidelberg in Germany

▶ Charles Weissmann of the University of Geneva reports the successful production of human interferon in bacteria

▶ Paul Berg, Walter Gilbert, and Frederick Sanger share the Nobel Prize in chemistry: Berg for his work on recombinant DNA, and Gilbert and Sanger for methods to map the structure of DNA

▶ Mount St. Helens in Washington State erupts, providing new geological data about volcanoes and the interior workings of the Earth

▶ Iraq, under the leadership of Saddam Hussein, invades Iran, beginning an eight-year war, during which Iran sustains more than 700,000 casualties

▶ Lech Walesa in Poland establishes the first labor union, Solidarity, in a Soviet-bloc country

1980–81

▶ First reported cases of AIDS (Acquired Immune Deficiency Syndrome)

1981

▶ Alan Guth postulates that the early universe went through an "inflationary" period of exponential expansion

▶ U.S. hostages are freed in Iran
▶ Sandra Day O'Connor is appointed the first female judge on the U.S. Supreme Court

1982

▶ Falklands War between Britain and Argentina
▶ First flight of the U.S. space shuttle

1983

▶ First CD (compact disk) player, using laser technology to play music
▶ Electroweak unified theory verified in collider experiments at CERN; attempts accelerated to arrive at a unified theory of all four forces
▶ U.S. biologists Barbara McClintock receives the Nobel Prize in physiology or medicine for her discovery of mobile genes in the chromosomes of corn
▶ Andrew W. Murray and Jack W. Szostak create the first artificial chromosome
▶ AIDS virus isolated
▶ Famine in Africa; years of drought result in widespread death from hunger, with 1 million dead in Ethiopia alone in the years 1984–85

1984

▶ Prime minister of India, Indira Gandhi, is assassinated
▶ Alec Jeffrey discovers the technique of genetic fingerprinting, using core samples of DNA
▶ Sheep embryos are successfully cloned
▶ Allan Wilson and Russell Higuchi of the University of California at Berkeley become first to clone genes of an extinct species

1985

▶ Mikhail Gorbachev takes office as general secretary of Communist Party in the Soviet Union; institutes a policy of "perestroika," involving sweeping economic changes, and "glasnost," a policy of openness toward other countries, including former cold war opponents such as the United States, Britain, French, and West Germany
▶ Hole in the ozone layer observed in satellite data from the area over Antarctica

1986

▶ Entire crew of seven dies in *Challenger* space shuttle disaster
▶ U.S. Department of Agriculture issues the world's first license to market a living organism produced by genetic engineering, a virus used as a vaccine to prevent herpes in swine
▶ Soviet Union launches *Mir*, the first space station permanently occupied by human passengers
▶ Haitian dictator Jean-Claude Duvalier is overthrown and flees to France, ending 28 years of rule by the Duvalier family
▶ Ferdinand Marcos, who had imposed martial law in the Philippines since 1972, is forced to flee with his wife, Imelda, when he declares himself winner of a rigged election; Corazón Aquino takes office
▶ Cooling system fails at a nuclear plant at Chernobyl, 60 miles from Kiev in the Soviet Union; the core melts down, and a radioactive cloud escapes. Immediate deaths mount to 30, and many more are afflicted with radiation-caused cancers. Soviet government attempts to seal the reactor by burying it under cement

1987

▶ Proton-decay experiments in the United States and Japan detect neutrinos broadcast by a supernova in the Large Magellanic Cloud, ushering in the new science of observational neutrino astronomy

1988

▶ Quasars are detected near the outposts of the observable universe; their red shifts indicate that their light has been traveling through space for some 17 billion years

1989

▶ The Cosmic Background Explorer (COBE) is launched from the space shuttle to probe the cosmic background radiation
▶ Henry A. Ehrlich announces a method for identifying (or at least ruling out) an individual from the DNA in a single strand of hair
▶ Ya-Ming Hou and Paul Schimmel discover how to decode part of the genetic code found in transfer RNA
▶ Rally of tens of thousands of students for democracy in China is quelled in a bloody confrontation in Tiananmen Square in Beijing

‣ Bloody revolution in Romania
‣ Berlin Wall is torn down
‣ Demonstrations in Hungary, Czechoslovakia, Poland, Albania, and Bulgaria lead to reform in those countries
‣ Loosened control by the Communist regime in Yugoslavia leads to ethnic violence

1990

‣ *Hubble Space Telescope* is launched
‣ Germany is reunited; first democratic elections held throughout Germany since 1932
‣ Iraq invades Kuwait
‣ Scientists from some 16 nations begin the Human Genome Project, an international cooperative effort to map the entire human genetic code
‣ The first successful attempt at human gene therapy uses a modified virus to transport a healthy gene for a needed enzyme into the cells of a woman whose immune system is in a very weakened state. The therapy works—providing a normally effective system—but requires regular repetition

1991

‣ The *Galileo* spacecraft takes a photo of Gaspra, the first photo ever taken of an asteroid in space
‣ Apartheid is dismantled in South Africa
‣ "Operation Desert Storm," a multinational military effort, pushes Iraq out of Kuwait
‣ Rajiv Gandhi, who succeeded his mother as prime minister of India, is assassinated
‣ Soviet Union breaks up after President Gorbachev resigns

1992

‣ Members of the *COBE* science team announce that "ripples" have been detected in the cosmic background radiation

1993

‣ Two groups of researchers announce identification of gene for colon cancer

1994

▶ Strong evidence for the existence of the "top" quark is discovered at Fermi National Accelerator Laboratory

1997

▶ The first successfully cloned mammal, a sheep named Dolly, is born in Scotland. To produce her, researcher Ian Wilmut and colleagues at Roslin Institute cloned DNA from adult sheep cells and inserted the DNA into a sheep egg, which was implanted in the uterus of another sheep

1998

▶ Dolly's first offspring, a normally conceived lamb, is born, showing that the cloned ewe can reproduce normally

1999

▶ Astronauts begin building an international space station that will take over the continuous human presence in space and establish a permanent space science laboratory to take the place of Russia's *Mir* space station, which must be abandoned

2000

▶ The first draft of the Human Genome Project is published, the record of the complete set of the approximately 31,000 genes housed in the 23 pairs of human chromosomes
▶ Information accessible on the World Wide Web reaches an estimated 1 billion pages

2001

▶ Terrorists cause three commercial jetliners to crash, destroying the twin towers of the World Trade Center in New York, severely damaging the Pentagon building in Washington, D.C., and killing thousands of civilians

2003

▶ Dolly, the cloned sheep, dies unexpectedly of pneumonia. Her life span is about one-half the life span of an average uncloned sheep

▶ The space shuttle *Columbia* explodes during reentry; all crew members die in the accident, and shuttle missions are placed on hold

▶ The United States wages war on Iraq

GLOSSARY

atom   The smallest chemical unit of an element, consisting of a dense, positively charged nucleus surrounded by negatively charged electrons. The Greek thinker Leucippus and his student Democritus originally conceived of the idea of the atom in the fifth century B.C. as the smallest particle into which matter could be divided. (The word *atom* comes from the Greek word *atomos*, which means "indivisible.") But in the 1890s and early 20th century, scientists discovered that the atom is made up of even smaller particles, which are strongly bound together.

baryon   One of a group of fundamental particles that theoretically are formed by three quarks joining together. (The term comes from the Greek word *barys* meaning "heavy.") Baryons include protons, neutrons, and several particles known as hyperons (lambda, sigma, xi, and omega), which have very brief lifetimes and decay into nucleons and mesons or other lighter particles. For every baryon, there is an anti-baryon.

chromosome   A linear body found in the nucleus of all plant and animal cells that is responsible for determining and transmitting hereditary characteristics.

cosmic ray   A stream of ionizing radiation that enters the Earth's atmosphere from outer space and particles (mostly muons) produced by collisions of these particles with the molecules of the upper atmosphere. The rays consist of high-energy atomic nuclei, muons, electromagnetic waves, and other forms of radiation.

DNA (deoxyribonucleic acid)   A nucleic acid that is the main constituent of the chromosomes of living cells; the molecule consists of two long chains of phosphate and sugar units twisted into a double helix with nitrogenous bases in between (adenine, thymine, guanine, and cytosine) joined by hydrogen bonds; the sequence of these bases determines individual characteristics.

fundamental interaction   One of the four forces found in nature: gravitation, electromagnetism, the strong nuclear force, and the weak nuclear force. People have known about the first two for a long time, since they function over long distances and are easily observed, but the strong and weak forces were not discovered until the 20th century, and their effects take place at the sub-atomic level.

fundamental particle   An indivisible subatomic particle; a member of one of the groups of particles called quarks and leptons.

gene   A hereditary unit that is located in a fixed place on a chromosome and has a specific influence on the physical makeup of a living organism. A gene is capable of mutation into various forms.

gluon   The term used to describe the "glue," or tiny carrier particle, that mediates the strong force, binding together the subatomic particles called quarks that make up the atomic nucleus (protons, neutrons, mesons, and so on). Gluons are theorized to exist in eight forms.

GUT (Grand Unification Theory)   A unified field theory attempting to explain all the fundamental interactions (gravitation, electromagnetism, and the strong and weak nuclear forces) under the umbrella of a single theory. Although no one has yet found a satisfactory theory, the search for it continues.

hadron   One of a group of fundamental particles that take part in all four of the fundamental interactions. Hadrons are composed of quarks.

half-life   The time it takes for one-half the nuclei in a given amount of a radioactive isotope to decay into another isotope or element. That is, after one half-life, one-half of the original sample of the radioactive elements will have transformed. Half-lives of different isotopes range from a few millionths of a second to several billion years.

hominid   A member of the family of two-legged primates that includes several human species, both extinct and living, among them *Australopithecus*, *Homo erectus*, and *Homo sapiens*.

Homo erectus   The genus and species names given to Eugene Dubois's Java man, Peking man, and other extinct, ape-like humans. Large (six feet tall), with heavy browridges and a brain measuring one-half to two-thirds the size of a modern human brain, *Homo erectus* lived between 500,000 to 1.6 million years ago.

lepton   A class of fundamental particles that are governed by the weak interaction and are not affected by the strong interaction; there are 12 known leptons: the electron, electron neutrino, moun, muon neutrino, tao, tao neutrino, and their antiparticles.

meson   A subatomic fundamental particle of the hadron class (formed from a quark and its antiquark, according to current theory). One type of meson's existence was first suggested by Hideki Yukawa of Japan in 1935 to explain how the parts of the nucleus are bound together, and this meson, known as the pi meson or pion, was discovered in 1947; others have been discovered since.

muon   A particle found in cosmic rays. The muon is classified as a lepton because it does not display the strong interaction; when a muon decays, an electron and a pair of neutrinos are left behind.

mutation   Any alteration in an organism that can be inherited, carried by a gene or group of genes.

nucleon   A proton or a neutron.

photon   The packet that carries electromagnetic force, having the properties of both a particle and a wave.

planetesimal   Formation material out of which the planets are made.

QCD   (See quantum chromodynamics)

QED   (See quantum electrodynamics)

quanta   Fundamental units, or "packets," of energy.

quantum chromodynamics (QCD)   The theory that explains the strong nuclear force (carried by particles called *gluons*) in terms of its effects in binding the subatomic particles called quarks in different arrangements to form the particles found in the atomic nucleus. According to QCD, protons, neutrons, and their antiparticles are composed of trios of quarks, while mesons are composed of one quark and one antiquark.

quantum electrodynamics (QED)   In the 1920s and 1930s, Paul Dirac, Werner Heisenberg, and Wolfgang Pauli proposed a set of equations that explained electromagnetic force in terms of the quantum nature of the photon. This set of equations, once it was developed further by Richard Feynman and others, provided the theoretical explanation for the interactions of electromagnetic radiation with atoms and their electrons and came to be called quantum electrodynamics or QED. QED succeeds in combining classical physics with quantum theory, explaining chemical reactions and many other observable behaviors of matter and at the same time encompassing classic electromagnetic theory.

quark   In nuclear physics, a subatomic particle, believed to be a fundamental nuclear particle, of which all hadrons are made. According to theory, quarks occur only in pairs or in threes, held together by the gluon, the carrier of the strong force. Quarks come in six types, known as "flavors," and the six flavors can also come in any of the three "colors." Although quarks may have properties that make them invisible, enough evidence points to their existence that most scientists accept the theory.

RNA (ribonucleic acid)   Found in all living cells, RNA consists of a single stranded chain of alternating phosphate and ribose units with the bases adenine, guanine, cytosine, and uracil bonded to the ribose. The structure and sequence of bases in this chain are determinants of protein synthesis.

strong nuclear force   One of the four fundamental interactions found in nature, operating only at the subatomic level; the strong nuclear force binds the particles in the nucleus known as hadrons—the neutron, proton, unstable particles called hyperons and mesons (some of which exist only as "virtual" particles).

subatomic   Describes units that make up the atom.

virus   A tiny agent of disease that consists of a core of nucleic acid surrounded by a protein coat. It is capable of replicating itself, but only in the presence of a living cell, and it produces disease by invading and destroying living cells and causing the release of a large number of new particles identical to the original one.

weak nuclear force   One of the four fundamental interactions found in nature, operating only at the subatomic level. The weak nuclear force is the force associated with radioactive decay and, together with the electromagnetic force, binds leptons (including electrons and muons).

FURTHER READING
AND WEB SITES

About Science and Science History

Cole, K. C. *The Hole in the Universe: How Scientists Peered over the Edge of Emptiness and Found Everything*. New York: Harcourt, Inc., 2001. A journey into the strange realms of the atom, guided by a "practical philosopher" who has both grace and a sense of humor.

―――. *Sympathetic Vibrations: Reflections on Physics as a Way of Life*. New York: William Morrow and Co., 1985. Well-written, lively, and completely intriguing look at physics presented in a thoughtful and insightful way by a writer who cares for her subject. The emphasis here is primarily modern physics and concentrates more on the ideas than the history.

―――. *The Universe and the Teacup: The Mathematics of Truth and Beauty*. New York: Harcourt Brace, 1998. Cole dispels "mathphobia" by engaging the spirit of mathematics and catching her readers up in an irreverent and humorous look at ourselves.

Corben, Herbert C. *The Struggle to Understand: A History of Human Wonder and Discovery*. Buffalo, N.Y.: Prometheus Books, 1991. Explores the history of scientific discovery and superstition and supernaturalism from prehistoric times to the present.

Dawkins, Richard. *Unweaving the Rainbow: Science, Delusion, and the Appetite for Wonder*. Boston: Houghton Mifflin, 1998. Dawkins counters late-20th-century attacks on science with well-reasoned arguments showing how science reveals the hidden beauties and the wonder of the universe.

Feynman, Richard P. *The Meaning of It All: Thoughts of a Citizen-Scientist*. Reading, Mass.: Addison-Wesley, 1998. Three lectures delivered by

Feynman at the University of Washington in 1963 on the religious, political, and social issues of the day: "The Uncertainty of Science," "The Uncertainty of Values," and "This Unscientific Age."

———. *The Pleasure of Finding Things Out.* Edited by Jeffrey Robbins. Foreword by Freeman Dyson. Cambridge, Mass.: Perseus Books, 1999. A collection of "short works," including interviews, speeches, lectures, and articles that depict the inside story of a life in science.

Gardner, Martin. *Fads and Fallacies in the Name of Science.* New York: New American Library, 1986 (reprint of 1952 edition). A classic look at pseudoscience by the master debunker. Includes sections of pseudoscientific beliefs in the 19th century.

Hann, Judith. *How Science Works.* Pleasantville, N.Y.: The Reader's Digest Association, Inc., 1991. Lively well-illustrated look at physics for young readers. Good, brief explanations of basic laws and short historical overviews accompany many easy experiments readers can perform.

Hazen, Robert M., and James Trefil. *Science Matters: Achieving Scientific Literacy.* New York: Doubleday, 1991. A clear and readable overview of basic principles of science and how they apply to science in today's world.

Holzinger, Philip R. *The House of Science.* New York: John Wiley and Sons, 1990. Lively question-and-answer discussion of science for young adults. Includes activities and experiments.

Internet History of Science Sourcebook. Available online. URL: http://www.fordham.edu/halsall/science/sciencesbook.html. Accessed June 23, 2003. Provides a wealth of links to educational sites tracing the history of science from "Egyptian mathematics" to "moral issues and modern science," sponsored by Fordham University in New York City.

People and Discoveries: A Science Odyssey. Based on the Public Broadcasting Service (PBS) television series and companion book, *A Science Odyssey: 100 Years of Discovery.* Available online. URL: http://www.pbs.org/wgbh/aso/. Accessed June 23, 2003.

Piel, Gerard. *The Age of Science: What Scientists Learned in the Twentieth Century.* An expansive, readable overview of the extensive strides in scientific understanding achieved between 1900 and 2000; written by the founder of *Scientific American.*

Silver, Brian L. *The Ascent of Science.* New York: Oxford University Press, 1998. A sweeping overview of the history of science from the Renaissance to the present.

Then and Now. This PBS Web site compares what we know now in science to what we knew 100 years ago. Available online. URL: http://www.pbs.org/wgbh/aso/thenandnow/. Accessed June 23, 2003.

timelinescience: one thousand years of scientific thought. National Grid for Learning (NGFL, managed by the British Educational Communications and Technology Agency). Available online. URL: http://www.

timelinescience.org/index.php. Accessed June 23, 2003. For each 100-year period from 1000 to 2000 c.e., this helpful resource provides a "Setting the Scene" section that discusses historical and social contexts, followed by a timeline that outlines key scientific discoveries.

Trefil, James. *The Nature of Science: An A–Z Guide to the Laws and Principles Governing Our Universe.* New York: Houghton Mifflin Company, 2003. Current and approachable, this book puts the information needed for science literacy all in one place.

Books about the Physical Sciences, 1946–Present

Ferris, Timothy. *The World Treasury of Physics, Astronomy, and Mathematics.* Boston: Little, Brown, 1991. Historical writings, essays, poetry. A wonderful anthology for both the science student and the general reader, sparkling with appreciation and wonder. A good book to give not only to science students and enthusiasts, but also to those skeptics who claim that science takes the poetry out of life.

ON PHYSICS, PARTICLE PHYSICS, AND THE QUANTUM

Boorse, Henry A., Lloyd Motz, and Jefferson Hane Weaver. *The Atomic Scientists: A Biographical History.* New York: John Wiley and Sons, 1989. Interesting approach to the history of atomic science. The development is followed through a series of brief but lucid biographies of the major figures.

Cropper, William H. *Great Physicists: The Life and Times of Leading Physicists from Galileo to Hawking.* New York: Oxford University Press, 2003. Lively coverage of late-20th-century pioneers in particle physics (Feynman and Gell-Mann) and astronomy, astrophysics, and cosmology (Chandrasekhar and Hawking).

Einstein, Albert. *Out of My Later Years.* New York: Philosophical Library, 1950. Essays on science, humanity, politics, and life by the gentle-thinking Einstein.

Farnes, Patricia, and G. Kass-Simon, eds. *Women of Science: Righting the Record.* Bloomington: Indiana University Press, 1990. Short one-to-three-page profiles of women who—often little recognized—have made contributions in archaeology, geology, astronomy, mathematics, engineering, physics, biology, medical science, chemistry, and crystallography. Written by scientists, this book offers a wealth of information and an eye-opener to the fact that many more women have made contributions in science than generally thought.

Feynman, Richard P. *The Feynman Lectures on Physics,* 3 volumes. Reading, Mass.: Addison-Wesley, 1963. A splendid series and Feynman at his finest.

————. *QED: The Strange Theory of Light and Matter.* Princeton: Princeton University Press, 1983. Vividly lucid and accessible to just about all interested readers. A slim and elegant example of a first-rate and original mind tackling a fascinating and difficult subject.

Gilmore, Robert. *Alice in Quantumland: An Allegory of Quantum Physics.* New York: Springer-Verlag, 1995. In which we watch Alice shrink to the size of a nuclear particle and then we travel with her to the realm of quarks, where the rules are all entirely different from what we are used to.

Glashow, Sheldon L. *Interactions: A Journey through the Mind of a Particle Physicist and the Matter of This World.* New York: Warner Books, 1988. Part autobiography, part science history, and all Glashow with his strong ego intact. Charming enough to get the reader over the difficult spots, both personal and scientific, providing a good look at the life, and particularly the youth, of one of the 20th century's major physicists.

Gleick, James. *Genius: The Life and Science of Richard Feynman.* New York: Pantheon Books, 1992. An uncommonly perceptive look at one of the most original minds of modern physics, written with the insights of a master science writer.

Han, M. Y. *The Secret Life of the Quanta.* Blue Ridge Summit, Pa.: Tab Books, 1990. Coming at the quanta from the practical rather than the theoretical end, Han concentrates on explaining how our knowledge of the quanta allows us to build such high-tech devices as computers, lasers, and the CAT scan—while not neglecting theory and the bizarre aspects of his subject.

Hazen, Robert M., and James Trefil. *Science Matter: Achieving Scientific Literacy.* New York: Doubleday, 1991. Includes good brief discussions on relativity and quantum physics.

Jones, Roger S. *Physics for the Rest of Us.* Chicago: Contemporary Books, 1992. Informative, non-mathematical discussions of relativity and quantum theory told as a straightforward matter, along with discussions on how both affect our lives and philosophies.

Lederman, Leon M., and David N. Schramm. *From Quarks to the Cosmos: Tools of Discovery.* New York: Scientific American Library, 1989. Takes a good look not only at the theorists but also at the experimenters and experiments in the development of our understanding of the atom. Well-done and easy-to-follow book.

Lederman, Leon, with Dick Teresi. *The God Particle: If the Universe Is the Answer, What Is the Question?* New York: Houghton Mifflin, 1993. A sprightly and often humorously personal look at the history of physics and particle physics. Easy to read, lucid, and informative.

McCormmach, Russell. *Night Thoughts of a Classical Physicist.* Cambridge: Harvard University Press, 1982. A fascinating novel treating the mind and emotions of a turn-of-the-century physicist in Germany who attempts to understand the disturbing changes happening in physics and the world around him.

Morris, Richard. *The Edges of Science: Crossing the Boundary from Physics to Metaphysics*. New York: Prentice-Hall, 1990. A tough-minded, and critical look at the current problems of physics.

Pagels, Heinz R. *The Cosmic Code: Quantum Physics as the Language of Nature*. New York: Simon and Schuster, 1982. Quickly becoming a standard reference for the history and problems of quantum physics. Brilliantly written and easy to read, offering a clear look at some of the quantum paradoxes.

Peat, David F. *Einstein's Moon: Bell's Theorem and the Curious Quest for Quantum Reality*. Chicago: Contemporary Books, Inc., 1990. A popularly written study of some of the major paradoxes of quantum theory.

Riordan, Michael. *The Hunting of the Quark: A True Story of Modern Physics*. New York: Simon and Schuster, 1987. A lively and engrossing history aimed at the general reader.

Segrè, Emilio. *From X-Rays to Quarks: Modern Physicists and Their Discoveries*. San Francisco: W. H. Freeman Co., 1980. Good study of the people and their discoveries by a key physicist.

Shapiro, Gilbert. *A Skeleton in the Darkroom: Stories of Serendipity in Science*. San Francisco: Harper and Row, 1986. Engagingly told stories of scientific discovery, including the discovery of cosmic microwave background radiation of the J/Psi meson, the development of the asteroid/comet impacts hypothesis, and the discovery of pulsars.

Von Baeyer, Hans Christian. *Taming the Atom*. New York: Random House, 1992. A well-told, easy-to-read look at the history and development of atomic physics. Von Baeyer also takes a look at developments in the field and experiments intended to help clear up the quantum mysteries.

Weisskopf, Victor F. *The Joy of Insight: Passion of a Physicist*. New York: Basic Books, 1991. Delightful and personal reminiscences by an easy-going and thoughtful physicist who knew many of the great quantum pioneers firsthand.

———. *The Privilege of Being a Physicist*. New York: W. H. Freeman Co., 1989. Reminiscences and random thoughts by a well-respected physicist.

ON ASTRONOMY AND COSMOLOGY

Bartusiak, Marcia. *Through a Universe Darkly*. New York: HarperCollins, 1993. A sparkling account of the history of the universe as we now think of it and the story of the people who have unfolded it.

Boslough, John. *Masters of Time: Cosmology at the End of Innocence*. Reading, Mass.: Addison-Wesley, 1992. A very good, critical look at the current problems in cosmology and a hard questioning look at the current theoretical search for the big answers.

Ferris, Timothy. *Coming of Age in the Milky Way*. New York: William Morrow, 1988. An exciting, readable account of some of the great discoveries of science from the time of the Greeks to the present. Draws on a deep appreciation for the beauty of science and its contributions to modern culture. Includes discussions of big bang theory, SETI, Guth's theories, and other areas of modern cosmology.

——. *The Whole Shebang: A State-of-the-Universe Report*. New York: Simon and Schuster, 1997. Ferris brings readers up to date on how scientists currently view the universe, given the vast amounts of new information gained in the past decade.

Hawking, Stephen. *A Brief History of Time*. New York: Bantam Books, 1988. This lucid, personal, and engrossing look at the "big picture" of modern physics by the brilliant scientist Stephen Hawking became a best-seller in 1988.

Lightman, Alan, and Roberta Brawler, eds. *Origins: The Lives and Worlds of Modern Cosmologists*. Cambridge, Mass.: Harvard University Press, 1990.

Overbye, Dennis. *Lonely Hearts of the Cosmos*. New York: HarperCollins, 1991. A highly readable look at the men and women in the forefront of modern cosmology.

Stewart, Ian. *Flatterland*. Cambridge, Mass.: Perseus Publishing, 2001. Uses imagination and a sense of humor while exploring our present understanding of the shape of the universe.

Books about the Life Sciences, 1946–Present

Chase, Allan. *Magic Shots*. New York: William Morrow and Company, Inc., 1982. The story of the quest for vaccinations to prevent infectious diseases in the 19th and 20th centuries, from Edward Jenner's smallpox vaccination to polio vaccines and the ongoing search for cancer vaccines.

Facklam, Margery, and Howard Facklam. *Healing Drugs: The History of Pharmacology*. New York: Facts On File, 1992. Part of the Facts On File Science Sourcebook series, this book tells the stories of Paul Ehrlich and his magic bullet, Best and Banting and their research on insulin, and Fleming's discovery of penicillin, as well as more recent drug research.

Kornberg, Arthur. *For the Love of Enzymes: The Odyssey of a Biochemist*. Cambridge, Mass.: Harvard University Press, 1989. One of the premier biologists of our time provides the 19th- and early 20th-century background for recent advances in biology, as a backdrop to his autobiographical account of his own significant work.

Moore, John A. *Science as a Way of Knowing: The Foundations of Modern Biology*. Cambridge, Mass.: Harvard University Press, 1993. A cultural history of biology as well as a delightful introduction to the procedures and values of science, written by a leading evolutionary-developmental biologist. Nontechnical and readable, it is an excellent source for the nonspecialist who wants to know more about how modern molecular biology, ecology, and biotechnology came to be.

Shorter, Edward, Ph.D. *The Health Century: A Companion to the PBS Television Series.* New York: Doubleday, 1987. An easygoing account of the scientific pursuit of keys to better health in the 20th century, set in the social context of the times.

ON GENETICS AND DNA

Bishop, Jerry E., and Michael Waldholz. *Genome.* New York: Touchstone/Simon and Schuster, 1990. The story of the heroic attempts to provide a complete map of all the genes in the human body told as an adventure story featuring a wide cast of interesting participants. Very readable and exciting.

Crick, Francis. *What Mad Pursuit: A Personal View of Scientific Discovery.* New York: Basic Books, Inc., 1988. Crick reminisces about the discovery of the double helix structure of DNA and in the process weaves a story of science, experiment, and theory—in the discipline of biology, and molecular biology in particular. Fascinating reading.

Keller, Evelyn Fox. *A Feeling for the Organism: The Life and Work of Barbara McClintock.* New York: W. H. Freeman, 1983. An unusually insightful biography of a highly independent scientist and her work, as well as a revealing look at the way science is done and the role played by those who buck the mainstream. Keller, who is trained in theoretical physics and molecular biology, brings a keen understanding of human dynamics in science to her account of this extraordinary renegade geneticist.

McCarty, Maclyn. *The Transforming Principle: Discovering That Genes Are Made of DNA.* New York: W. W. Norton and Company, 1985. A first-person account by one of the three scientists that discovered in 1944 that DNA is *the* genetic material, giving birth to molecular biology and modern genetics.

Newton, David E. *James Watson and Francis Crick: Discovery of the Double Helix and Beyond.* (Makers of Modern Science Series.) New York: Facts On File, 1992. Written for young adults, this dual biography traces the paths of Watson and Crick through the exciting years of their teamwork on the structure of DNA and also explores their later work, done separately.

Porter, Roy, ed. *The Cambridge Illustrated History of Medicine.* Cambridge, Mass.: Cambridge University Press, 2001. In essays written by experts in the field, this illustrated history traces the evolution of medicine from the contributions made by early Greek physicians through the Renaissance, Scientific Revolution, and 19th and 20th centuries up to current advances. Sidebars cover parallel social or political events and certain diseases.

Portugal, Franklin H., and Jack S. Cohen. *A Century of DNA*. Cambridge, Mass.: The MIT Press, 1977. Provides a thorough look at the background leading up to the discovery of the role played by DNA in heredity.

Ridley, Matt. *Genome: The Autobiography of a Species in 23 Chapters*. Ridley tells how the Human Genome Project mapped the approximately 31,000 genes found on the 23 pairs of human chromosomes. He picks one newly discovered gene from each of the 23 pairs of chromosomes and takes the reader inside its story—and the story of how scientists solved some of the mysteries surrounding genetics and the nature of life.

Watson, James D. *The Double Helix*. New York: Atheneum, 1968. A now-classic, highly personal account of the search for the elusive structure of DNA, as engrossing now as when first written. Science research as a battlefront in one of the first and best "warts-and-all" looks at how science is done.

Watson, James D., and John Tooze. *The DNA Story: A Documentary History of Gene Cloning*. San Francisco: W. H. Freeman and Co., 1981. An offbeat and very compelling look at the history of DNA research told through the use of newspaper clips, personal correspondence, official documents, and narrative. Well done and interesting, but it does require a little background on the part of the reader to help put all the pieces into perspective.

Watson, James D., with Andrew Barry. *DNA: The Secret of Life*. New York: Alfred A. Knopf, 2003. Fifty years after the author and his colleague Francis Crick discovered the structure of DNA, Watson provides the panorama of the genetic revolution—journeying from Mendel's vegetable patch to Watson and Crick's discovery of the double helix and bringing readers up to the moment with an account of the human genome and beyond.

ON EVOLUTION

Morris, Richard. *The Evolutionists: The Struggle for Darwin's Soul*. New York: W. H. Freeman and Company, 2001. Contains good descriptions of Darwinism and Darwin's development of evolutionary theory, as well as discussions of 21st-century views spearheaded by Richard Dawkins and Stephen Jay Gould.

Eldridge, Niles. *Life Pulse: Episodes from the Story of the Fossil Record*. New York: Facts On File, 1987. A little tough going and dry but well worth the effort for the serious student.

Milder, Richard. *The Encyclopedia of Evolution*. New York: Facts On File, 1990. Just what the title says, written in an easygoing, informal style that makes it a joy to use for research or just endless hours of browsing fun. Plenty of surprises, too, including looks at popular films dealing with the subjects and lots of little-known oddities.

Reader, John. *The Rise of Life*. New York: Alfred A. Knopf, 1986. Beautifully illustrated popular-level book covering the origins and evolution not only of humans but of all life forms. Very well done.

ON THE SEARCH FOR HUMAN ORIGINS

Burenhult, Gören, gen. ed. *The First Humans: Human Origins and History to 10,000 B.C.* Volume 1 of the Landmark Series from the American Museum of Natural History. New York: HarperSanFrancisco (a Division of HarperCollins Publishers), 1993. Originally published by Weldon Own Pty Limited, McMahons Point, Sydney, Australia, and Bra Böcker AB, Sweden, 1993. Beautifully organized, edited, and illustrated. Charts, maps, and illustrations all work hand in hand with a highly readable narrative to make this an indispensable up-to-date volume for any personal or school liberty.

Lambert, David, and the Diagram Group. *The Field Guide to Early Man*. New York: Facts On File, 1987. Well-designed and carefully illustrated "hand-book" on all aspects of early humans. A wonderful book for finding facts, or just reading for fun. Easy to read and endlessly fascinating.

Lewin, Roger. *Bones of Contention: Controversies in the Search for Human Origins*. New York: Simon and Schuster, 1987. Although primarily concerned with the controversies and developments in the latter half of the 20th century, this book does have good, readable background material about the search for human origins during the period from 1895 to 1945, as well.

Spencer, Frank. *Piltdown: A Scientific Forgery*. London: Natural History Museum Publications, Oxford University Press, 1990. Exhaustive but highly readable look at the Piltdown hoax and its discovery. Covers just about everyone involved in the story, including the most likely suspects. Illustration and seldom-seen photographs help bring the story to life. A must for anyone interested in science and the Piltdown mystery.

Willis, Delta. *The Hominid Gang: Behind the Scenes in the Search for Human Origins*. Introduction by Stephen Jay Gould. New York: Viking, 1989. Fascinating, on-the-spot examination of how anthropology is done in Africa by Richard Leakey and his crew of trained specialists, recorded with a skeptical eye by photojournalist Delta Willis.

INDEX

Italic page numbers
indicate illustrations.

A

aces (subatomic
particles) 40
acquired
immunodeficiency
syndrome (AIDS) 147,
151–156, *154*
adenine (nitrogen base)
130
Africa
AIDS in 152
as source of human
evolution 179
The Age of Aquarius 198
AIDS. *See* acquired
immunodeficiency
syndrome
alanine (amino acid) 142
alternative health
movement 195, 201
Alvarez, Luis Walter
116–117
Alvarez, Walter 116–117
amino acids 135, 140,
142
Anderson, Carl 7–8, *8*,
12
Antarctica, ozone hole
over 119
antibiotics, bacterial
resistance to 156–157
antimatter 7, 22
antiparticles 76
antiprotons 22

apes, evolution of 168
Apollo (asteroid group)
93
Apollo spacecraft 190
Apollo 17 80
The Aquarian Conspiracy
(Ferguson) 198–199
Arber, Werner 157
Arecibo, Puerto Rico,
radio antenna at
60–61
argon gas, on Mars 90
Ariel (moon of Uranus)
102
Aristotle (Greek
philosopher) 138
Arp, Halton 63–64
Arp 220 (galactic
merger) 54
Asia, AIDS in 152
asteroid belt 92
asteroids 87, *92*, 92–93
astrology 198
astronomy 47–48
radio 59–62
Aten (asteroid group) 93
atom(s) 4–6, 9
Standard Model of
43–44, 44*f*, 76
atomic bomb 12–13,
185–186. *See also*
Manhattan Project
aura (of person) 200
australopithecines 169,
175, 178–180
Australopithecus
aethiopicus 180

Australopithecus
afarensis 175–177,
176, 180
Australopithecus
africanus 169, 180
Australopithecus
anamensis 180
Australopithecus
bahrelghazali 180
Australopithecus
boisei 172, 178,
180
Australopithecus
robustus 178, 180
Avery, Oswald 126
axions (hypothetical
particles) 74
azidothymidine (AZT), in
AIDS treatment 154

B

bacteria 156–157
bacteriophages 156–157
Baltimore, David 149
Bardeen, John 10, *11*, 24
baryons (subatomic
particles) 38, 39–40,
42
base-pairing, in DNA
130
BCS theory, of
superconductivity 24
Beagle-2 (spacecraft) 91
Beckwith, Jonathan 157
Becquerel, Henri 31
Bednorz, Georg 24
Bell, Jocelyn 62, 64

235